Compelled to Serve

The Story of American Assemblies of God Missions in Early 20th Century China

Michael McAteer

Book 6 of the Pentecost Around the World Series

WIPF & STOCK · Eugene, Oregon

Wipf and Stock Publishers
199 W 8th Ave, Suite 3
Eugene, OR 97401

Compelled to Serve
The Story of American Assemblies of God Missions in Early 20th Century China
By McAteer, Michael

Softcover ISBN-13: 979-8-3852-7607-3
Hardcover ISBN-13: 979-8-3852-7608-0
eBook ISBN-13: 979-8-3852-7609-7
Publication date 2/17/2026
Previously published by APTS Press, 2025

This edition is a scanned facsimile of the original edition published in 2025.

Table of Contents

Publisher's Preface

to the Pentecost Around the World Book Series

We are pleased to announce that this new book, *Compelled to Serve: The Story of the Assemblies of God in Early 20th Century China* by Michael McAteer, is the sixth volume in our Pentecost Around the World series. The purpose of this series is to provide a place for historical reflection on what God is doing through the Pentecostal Movement, particularly in the Asia Pacific and Pacific Oceania regions of the world.

The five previous titles are: *Reflections of an Early American Pentecostal* by Stanley Horton; *The Cross Among Pagodas: A History of the Assemblies of God* in Myanmar by Chin Khua Khai; *Pentecost to the Uttermost: A History of the Assemblies of God in Samoa* by Tavita Pagaialii; *Pentecostal Pioneer: The Life and Legacy of Rudy Esperanza and the Early Years of the Assemblies of God in the Philippines* by Dynnice Rosanny D. Engcoy; and *From Seedtime to Harvest: The History of the Assemblies of God in Cambodia* by Joshua J. Lovelace.

Unfortunately, the first two books are no longer available. The rest are available for purchase through our website, www.aptspress.com.

If you have any questions or comments, you are welcome to contact us through our website, www.aptspress.com.

We hope you enjoy this book.

THE PUBLISHER

Foreword

"I feel as if I could not live if something is not done for China."
J. Hudson Taylor

In the early 1980s, a young couple from Arkansas felt a clear and compelling call to missionary service, sensing a profound witness of the Spirit of God. Missionary Hudson Taylor's life and writings impacted the trajectory of their ministry. Forty-one years later, Mike and Jane Ann McAteer have made an eternal impact on the people of China and the diaspora. That influence includes church planting, teaching at Bible school and seminary levels, mentoring young hungry believers in the Christian life, and coaching and guiding new missionaries. Moreover, as a faithful witness of the gospel of Jesus Christ, Mike also earned a Doctorate in Applied Intercultural Studies. His passion for missiology is reflected in this outstanding work.

Their ministry led them to live in two of the busiest cities in China, provided them with the opportunity to learn one of the most challenging languages in the world, and enabled them to raise three daughters to adulthood in cross-cultural environments. Mike's firsthand, on-the-ground experiences, teaching gift, and language ability have continued to open doors for expanded ministry abroad and in the United States.

Mike utilizes his experience and expertise to teach at the Assemblies of God Theological Seminary, traveling the world to visit seminaries, teach classes, and minister in churches. Prayer is a vital part of Mike's and Jane Ann's lives. They lead a weekly prayer meeting, where mostly retired missionaries gather to pray for unreached people groups, the lost, missionary families, including their children, and for open doors for the gospel.

My wife, Sandie, and I had the opportunity to visit them when they lived overseas, and we saw firsthand their love for the Lord, their commitment to the Chinese people, their love for family, and their passion for seeing people come to Christ. We can testify that this couple walks in integrity and in the light of the Lord Jesus.

Fascinating—that's how I describe this book. The alignment of these pioneer missionaries with the developing Pentecostal missiology of AGWM demonstrates a strategic and Spirit-led orientation. Mike has done the Christian missions world an important service through his research and excellent descriptive writing. I highly recommend *Compelled to Serve: The Story of American Assemblies of God in Early 20th Century China.*

Greg Mundis, D.Min.
Former Executive Director
Assemblies of God World Missions

Chapter One

INTRODUCTION

Wayne W. Warner and Darrin Rodgers (2017, 44) wrote: "With each passing year of time it becomes more apparent that we must preserve the story of the Pentecostal revival out of which the Assemblies of God movement was born." Allan Anderson (2004, 175), in the same vein, stated: "We have taken for granted an obscure history of Pentecostalism for so long that the multitudes of nameless people responsible for its grassroots expansion have passed into history unremembered and their memory is now very difficult to retrieve."

Several years ago, my Chinese friend, Li Yun,[1] and I lamented the fact that so many Chinese Christian testimonies remain undocumented. With an increasing number of those who survived the turbulent early years of China's Communist Party and the Cultural Revolution steadily passing into eternity, the importance of recording these irreplaceable and heroic stories, before they are lost to us forever, has never been more urgent.

On one of my first trips to the People's Republic of China, I experienced a special opportunity to sit in a restaurant's private dining hall and listen to Allen Yuan,[2] a minister, his wife, and

---

[1]Names are changed for security reasons.

[2]Allen Yuan was born in 1914. For a time, he worked closely with a Norwegian AG pastor named Arnult Solvoll. They split ways when they disagreed about keeping their church plant (in Beijing) closely tied to the Norwegian AG organization. Solvoll pushed

their daughter share testimonies. Also, I have worked alongside David Plymire, Robert Bolton, and Jim Andrews, whose parents served as pioneer missionaries in early twentieth-century China. During my own family's candidate orientation, we met Ruth Melching, a retired China missionary, and invited her to come to our commissioning service and pray over us as we prepared for ministry in the Chinese world. Shortly after arriving in Taipei, Taiwan, we met Matthew Lee, who had served in pre-Communist China.[3] Being young and naïve, I failed to grasp the unique opportunity to listen to stories that helped define our Pentecostal legacy in the Chinese world.

Stories fascinate me. From a young boy, the narratives of the Old Testament, along with the Gospels and Acts, continue to be why I love to read the Bible. Sitting in church services as a child, I could daydream through the preacher's homiletic outline, but when the speaker began to tell a story I was hooked, listening with undivided attention.

Pentecostals are frequently criticized for placing an overemphasis on the Lukan narrative rather than the didactic teachings of the Pauline letters. Today, however, many Pentecostal scholars such as Roger Stronstad (1984), Robert P. Menzies (1994), William W. Menzies (2000), and James B. Shelton (1991) embrace the belief that Luke chose to use the narrative method to teach theology.[4]

---

for this, which would have enabled the young church to receive financial assistance from the AG. Yuan rejected the idea, desiring for the church to be empowered to stand on its own feet from its inception, completely independent of any foreign association. Yuan's decision later enabled him to defend his church as being totally indigenous and free from foreign control. However, since he refused to join the Three Self Patriotic Movement (TSPM), the church's indigenous status did not protect Yuan from a lengthy imprisonment later on. Lydia Lee has written a biography of Yuan's life (Lee 2001).

[3]Matthew Lee helped to translate the hymnal *Salvation Songs*, which has been used by Assemblies of God Chinese churches.

[4]Roger Stronstad (1984) *The Charismatic Theology of St. Luke*; Robert Menzies (1994) *Empowered for Witness*; and the book he co-authored with his father, William Menzies (2000) entitled, *Spirit and Power*; and James B. Shelton (1991) *Mighty in Word and Deed* are just a few of the books that could be cited here.

The Importance of Narrative in Missiology

Ralph Winter practiced analyzing history for insights into the ways God used men and women for the advancement of his Kingdom. In teaching the course, "Historical Development of the Christian Movement" at Fuller Seminary, Winter expected his students to read history analytically, recognizing trends and applying historical narrative in devising strategies for contemporary missions (Gill 2016, 3).

This project grows out of the conviction that the preservation of Assemblies of God history through biographical narrative, provides encouragement as believers review the roots from which they have come. At the same time, the historical narrative challenges leaders as to future direction. The angel of the Lord questioned Hagar as she was fleeing from Sarai: "Hagar, . . . where have you come from and where are you going (Gen 16:8)?"[5]

Similarly, Moses told the Israelites that when their children questioned the meaning of the testimonies, statutes, and rules given by God, the parents should rehearse the acts of God in delivering Israel from Egypt.[6] In other words, tell the children the stories. In doing so, they would place the current generation in the meta-narrative of what God is doing—His plans and purposes.

Dwight Baker (2016, 5-7), in his article "Aspects of the Role of History in Missiology," pictures missiology as a multi-legged stool with three primary legs: theology, anthropology, and history. Although he feels one should always exercise caution in devising mission strategy solely from history, he does admit that the study of mission history certainly provides a background from which such decisions can be made. Baker also claims that neglecting the scholarly research and writings about missionaries is too steep a

---

[5]Unless otherwise indicated, all Scripture references are from the English Standard Version (ESV).

[6]Deut 6:20-25. This theme is seen throughout Deuteronomy. In Deuteronomy 8, Moses admonished Israel to remember how God led them through the wilderness, how he fed them with manna, and how their clothing did not wear out. In chapter 9, the events of the giving of the Law and the sin of worshiping the golden calf are recounted to encourage the people to be faithful and to obey. God constantly encourages, admonishes, and teaches his people through the stories of their past.

price to pay that and such neglect causes us to "lose our grounding and frame of reference" (D. Baker 2016, 7).

The Biographical Narrative Lens

This study zeroes in on six biographical narratives (a study of eight missionaries), all but one of whom were officially associated with the Assemblies of God (AG). The remaining one served as an independent missionary with close ties to the AG. W. W. Simpson, his son Willie, and Victor Plymire served in northwest China. Marie Stephany and Anna Ziese ministered only a few miles apart in Shanxi province. Les and Ava Anglin were based in the northeast part of China. The Bakers and Boltons dedicated their lives to work in southwest China.

A study of Assemblies of God missions must include a study of the councils where delegates debate ideas and define policies. However, this study specifically takes a biographical narrative approach. When beginning this study, I anticipated difficulty in finding sufficient primary source material. I had heard that in the early days of AG history, there was a scarcity of Pentecostal missionary writing. Assemblies of God missionaries were compelled to act by their beliefs; the coming of the Lord could occur at any moment, they must obey Jesus' commission to carry the gospel to the ends of the earth, and that millions of souls hung in the balance between heaven and hell. Time was of the essence and the work must be done while it was still day, for the night would come when no one could work.

In light of such convictions, I anticipated difficulty in finding much reflective or descriptive writing. Yet many AG leaders and missionaries did write. J. Roswell Flower (1920) and Alice Luce (1921a, b, c) wrote missiologically and paved the way for the writings of Melvin Hodges, Morris Williams, J. Philip Hogan, and others.[7] In addition, early pioneers promoted their work through

---

[7]Flower frequently wrote articles for *The Pentecostal Evangel* concerning Assemblies of God missions. One such entry was his October 16, 1920 "Report of Missionary Treasurer for Year Ending September 1, 1920." Alice Luce (1921) wrote three articles on

such publications as *The Apostolic Faith, Word and Witness, The Pentecost, Latter Rain Evangel, Glad Tidings Herald, The Pentecostal Evangel*, and *Midnight Cry.* These men and women served in the missiological laboratory as the commitment to follow Pauline methods (as espoused by Roland Allen,[8] Alice Luce, and Melvin Hodges) was worked out in practical experience. How would the tension between the primacy of evangelism and social concern be managed? How would discipleship and planting of indigenous churches work in different cultural contexts? Would God indeed confirm the preaching of his word with accompanying signs and wonders?

Kenneth Scott Latourette (1970a) suggested seven questions for an examination of Christianity's growth through church history:

> (1) What was the Christianity which spread? (2) Why did Christianity spread? (3) Why has Christianity suffered reverses and at times met only partial successes? (4) By what processes did Christianity spread? (5) What effect has Christianity had upon its environment? (6) How did the environment affect Christianity? (7) What bearing did the processes by which Christianity spread have upon the effect of Christianity on its environment, and of the environment upon Christianity? (Latourette 1970a, x-xv).

Vern Middleton (2011, 158) notes that Donald McGavran (1990) asked related questions in his studies on church growth: (1) How is the church growing? How has it grown? Why is it growing?

"Paul's Missionary Methods," which appeared in the January 8, 1922, and February 5, 1921 issues of *The Pentecostal Evangel.* Melvin Hodges wrote *The Indigenous Church and the Missionary* (1978) as well as *A Theology of the Church and Its Mission* (1977). Morris Williams (1986) addressed the issue of partnership in his book, *Partnership and Mission.* J. Philip Hogan's many writings are examined in Everett Wilson's *Strategy of the Spirit* (1997) as well as Klaus and Petersen's (2006) *The Essential J. Philip Hogan.*

[8]Roland Allen's two books, *Missionary Methods: St. Paul's or Ours?* ([1912] 1962) and *The Spontaneous Expansion of the Church and the Causes Which Hinder It* ([1927] 1960), greatly influenced the development of AG missiology. Chapter 10 addresses this further.

(2) Where and why has it stopped? (3) What mission procedures help and hinder church growth? (4) How can we get more church growth?

These questions assist in the examination and evaluation of the missionaries included in this study. The Chinese context interacted with the work of the Holy Spirit in these missionary lives. Distance between the present time and the historical context proves long enough to allow a critical evaluation of the methodology and potential application for the present.

Reasons to Adopt a Biographical Narrative Approach

Although these questions are indirectly addressed by this project, this study follows the example of Gary B. McGee's book, *People of the Spirit* (2004) and Ruth Tucker's (2004) book, *From Jerusalem to Irian Jaya.* Biographical narrative chooses to emphasize people rather than events. Any movement's history can only be understood when looking at the "lives of the people who made it happen" (McGee 2004, 13-14). The men and women responsible for planting the foundations of the AG work in China should not be forgotten. Their lives challenge succeeding generations to hear and obey the call of God. By recounting the "struggles, emotions, adventure, romance, and sorrow" (Tucker 2004, 13) of our predecessors, the biographical narrative draws a younger generation into the meta-narrative of what God is doing. This younger generation needs this connection with the past so they can see how God led and used earlier generations (McGee 2004, 13-14). The stories of how God used men and women "of like passions" (James 5:17 KJV) inspire and encourage believers as they press forward in obedience to God's call today.[9]

Details included in the biographical sketches permit us to study these pioneers' methodology and ecclesiology. The

---

[9]Several years ago, I taught a mission history class at a church in Hong Kong. Dates and events left a glazed look in the eyes of the students. But when I recounted personal events in missionaries' lives, students became fully engaged. I have noticed similar responses as I have shared these stories with churches and individuals while researching this project.

longer the wait to research the archives and interview surviving witnesses, the more difficult the task becomes and the more likely that the early pioneers' stories will pass into history forgotten and buried. It is time to dig them out and let a new generation examine their lives: their calls, their struggles, their challenges, their dreams, their victories, and yes, even their shortcomings. Through studying their missiology, one can see both how their praxis was influenced by the developing AG mission theology as well as how their methodology contributed to the development of the Assemblies of God World Missions' (AGWM) "reach, plant, teach, serve" philosophy of ministry.[10]

J. Philip Hogan responded to Miriam Adeney's article entitled "McMissions," in the November 11, 1996 issue of *Christianity Today,* with a letter to Loren Triplett, AGWM Executive Director:

> Brethren, please hold the line which says there is yet no substitute for a man [or woman] whose heart is on fire, who accepts missionary appointment as a career, and who goes and learns a language, identifies with a culture, and is determined to plant the local unit of the body of Christ in lands afar. (Hogan 1996, 1-2)

Indirectly, Hogan's letter shows the importance of missionary biography. "Hearts on fire," "learning a language," and "identifying with a culture," speak to missionary calls and commitment and incarnational living, which serve as a cornerstone of successful missions. Without this missiological heritage, "we [believers] no longer know who we are—as individuals, as families and

---

[10]RPTS: Assemblies of God World Missions (AGWM) philosophy has adopted four pillars: "Reaching, Planting, Teaching, Serving." In brief, they describe a methodology calling for evangelizing the lost so that all may hear, planting indigenous churches, discipling and teaching those who have been reached, and ministering holistically to people, both inside and outside the established church. Beginning in January 1981 these pillars appeared in every issue of *Mountain Movers* as the missionary strategy of AGWM. Later in 2013, Randy Hurst wrote "All He Commands" which described these four pillars in depth. Hurst's article appeared in the January 6, 2013 issue of *The Pentecostal Evangel*, 10-13.

communities, as a people, or as the people of God" (D. Baker 2016, 7).

History may not give a precise strategy or plan. As L. P. Hartley (1953, 17) noted in *The Go-Between*, "The past is a foreign country; they do things differently there." Many of the challenges of early twentieth-century China no longer exist. But new challenges have risen, and knowledge of our mission history helps us to "sharpen our perception" and "make us more alert to crux issues" (D. Baker 2016, 9).

The pre-1952 missiological and ecclesial praxis of these missionaries influenced the formation of the Assemblies of God in China. That methodology, furthermore, has influenced the post-1952 Chinese Christian community. This project represents a small step toward the study of Pentecostalism in China and the development of a Chinese missiology.

Limitations and Boundaries of the Project

This project primarily limits itself to the study of Assemblies of God USA missionaries in China up to 1952. Although the Assemblies of God was not officially organized until 1914, several of the first AG missionaries in China had already been serving in China under other organizations. In such cases, the entire body of work of these missionaries will be included in the narratives. Although the Chinese Communist Party came to power in 1949, resulting in a mass exodus of foreign missionaries in that year, there were several who remained in China until 1952. Thus, that year has been chosen as the terminus of this study.

Much of the archival material examined is autobiographical in nature or has been written by close colleagues and friends. I assume and accept that there may be a high hagiographic element in the archival material. However, this does not minimize the importance of the biographical narrative, or the conclusions drawn from the evidence.

Outline of the Project

The Context

Chapters 2 and 3 will investigate the religio-socio-political context leading into the period of study. This requires a look at the previous waves of Christian missions work in China as well as the status of Christianity in the Middle Kingdom at the turn of the twentieth century. Many people mistakenly assume that it has only been since the establishment of the People's Republic of China in 1949 that Christianity has been unwelcome in China. Actually, China has always given a cool reception to those missionaries bringing the Christian message to her people.

China's recorded history dates back to the Shang dynasty over 3,500 years ago. The socio-political context in Chapters 2 and 3 will primarily focus on the nineteenth century, thus enabling an understanding of China confronting these early pioneer AG missionaries. The religious context covers the prior attempts at the evangelization of China from the early Nestorians to the modern era, which began with Robert Morrison's arrival in 1807. Nineteenth- and early twentieth-century missionary activity in China was forced to contend with the Opium Wars, the Taiping Rebellion, the rise of nationalism and anti-foreignism, the Boxer Rebellion, the collapse of the Qing dynasty, and the struggle for political power by warlords—the Nationalists, the Communists, and the Japanese. The evolving methodology of American AG missionaries was birthed and grew amid these turbulent times.

The Six Narratives

There are several reasons behind the selection of these six narratives. First, for all but two of these, I have had either a personal acquaintance with family members of those selected or have frequently traveled in the areas where they served, so my historical analysis benefits from knowing the persons and the contexts in which they lived. Second, the Flower Pentecostal Heritage Center (FPHC) and Assemblies of God World Missions (AGWM) Archives, both located in Springfield, Missouri, contain a large number of personal letters and writings both by and about these six missionaries. Third, their lives highlighted the methodological questions that confronted AG mission leaders and missionaries in those days, concerning their approach to the work at hand, within the context of their daily circumstances. Would evangelism be primary? What about compassion work, the establishment of orphanages, famine relief, and so on? How could indigenous churches be planted and what of the need for the training of indigenous leaders? Consider the tension between urban and rural evangelism. Could signs and wonders be expected to follow the preaching of the gospel? What about partnerships and teams? These six missionaries exemplify the success of AG missions to China in the early part of the twentieth century.[11]

The first subject, H. A. Baker, was not officially an American AG appointed missionary. Early on, Baker decided not to officially join any mission organization. Nevertheless, he was selected for inclusion here for several reasons. Most importantly, he was devoutly Pentecostal and, except for some aspects of his eschatology, taught and ministered in accordance with AG mission principles. The geographical area where Baker served corresponds to the scene of much American AG mission activity through the years. David Plymire remembers that Baker had good relationships with other AG missionaries in the area.[12] Later, when Baker relocated for ministry in Miaoli, Taiwan, he worked closely with the Finnish AG.[13] His son, James Baker, served as an American AG appointed missionary in China, Hong Kong, and Taiwan. Both the FPHC and AGWM Archives contain a large amount of material on Baker's work, which would seem to indicate that there was, at the very least, an informal relationship with the American AG. Moreover, Gary B. McGee's (2004) book, *People of the Spirit: The Assemblies of God*, contains a biographical summary of his life and work. Baker's combination of orphanage work and his evangelistic church planting ministry among the mountain tribes demonstrated how a

---

[11]A more detailed account along with citations is included in Chapter 3.

[12]David Plymire, conversation with author, Springfield, Missouri, January 25, 2019.

[13]Ibid.

healthy relationship between evangelism and compassion ministry could work. Furthermore, his methods of training indigenous leadership exemplified the importance of mentoring and training national leadership.

Victor Plymire served among the Tibetans of northwest China. He established his mission base in Tangar (current Huangyuan) in Qinghai province. His home still stands, and the graves of his first wife and son, who died of smallpox in 1927, are located outside of the city on the side of a mountain. Victor Plymire and his son David represent over 110 years of continuous ministry to the Chinese (1908-2019).

Les and Ava Anglin served in Tai-an in Shandong province. A chance meeting with a young beggar during one of Leslie's evangelistic meetings changed the course of their lives and led to the establishment of the Home of Onesiphorus. The Anglins modeled a holistic ministry that included feeding and sheltering widows, orphans, and the destitute as well as providing education that included vocational training. The Anglins' ministry influenced the entire community, and the work they established continues today.

Marie Stephany headlines a group of single women who served in Shanxi province. Stephany, who was later joined by Alice Stewart and Henrietta Tieleman, evangelized, planted churches, and ministered among opium addicts and orphans in Ta Ch'ang, Shanxi. When I walked through the streets where Stephany's team witnessed the love and power of Jesus to lost and hurting souls, an older Christian woman identified herself as the daughter of one of Marie's orphans. She continues to host meetings in her home. Her daughter and granddaughter are both Christians. This family represents four generations whose lives were forever changed by Marie's orphanage work. A few miles away, in Taiyuan, the provincial capital, Anna Ziese developed an extensive prison ministry. These women missionaries instituted a Bible school program that preceded Truth Bible Institute in Beijing. B. T. Bard, who would later serve as the principal of Truth Institute, filled in for Stephany during her furlough back to the USA. Although most missionaries left China in 1949, both Stewart and Tieleman remained until 1952. They later ministered in Taiwan and helped plant one of Taipei's largest AG churches. Anna Ziese never left China and died of natural causes in Taiyuan in the late 1960s.

William Wallace Simpson first arrived in China in 1892. Like several others who are on the list of AG missionaries in China, he began his China work with the Christian and Missionary Alliance. Simpson's burden for the Tibetans carried him to the Gansu/ Tibetan border region where ministry expanded to include the Chinese with a strong emphasis on the baptism of the Holy Spirit. However, Simpson suffered a terrible sacrifice. Bandits, on a road in the Gansu province, killed Simpson's son, Willie, in the early 1930s. Simpson was forced to leave China in 1949 at the age of 80. Several of the sermons he preached in American churches in the early 1950s are preserved in both the FPHC and AGWM Archives. In several of these, Simpson continued to ask for prayer that he might be able to return to China. Many churches in southern Gansu province today still claim the name of Assemblies of God, and books of Simpson's sermons can still be found and are read in these churches.

Leonard and Ada Bolton served among the Lisu of southwest China. Their son and daughter-in-law, Robert and Evelyn Bolton, served for many years among the Chinese in Taiwan. They, along with Robert's sister, Elsie Bolton Ezzo, have written extensively about their parents' work in China.

On one of Leonard's deputation cycles, he was invited to share his mission story at a convention in Lincoln Park, Michigan. A young pastor couple, Philip and Virginia Hogan, spent several hours following the service talking with Leonard about the needs of China. The Hogans later applied for a missionary appointment to work with the Chinese. Later, Philip Hogan served as Executive Director for the Assemblies of God world missions program from 1959-1989.

Many other missionaries could have been added to the narrative section of this paper, but space prohibits their inclusion. These six have been chosen because they provide a thorough sampling of both the methodology and ecclesiology of the group as a whole.

Analysis of the Narratives

Chapter 10 analyzes and summarizes the findings from the biographical narratives. As early as 1914, the AG had committed itself to the "greatest evangelism the world has ever seen."[14] The influence of writers such as Roland Allen and Alice Luce led to the adoption of Pauline methods as a missionary model. But what did the missiological writings of Allen[15] and Luce, among others, actually propose? Did the Assemblies of God missionaries in China follow the Allen/Luce model? In what ways did they deviate from that model and were there significant adaptations made contributing to the evolving AG missiological philosophy?

Summary

Beginning in 1949, foreign missionaries were expelled from China. Many people in the West questioned whether the church in China would be able to survive the anticipated persecution and oppression. The church in China not only survived but has thrived, growing and developing its own missionary passion.

Chapter 12 examines the challenges to the church in China today. Does the Pauline/Allen/Luce methodology employed by AG pre-1952 American missionaries in China apply to the modern Chinese church? The chapter also concludes with possible applications for the Chinese context. This project provides a descriptive foundation upon which future studies can build and gives some suggestions for such study.

This historical study describes men and women who, despite living in perilous times and a changing world, believed God had called them. They responded obediently, sacrificing a great deal in the process. They also responded to human needs with works of compassion. Some of them saw a great revival as a result of their obedience. Communities and people groups were changed.

---

[14]*General Council of the Assemblies of God Minutes*, Monday, November 23, 1914. This council was held at the Stone Church in Chicago.

[15]Unless otherwise noted, all references listed as Allen refer to Roland Allen.

Others saw little or no fruit from their labor, yet they forged ahead believing that by breaking up the spiritual ground and planting the seed of God's Word, they were preparing for the day when there would be a spiritual harvest.

These men and women proclaim, with the Apostle Paul, that they have fought a good fight, finished the race, and kept the faith (2 Tim 4:7). They have joined the cloud of witnesses eagerly watching current believers as they pick up the torch, endeavoring to serve God's purpose for their generation (Heb 12:1; cf. Acts 13:36).

Chapter Two

RELIGIOUS AND SOCIO-POLITICAL CONTEXT

Nestorian Christianity in the Tang Dynasty

Over the past 1,300 years, Christian missionaries have brought their message to China, predominantly in four separate movements. The first was a Nestorian missionary named Alopen, who came to China in CE 635. He arrived at an auspicious time, and the Tang emperor extended him a favorable reception. For the next two hundred years, Nestorian Christianity enjoyed the blessing of the royal court with the exception of Wu, the Empress, and Wuzong, the Emperor. Officials referred to it as "The Luminous Religion." Favor ended in CE 845 when Wuzong decided to expel all foreign religions from China in favor of indigenous Taoism. Although the primary target was the more established Buddhism, all religions were affected (Sunquist 2001, 139).[16] It took more than

---

[16]Both religious and economic reasons contributed to Wuzong's persecution. As to religion, he was a devout Taoist and pursued immortality elixirs, ironically resulting in his death at age thirty-three. Economic pressures on the government also contributed to the persecution. Buddhist monasteries controlled huge wealth and a large number of monasteries had become tax havens since people who declared themselves to be monks or nuns were tax-exempt. In 830 CE, over 700,000 men and women had declared themselves to be Buddhist monks/nuns. Almost all were well-educated, exempt from taxation, and dependent on donations from the community for their livelihood. This represented about 2 percent of the population. Wuzong declared that all Buddhist monks/nuns under the age of fifty had to leave the monasteries and resume other work. Three years later, he ordered all tax-exempt Buddhist monasteries to be closed. Later he did

four hundred years for Buddhism to return to its pre-Wuzong strength in the number of monks, nuns, and monasteries. If Buddhism was affected to that degree, one can only imagine the effect upon the small Nestorian church (Moffett 1998, 303-304).

Nestorianism slowly disappeared from the Chinese landscape as monks and priests were systematically secularized. Traces of its survival could be found among the minority ethnic groups of northwest China, although some scholars contend that they were slowly absorbed into the expanding Muslim community (Sunquist 2001, 139).[17]

Christianity Under the Mongols

Christianity's second entrance into China came under Mongol rule in the Yuan dynasty of the thirteenth and fourteenth centuries. Once again, the ruling dynasty, although predominantly shamanistic, displayed a tolerant attitude toward other faiths.

The Catholic Church sought a formal relationship with the Mongol court, sending two Franciscan representatives, John of Plano Carpini and William of Rubruck, to visit the Mongol capital.[18] In 1296, Kublai Khan sent letters to the Pope via the Polo brothers requesting that one hundred well-educated missionaries travel to China and teach the Christian faith. However, the Church fell well short of meeting that request. It fell upon John of Montecorvino to represent the Catholic faith in China. He built a church in the capital and, by 1305, reported six thousand converts. By the time of his death in 1328, he estimated that number had grown to over ten thousand (Sunquist 2001, 139).

---

allow a limited number to re-open (Burnett 2008, 147). Other religions were also affected by Wuzong's decrees, with monasteries/temples closed and priests/monks forced to return to lay life. Sacred books were burned at this time as well (Sunquist 2001, 139).

[17]See also Clark (1969), Moffett (1988), and Jenkins (2008).

[18]This could very well have been an example of "the enemy of my enemy is my friend" diplomacy. The Catholic Church was increasingly concerned about both the military power and religious influence of the Islamic world. If relationships were established with the Mongol military power, they could potentially be useful in negating the Muslim threat to Europe.

The fall of the Yuan dynasty brought the second collapse of Christianity in China. The church once again relied upon the favor of the imperial court, and in the case of the Mongols, the local Han Chinese viewed them as foreign oppressors. To the Chinese, Christianity appeared as a foreign religion supported by a foreign government (Moffett 1998, 474).

In *The Lost History of Christianity*, Philip Jenkins (2008, iii) traces what he calls "the thousand-year golden age of the church in the Middle East, Africa, and Asia—and how it died." Jenkins' thousand-year golden age covers the first two Christian movements in China. Jenkins attributed several reasons for the decline of Christianity during this period. Geographical distance from the sending organizations, combined with centuries of opposition and persecution, and the failure to effectively indigenize the faith—all played a role in Christianity's demise. Jenkins (2008, 321) states: "The key difference making for survival is rather how deep a church planted its roots in a particular community, and how far the religion became part of the air that ordinary people breathed."

Jenkins (2008, 253), however, cautions the observer to be careful in "describing a religion as extinct" because "churches end, but The Church goes on." In 1500, all outward appearances suggested that the Nestorian and Catholic attempts to plant Christianity in the Chinese soil of the Tang and Yuan dynasties had abysmally failed. However, the seeds planted still lay in the spiritual soil, awaiting God's opportune moment. One cannot speak authoritatively of what may happen years into the future. As Jenkins (2008, 255, 256) noted, "*Forever* can be a risky term and so can *extinction*." Nestorians planted, Catholics watered, and, ultimately, many churches benefited.

The Jesuits and the Rites Controversy

The coming of European powers to China in the sixteenth century coincided with the height of Chinese xenophobia. The Europeans desired trade but found a China that considered itself the center of the world.[19] Surrounding countries would send emissaries bringing gifts, which Chinese officials frequently viewed as tribute. China felt totally self-sufficient in all areas as well as culturally superior to outsiders. Any trade concessions were, from the Chinese point of view, examples of the emperor's mercy and charity.

At the same time that European countries sought to break into the China market, Jesuit missionaries pioneered the third attempt to plant Christianity in China. Although coming on Portuguese ships, the early Jesuits were primarily Italian and devoid of the intense nationalistic rivalry that had developed between Portugal and Spain.

Alessandro Valignano

The Portuguese had established a presence in Macau and Alessandro Valignano was the designated visitor to all the Jesuit missionaries in Asia. Therefore, he spent ten months in Macau studying conditions in China. In 1579, he cried out as he looked at the Chinese mainland, "Rock, rock, oh when wilt thou open, rock."[20]

Students of missionary methodology can profit from carefully studying the Jesuits' approach to China. Valignano played an influential role in the development of that methodology. His mission strategy called for a contextualized approach as well as the development of an indigenous priesthood. From the beginning, Jesuit missionaries were instructed that their initial priority was language learning.[21]

Valignano's vision for China received a frosty reception from other missionaries. Priests in Macau told him it was impossible to convert the Chinese, so they limited their work in the colony to

---

[19]The Chinese name for China is 中国, translated literally, it means Center Country or the Middle Kingdom.

[20]This quote is often attributed to Francis Xavier. Stephen Neill (1964, 139), however, says that it should be credited to Valignano.

[21]Valignano's ideas on indigeneity preceded those of Henry Venn, Rufus Anderson, Roland Allen, Alice Luce, and Melvin Hodges by two to three centuries.

the Portuguese and other foreigners. Valignano, however, was not easily discouraged.

The failure of previous attempts to evangelize China, Valignano concluded, came as a result of the methods adopted. He wrote that the successful evangelization of China would require innovative approaches. Valignano believed that the Chinese respect for education provided a way to present the gospel message to them. He was also convinced that presenting that message from the position of cultural and/or racial superiority would automatically result in the rejection of their message. He instructed all China Jesuit missionaries to learn to read, write, and speak Chinese as well as to become familiar with all aspects of Chinese culture (Ronan and Oh 1988, 33).

Similarly, the first two Jesuit missionaries to China, Michele Ruggieri and Matteo Ricci, felt that successful propagation of the gospel in China would require the missionaries to become Chinese. They proposed a plan to transform European Christianity into one more suited for a Chinese setting. This proved hard to explain to people in Europe and resulted in censorship of the early Jesuit letters due to prevailing European attitudes of racial and cultural superiority (Rientsra 1986, 8).

Matteo Ricci

Matteo Ricci (1552-1610) was well-suited to take advantage of Valignano's suggestions of adopting an educational approach. He was well-trained in mathematics and astronomy. Upon his arrival, he diligently studied the Chinese language and Confucian classics and became an expert in both areas. Slowly he won the respect of the Chinese literati and officials. He became convinced that the Chinese could become Christians without making a complete break with Confucianism (Latourette 1975, 939).

Ricci and Ruggieri began their work in China by attempting a Buddhist route into enculturation. They shaved their heads and adopted the attire of Buddhist monks. Two years of work saw several converts to Christianity as well as the dedication of a small church. However, Ricci soon came to believe that Confucianism provided a better bridge. Consequently, he switched from the clothing of Buddhist monks to the attire of a Confucian scholar. For Ricci, the switch provided a unique opportunity for evangelism. If the Chinese viewed Confucianism as a philosophy, then it would be possible for them to accept Christianity as a religion while maintaining their other traditional Confucian beliefs (Tucker 1983, 64).

Ricci realized that the Chinese viewed everything foreign with suspicion. He decided to do everything possible to make Christianity as "little foreign as possible" (Neill 1964, 140). Thus began the Jesuit journey toward cultural accommodation.

Ricci patiently invested time in language and culture learning and attempted to make the gospel Chinese. He received approval to live in the southeastern corner of China. Ricci's humility, combined with his commitment to proficiency in the Chinese language and incarnational living, resulted in his receiving permission to live in Beijing. Much can be learned from Ricci's formal request to the emperor, due to the insight into the way China saw itself in regard to the rest of the world.

> Li Ma-tou, your Majesty's servant, come from the Far West, addresses himself to your Majesty with respect, in order to offer gifts from his country. Your Majesty's servant comes from a far distant land which has never exchanged presents with the Middle Kingdom. Despite the distance, fame told me of the remarkable teaching and fine institutions with which the Imperial Court has endowed all its people. I desired to share these advantages and live out my life as one of your Majesty's subjects, hoping in return to be of some small use. If your Majesty does not reject an ignorant, incapable man, and allows me to exercise my paltry talent, my keenest desire is to employ it in the service of so great a prince (Neill 1966, 119, 120).

Ricci accompanied his request with several gifts, including two clocks, for the emperor. Maintaining and repairing these clocks, which was necessary four times a year, created Ricci's residency platform (Covell 1986, 42). Ricci remained in the capital for the next ten years, during which time he gradually formed the nucleus for a Chinese church and engaged in writing and translating materials.

Ricci's basic methodology could be summarized in four brief statements: (1) accommodate and adapt; (2) start evangelism with community influencers; (3) use all means, including science and technology, to create influence; and (4) be open and tolerant of Chinese morality and ritual practices (Bays 2012, 21, 22).

The Jesuit approach to ancestor veneration and the Confucian rites exemplified this methodology. During the sixteenth century, these rites were observed in three separate contexts. At the highest level, the emperor would perform the rites biannually accompanied by animal sacrifices to legitimize his rule and reinforce his claims to be the "son of Heaven." In this capacity, they served both a civil and political function. Opposing these ceremonies was considered a treasonous act (Lowe 2001, 39).

In a second context, regional and local magistrates conducted rites and ceremonies, making offerings to both Confucius and localized gods. Because of the association of Confucius with the literati, all successful candidates at civil service exams were expected to make obeisance to Confucius in the halls next to the examination centers. In addition, individuals appointed to government positions were expected to perform the rites, including sacrifices to Confucius, twice yearly. Twice a month, less elaborate ceremonies incorporating local gods into the rituals were performed. Opposing these ceremonies would alienate the local and regional civil and political leaders (Lowe 2001, 39).

At the lowest level, the Chinese populace venerated their ancestors daily while more extensive rituals were performed twice a month. Twice a year, people presented offerings at the grave sites of deceased ancestors. Funeral offerings were the most elaborate of all. "To oppose these rites would be to reject a central element of Chinese culture" (Lowe 2001, 39, 40).

Ricci was aware that he faced a seemingly insurmountable obstacle. If he opposed the rites, his mission would probably have few converts and would continue to operate without the favor of either the civil/political leaders or the local populace. However, to fully embrace the rites would place the Jesuit mission on dangerous grounds and open it to the accusation of compromising the Christian message.

Furthermore, Ricci argued that the Confucianist rituals of the sixteenth century (neo-Confucianism) differed from the original system celebrated in the times of Confucius. Ricci contended that Taoist and Buddhist influences during the Tang and Sung dynasties had corrupted the original ceremonies (Ronan and Oh 1988, 43-44).

The idea of one true God, Ricci argued, was not alien to the Chinese. He claimed that the Chinese classics left no trace of polytheism. However, Ricci neglected to call attention to other troubling facts that came out of the classical period:

> They recognized a Supreme Being as a personal being. The offering of sacrifices to this Supreme Being was reserved for the emperor, and ordinary citizens could not presume to arrogate this privilege for themselves. It is true that besides the Supreme Being the emperor offered sacrifices to the spirits of the mountains, rivers, and famous men and that the people were allowed and even urged to offer sacrifices to the tutelary spirits of their villages and individual families to their ancestors. But all these spirits were subordinated to the Supreme Being, so that the original religion of China before the advent of Taoism and Buddhism was monotheism (Ronan and Oh 1988, 42, 43).

Ricci and the other Jesuits did not deny that there were troubling aspects of the rites that did appear to be superstition and contrary to the Christian faith. However, they contended that Buddhist and Taoist additions could be eliminated, leaving a core that could be kept allowing Christianity to "perfect Confucianism" (Cary-Elwes 1957, 147, 148).

Ralph Covell (1986, 63) summarizes the Jesuits' adapted position. First, ancestral tablets for Christians could contain the same basic features as those used by non-Christians. However, the wording on the tablets would convey Christian messages. The center of the tablet was inscribed with the admonition to "worship the true Lord, creator of heaven, and earth, and all things, and show filial piety to ancestors and parents" (Covell, 1986, 63). Second, the right side of the text explained that the Heavenly Lord (天主) has created everything and has the authority to punish evil and reward good (Covell 1986, 63). Finally, the left side referenced departed parents:

> It is through father and mother that one receives his greatest favors from God. After death, whether they receive punishment or reward, they will not return home. Therefore, the filial son or kind grandson sets up a tablet or picture by no means that their spirits might dwell therein, but to serve as a reminder of his debt (Covell 1986, 63).

The Jesuits included certain "non-negotiables" that would be taught concerning the use of these "Christianized" tablets, the more important being: (1) no spirit money to be burned before the tablet, (2) food placed before the tablets provided no nourishment for the dead, (3) no prayers should be made to the dead, and (4) ceremonies honored the dead rather than worshipped the dead (Covell 1986, 63).

Ricci's attempts at accommodation indicate that the Jesuits only intended to tolerate the rites temporarily with the hope of recasting them in a biblical fashion. Also, the Jesuits did not impose their views on missionaries whose consciences would not allow them to support these methods. Keep in mind that without the Jesuit method, these other missionaries probably would not have been able to reside in China. In seeking to secure an open audience for the gospel message, Ricci adopted a pragmatic approach that accepted the Confucian rituals and ceremonies, hoping these would be purged by the cleansing elements of the biblical message (Ronan and Oh 1988, 47, 48).

The Coming of the New Orders and the Rites Controversy

For several years, the Jesuits were the only mission group in China, so this model had few problems. The papal order of 1585 opened China only to the Jesuits. However, everything changed in

1600, as the Franciscans and Dominicans also received approval for missions work in China (Latourette 1970b).[22]

The practices of the Jesuit converts horrified these newcomers, who felt that the Jesuits were condoning a semi-pagan Christianity and had compromised their faith to avoid persecution and to secure good standing with the civil authorities (Neill 1964, 163).

Biblical interpretation and missionary methodology, however, fail to adequately describe the whole picture. Internal church jealousies between the Jesuits, Dominicans, and Franciscans had already adversely influenced mission work in Japan. The national interests of France, Italy, and Portugal colored the viewpoints of missionaries from the respective countries. In China, the Jesuits had monopolized the Catholic missions work for many years, and now the incoming mendicant orders quickly found fault to confirm their already prejudiced views (Tucker 1983, 65).

In 1742, a papal bull by Benedict XIV, the pope, finally put the controversy to rest for the Catholics. The church rejected the Jesuit position. All further discussion and debate on the matter was forbidden. All missionaries in China were required to take an oath of submission to the decision. The oath closed with the statement, "I will never allow the Rites and Ceremonies of China . . . to be put into practice by these same Christians. . . . So may God help me and his Holy Apostles" (Luttio 1968, 302, 303).

Several years before Benedict's decree, however, Kangxi, the emperor, had resolved the China side of the issue. In December 1706, he decided that only those missionaries who agreed with the practices of Matteo Ricci would be permitted to remain in China. Kangxi's son, the Yongzheng emperor, made Christianity an illegal sect in 1724. The number of Catholic missionaries serving in China was greatly reduced by 1800, with only about twenty-five foreign priests remaining in the country. The decreasing number of foreign Catholic priests, however, led to an increase in the number of Chinese priests who arose to serve the Catholic constituency. In contrast to the previous Christian movements, the change in the

---

[22]Latourette's (1970b), Chapter XIV, "The Chinese Empire, Formosa, Tibet, and Korea," depicts the status of Christianity during this turbulent time (pp. 336-366).

imperial attitude toward Christianity did not result in the collapse of the Christian church, although it did lose its standing with the educated elite of China (Bays 2012, 30, 31). Christianity no longer enjoyed the favor of the court and was once again viewed as a foreign religion with foreign ties. Harassed by officials, it appealed primarily to those on society's periphery (Ross 1994, 198).[23]

One key observation stands out concerning this century-long controversy. The Catholic Church failed to see the importance of building an indigenous work in China that included self-theologizing. Theologians in Rome felt they were in a better position to make decisions on matters relating to the Chinese, as noted by Neill (1964, 165): "Roman practice, nearly as it was at Rome, was to be in every detail the law for the missions."[24] This policy became the standard for Roman Catholic practice for the next two hundred years. With the expulsion of so many foreign priests, the various Catholic groups in China were forced to plan for an increase in the number of Chinese clergy. With the absence of foreign management, churches came under local leadership (Bays 2012, 31).[25]

Protestants and the Rites Controversy

The debate on ancestral and Confucian rites was not confined to the Catholic Church. The controversy continued among Protestant missionaries beginning in the late nineteenth century and persisted into the twentieth century as a point of discussion in Protestant missionary conferences. W. A. P. Martin and Hudson

---

[23]Covell (1986, 64) writes that Kenneth Scott Latourette did not view the Rites Controversy as being harmful to the church. He argues that, even with the emperor's favor, there would have eventually been conflict between the Christian church and Chinese culture and a resultant persecution. Latourette also affirmed his conviction that the accommodation required to make Christianity acceptable to the average Chinese would have sacrificed its integrity and unique message.

[24]The Catholics were not the only ones plagued with hesitancy for releasing the Chinese church to self-theologize. Protestants have also faced the same challenge.

[25]The number of Catholic adherents remained the same from 1700 to 1800. A gain in the second half of the century offset the loss during the first half. By 1800, Chinese priests had risen to forty or fifty (Bays 2012, 31).

Taylor took opposite stances on the rites during the opening salvos of the Protestant chapter (Sunquist 2001, 20-21).

Similar divisions occurred in the Protestant debates. Those opposed were driven primarily by a concern for purity in doctrine and practice, not wanting to compromise the Christian message. Those who wished to be more culturally accommodating emphasized the obstacles to conversion posed by prohibitions concerning ancestral ceremonies (Lowe 2001, 47, 48).

In the conference of 1890, William Martin admitted that most Chinese believed that the spirits of the dead resided in the ancestral tablets. However, he argued for accommodation based on both pragmatic and moral grounds. Pragmatically, Martin argued that trying to end the rites is like trying to move a mountain. The rites rise out of the deeply rooted emphasis on filial piety. Morally and religiously, the rites promote and strengthen family ties and serve as a restraint against evil. They support a belief in the afterlife. Martin argued, rather than doing away with the rites they should be modified or reinterpreted with new Christian meanings (Lowe 2001, 47-48).

Many at the 1890 conference, including Hudson Taylor, strongly opposed Martin. H. Blodget presented a paper at the Shanghai meeting sharing the opposing viewpoint. Blodget argued that the Chinese classics show that ancestor veneration assumes an ongoing reciprocal relationship between the living and the spirits of the dead. He continued by saying that rather than showing respect and honor to the deceased ancestors, a belief in and fear of the spirits served as the motivation behind the rites. Blodget believed that underlying the rites was an implied belief in communication between the living and the dead. He urged that the only safe course of action was a complete and total severance from the "evil practice" (Lowe 2001, 49, 50).

Y. K. Yen, a Chinese participant in the conference, contended that Martin's view contained a fatal fallacy. Yen claimed that the association had become so hereditary among the Chinese that to prostrate and to make offerings brought to mind the feeling that the spirits were present, heard their prayers, accepted their gifts, and, in return, would care for them. In short, the spirits could do what Christians believe God can do for them. New forms to express reverence for ancestors needed to be adopted (Lowe 2001, 49-50).

Closing Thoughts on Ancestor Veneration

A close look at the entire Rites Controversy and the Jesuit methodology brings several questions to the surface. These questions force missiologists to join missionaries worldwide and throughout time who were forced to address such issues of eternal impact. How they answered these questions was influenced by what Chuck Lowe (2001, 52) calls "social location." Missionaries sympathetic to the rites were predominantly intellectuals who collaborated primarily with other intellectuals. Those opposed tended to work with the masses, who were generally less educated (Lowe 2001, 52).

There is no doubt that Ricci's attitude toward the rites was influenced by the Chinese literati. They declared that bowing to Confucius simply honored and respected him as a great teacher. Bowing did not imply any prayers for special blessings. It was a civil ritual and not a religious one (Ronan and Oh 1988, 46). Even the neo-Confucianists agreed. According to them, only Confucius' name and memory remained. The same could be said of all the ancestors. Their souls long ago disappeared into nothingness. Believing this, prayers to the ancestors were a useless exercise (Ronan and Oh 1988, 46, 47). Ricci was also greatly influenced by his target audience:

> The intention of the participants determined how the rites would be interpreted. Acts are not idolatrous, he reasoned, so long as they seek merely to honor the ancestors, without providing for their material needs in the afterlife or seeking their help to over-come obstacles in this life. . . . On these grounds, he considered it possible to be both Confucian and Christian; both to venerate ancestors and to worship God. (Lowe 2001, 41)

However, those working predominantly with the masses, especially in the countryside, observed a completely different interpretation of the rituals and ceremonies that led them to view any participation in them as idolatrous and a compromise of the gospel message.

Missionaries on both the Catholic and Protestant sides faced several questions that determined both their methodology and ecclesiology. The six American AG missionaries to be examined in ensuing chapters were also forced to address these and comparable questions as they worked out their missiological praxis:

- How does one effectively communicate the gospel without compromising the integrity of the message?
- How does one guard against syncretism?
- How important is cultural sensitivity in mission endeavors?
- To what extent should the missionary identify with his or her target audience?
- What emphasis should be given to the development of an indigenous theology?
- How does one work toward developing such a theology that remains faithful to biblical principles?[26]

---

[26]Paul Hiebert's (1987) "Principles of Critical Contextualization," as good as they are, probably would not have resolved this issue nor would Gailyn Van Rheenen's (2002) "Missional Helix." Most missionaries of this era viewed Western civilization as a goal to work toward. The very possibility of an open dialogue between Western missionaries and Chinese Christians was remote. In addition, the gap between the literati and the commoner was simply too great. Would open discussion of a biblical exegesis on related Scriptures have been possible? Would the Western missionaries have dominated the discussion? Exegesis of culture would have resulted in a vastly different point of view depending on social location New contextualized practices with new forms would have varied from place to place. Would this have been bad? Or would it have further widened the gap between the various factions? Even the willingness to consider such a dialogue as equal partners at the table might have provided interesting answers.

Chapter Three

RELIGIOUS AND SOCIAL CONTEXT: THE NINETEENTH CENTURY

Protestantism and the Nineteenth Century

As seen above, the expulsion of Catholic missionaries from China in the eighteenth century and the declaration that Christianity was a heterodox sect did not destroy the tender plant. By 1800, there were approximately 200,000 believers, and the number of Chinese priests was approaching fifty. With the coming of the nineteenth century, new forces brought new challenges. Robert Morrison's arrival in China in 1807 marked the beginning of a Protestant era. In addition, European powers, intent on trade, confronted a weakening dynasty. In China, the nineteenth century included wars, rebellions, imperialism, the growth of anti-foreign sentiment, and natural disasters. To understand the China awaiting pioneer AG missionaries of the next chapter, one must examine these historical events.

Robert Morrison

Robert Morrison's arrival in Macau in 1807 marked Christianity's fourth attempt to enter China. At twenty-one, Morrison was deeply moved by reading Christ's command to "go into all the world and preach the gospel" (Mark 16:15 NASB 2020). His reading of the Great Commission, combined with his awareness that millions of people outside his corner of the world had never heard the gospel, compelled him to ask the London Missionary Society to send him "where the difficulties were greatest, and most insurmountable" (Moffett 2005, 286).

Morrison's difficulties came from several fronts. First, the British East India Company refused him passage on British ships sailing for China. Morrison decided to travel to the United States. Once in New York, he booked a passage on an American ship bound for China. The ship owner asked him, "And so, Mr. Morrison, you really expect that you will make an impression on the idolatry of the great Chinese empire?" Morrison's well-known reply was, "No, Sir. I expect God will" (Moffett 2005, 287).

The second difficulty was establishing residency in China. Reacting to the Pope's attempt to dictate China's domestic policy on religious matters, in 1720, Emperor Kangxi decreed that missionaries could not reside in China. In 1793, Emperor Qianlong warned a British ambassador that "no propagation of the English religion in China would be permitted" (Moffett 2005, 287). The penalty for preaching the gospel was death. Consequently, Morrison spent the first two years wearing Chinese clothes, attempting to avoid attracting attention. Instead, he concentrated on learning Chinese. In 1809, Morrison's proficiency in speaking Chinese attracted the attention of the East India Company that hired him as a translator. This, however, only partially solved his residency difficulties. Even though he had become a legal resident, Morrison was restricted to operating in Guangzhou.[27] At that time, all foreigners in China were limited in their movements and closely watched. The government confined them to a small plot of land along the river in Guangzhou and they could only reside in that area during the prescribed trading season. When that was over, all foreigners were required to return to Macau (Bays 2012, 44, 45).[28]

---

[27]Canton.

[28]Jonathan Spence (1996) gives a good description of the restrictions placed on the Western traders in Guangzhou in his book, *God's Chinese Son*. The Chinese confined them to a small parcel of land by the river. Only 270 steps were required to traverse the allotted space from east to west. Going from north to south was even shorter. No women were allowed to be with them, those who were married had to leave their wives in Macau

Third, Chinese law forbade evangelism, and the East India Company would not permit their employees to engage in any activity that might jeopardize the company's prospects of making money. Consequently, Morrison used his time to translate the Bible and prepare a Chinese-English dictionary. From a twenty-first-century perspective, we applaud this strategic decision. Protestants of all denominations have underscored the necessity of every people group having the Bible in their language. For Morrison, work in this area was just as much a practical decision as a strategic choice (Bays 2012, 44, 45). In retrospect, the restrictions placed upon Morrison, instead of being a hindrance to the spread of Christianity, advanced the missionary cause with the translation of the Bible into Chinese.

When Robert Morrison died (1833), only ten Chinese Christians were identified as having converted to Christianity through his ministry. Nevertheless, during his twenty-five years of missionary service, he completed his Bible translation and organized an English-Chinese dictionary. These two accomplishments laid a foundation upon which other missionaries could build.

The Opium Wars and the Unequal Treaties

China's population more than doubled in the 100 years between 1700 and 1800, increasing from 150 million to over 300 million. By 1850, it had grown to 430 million (Jones and Kuhn 1978, 108-109). Cultivable land had not significantly increased, putting pressure on the country with so many more mouths to feed. When natural disasters hit the country, entire provinces were devastated. Millions became marginalized and the number of cheap laborers soared. Bandits roamed the countryside. The need to employ constantly growing numbers of workers discouraged mechanization and industrial development, resulting in China

during the trading season. Twice in 1830 a few husbands attempted to smuggle their wives into the foreign compound, but locals ferreted out their presence. Local officials threatened to close all foreign trade if the "foreign devil women" did not return to Macau (Spence 1996, 4).

falling even farther behind the European powers who were knocking at her door demanding entrance for trade. Chinese officials continued to maintain the old "Middle Kingdom" mindset where China occupied the world's central, most critical position. China's ruling class met the imperialistic onslaught of the West with both xenophobic and ethnocentric attitudes (J. Spence 1990; Fairbank 1992).

As China entered the nineteenth century, it was completely unprepared to meet the challenges of the new era. Stephen Neill (1966, 123) argues that, in many respects, China had retreated rather than advanced: "China knew nothing of the outside world and had no desire to learn." Stephen Platt (2018, xxvii) offers a contrasting view, stating that coastal officials and those interacting with the incoming foreigners knew that China had fallen far behind the West. However, they believed that if trade stabilized, conflict could be avoided.

Yet, several things remained obvious. The emperor and his leading officials, locked away in the imperial palace, retained the maintenance of domestic harmony as the top priority. They viewed change as an evil to be resisted at all costs. The inventive genius of Chinese minds from centuries prior had atrophied. A few discoveries were made. The emperor controlled all government decisions, and access to the emperor was tightly regulated. Corruption prevailed. With ever-increasing numbers of foreigners seeking entrance to China for trade, China could no longer hide its military weakness. Provincial governors raised armies on their own and paid for them as needed. The seeds of warlordism awaited the collapse of the Qing dynasty for the reaping of a bloody harvest. With no imperial army, China was incapable of resisting any attacks mounted from outside the country (Neill 1966, 122-123).

The Western powers that approached China desiring trade agreements found an unbending imperial order. The West expected to find China abiding by commonly accepted principles of international law and trade only to find irreconcilable and opposing viewpoints. China believed it was self-sufficient and in need of nothing. She continued to believe that the "barbarians" had nothing of value to exchange. The very word "treaty" ran against the Chinese worldview as that would imply equality and mutual obligations. The Chinese court could not accept such a concept (Neill 1966, 126-127). The tense relationships only needed a spark to accelerate the path to conflict.

Platt (2018, xxiii) states: "No event casts a longer shadow over China's modern history than the Opium War." The war itself, compared to the later Taiping Rebellion or the war with Japan the following century, was contained to relatively minor skirmishes. Nevertheless, the Chinese remember the war as the beginning of the "Century of Humiliation" when various foreign countries sought to carve up the country by bullying China's leaders to accept unequal treaties. Modern Chinese nationalism traces its birth to this time (Platt 2018, xxiii).

The Opium War placed the missionaries in a quandary. They naturally opposed the opium trade on moral grounds but also chafed under the restrictions of the Chinese regulations that prohibited them from traveling throughout China, limiting their evangelism opportunities. Elijah Bridgman, following the example of the early apostles who had responded to the Sanhedrin's threats by saying, "We must obey God rather than men" (Acts 5:29), expressed the feelings of many of the missionaries. "If laws are enacted requiring what is wrong, no one is bound to obey them," Bridgman declared (S. Miller 1974, 251). Some missionaries began taking illegal trips along the coast, distributing tracts, and preaching to the locals. Stevens and Medhurst, two early American missionaries, boasted of ignoring the Chinese authorities on one itinerary, even to the point of "disrupting schools and court proceedings to deliver their message of salvation" (S. Miller, 1974, 251). It is no surprise, then, that missionaries "resorted to legalistic justifications for the war that avoided the opium issue" (S. Miller 1974, 252), feeling that God was sovereignly overriding Chinese officialdom to open the doors for gospel proclamation.

The East India Company was heavily involved in the opium trade. Despite a surprisingly large amount of moral opposition to the ensuing Opium Wars in Britain and America, the company's business interest to forcefully open the gates of free trade won the day (Platt 2018, xxvi-xxvi). Still, bystanders were perplexed, to say the least, by this hypocritical stance. "It seemed paradoxical ... that a liberal British government that had just abolished slavery could

… fight a war to support drug dealers, or that proponents of free trade would align their interests with smugglers" (Platt 2018, xxv).

During the mid-1800s, on two occasions, Great Britain led several Western countries in the fight to open up the Chinese markets. These two "Opium Wars" resulted in the signing of what became known as the "Unequal Treaties." Because of their fluency in Chinese, missionaries were asked by their governments to assist with the translation and negotiation of those treaties. Naturally, these missionaries requested the inclusion of such terms as the opening of more cities where missionaries could live, approval for travel further inland, rights to buy property and build churches, and protection for their Chinese converts. Hearing of these agreements, Christians in the West rejoiced at the providential hand of God in arranging these favorable terms as part of the treaty settlements.[29]

In sharp contrast to the rejoicing in the West, the Chinese felt that foreign governments had humiliated China and imposed their will over China's domestic issues. Although opium had been used medicinally in China for centuries, the number of Chinese opium users increased dramatically beginning as early as the seventeenth century. In 1729, the Qing Dynasty prohibited the importation of opium. In the opening years of the nineteenth century, the smuggling of the drug through Macau had risen to 4,000 chests per annum.[30] By 1819, the opium trade boomed to the point where one agent stated: "Opium is like gold. I can sell it any time" (Wakeman 1978, 172). In less than twenty years, the value of imported opium into China was over $18 million, "making it the world's most valuable single trade commodity of the century (Wakeman 1978, 172). Millions of Chinese were addicted. One Chinese official wrote a letter to Queen Victoria in

---

[29]Several authors have written about the events outlined in the previous paragraphs. Stuart Creighton Miller's (1974) chapter entitled, "Ends and Means: Missionary Justification of Force in Nineteenth Century China," in *The Missionary Enterprise in China and America*; Stephen Platt (2018) in *Imperial Twilight: The Opium War and the End of China's Last Golden Age* gives a detailed account of the events leading up to the conflict as well as the aftermath. Fairbank (1992) and Spence (1990) remain standard reference works.

[30]One chest usually weighed 140 pounds.

protest requesting her intervention (Wakeman 1978, 191). While the number of drug addicts soared, China's trade deficit with the West impoverished the nation (Spence 1990, 149). The same boats that brought opium to China also brought missionaries, taking advantage of the new treaty terms. In some cases, while workers unloaded opium on one side of the boat, the missionaries were disembarking from the other.

Bridgman, among others, justified the war by claiming that Chinese laws violated the higher laws of God. Bridgman opined: "The agency in these great moments is human; the directing power divine. The high governor of all the nations has employed England to chastise and humble China. He may soon employ her to introduce the blessings of Christian civilization and free intercourse among her millions" (S. Miller 1974, 255).

The American medical missionary Peter Parker added his voice to the common missionary opinion that the war was the way for "the God of nations to open a highway for those who would preach the word" (S. Miller 1974, 254). The question remains as to whether the temporary gains from the treaties concluding the conflict were worth the heavy price exacted later when the fruits of Chinese nationalism ripened for harvest.

Post Opium War Years and the Unequal Treaties

The Opium Wars and unequal treaties aroused great animosity among the Chinese. It is easy to react in moral outrage to a war fought to force a weaker country to accept the importation of opium, which led to the addiction of millions as well as their impoverishment. Opium was not the actual cause but only the occasion of the war (Neill 1966, 130), and fault can be found on both sides.

The first Opium War (1839-1842) ended with the Treaty of Nanjing.[31] Neill claims that the term "unequal treaty" begs the question of how all treaties ending wars could be classified as "unequal." He takes exception to the term, claiming that compared

[31]Nanking is the older spelling of the city that is known as Nanjing today.

to other treaties of the time, it seemed "exceptionally mild," doing "little more than guaranteeing foreigners in China such rights as they enjoyed in almost every part of the world" (Neill 1966, 132, 133). Neill's chapter on colonialism in China holds a strong Western bias and portrays the Western interpretation of the conflict. Regardless of how justifiable the fighting may have been from Britain's point of view, China viewed it as a national embarrassment and humiliation. Even today, China remembers her victimization at the hands of international imperialists. This treaty was "dictated by barbarians on the sacred soil of China itself. The outrage was never forgotten or forgiven" (Neill 1966, 133).

The Treaty of Nanjing included the following major provisions:

- Five port cities (Guangzhou, Xiamen, Fuzhou, Ningbo, and Shanghai) were to be opened to allow foreign residence.
- The principle of extraterritoriality (exemption from local laws and/or jurisdictions) would be applied to all foreigners in China.[32]
- Hong Kong would be ceded to the British in perpetuity.
- Merchants who had experienced loss in the confiscation and destruction of their opium supplies would receive compensation (J. Spence 1990, 158-160).

The three decades preceding the first Opium War witnessed a degeneration of Chinese/Western relations. Foreign traders chafed under strict travel restrictions and limitations on their freedom. They were permitted to reside on a slight stretch of land along the river in Guangzhou, but only during the trading season. Not only were they restricted from traveling to other cities in China at other times, but they were also banned from entering the city of Guangzhou itself. Customs charges were levied on the whim of the local officials. Accusations and complaints against foreigners were taken up in Chinese courts of law, and no appeals were

---

[32]Extraterritoriality allowed all foreigners the right of protection by their consuls for acts committed in China as well as trial in their own consular courts rather than being judged by Chinese law.

allowed for foreigners. All terms of the Treaty of Nanjing reflect the dissatisfaction with Chinese restrictions enforced since the beginning of trade (Neill 1966, 127).

Missionaries suffered on two fronts. The same restrictions limiting the traders' activities also applied to them. Christianity was an outlawed religion. The closing years of the eighteenth century brought a countrywide search for foreign priests, the razing of churches, and the persecution of Chinese Christians (Moffett 2005, 132). When Morrison arrived in China, finding a teacher to learn the Chinese language proved difficult, since a Chinese teaching the language to a foreigner placed the teacher at risk of execution. Literature distribution in Guangzhou was forbidden. Missionaries caught propagating the Christian faith risked deportation. In addition, the agents and Chinese merchants responsible for their conduct risked imprisonment or worse (Covell 1986, 71).

On a second front, traders worried that the missionaries' activities might jeopardize their fragile position in doing business in China. As mentioned above, Morrison was forced to pursue mission work discretely when he arrived in Guangzhou. He earned a position with the East India Company through his skill in speaking the Chinese language. His value to the company outweighed the risk presented by his Christian faith.

The Second Opium War (1856-1860) concluded with the Treaties of Tianjin (1858) and Beijing (1860). Once again, China proved helpless in defending itself. The second war ended with two extremely embarrassing events, causing great loss of "face."[33] Lord Elgin, representing Great Britain, made a state entry into the Court of the Board of Ceremonies. Up to that point in time, no foreigner had ever set foot on this floor. Elgin came to dictate the terms that the Chinese must accept for their surrender. He also ordered the burning of the Summer Palace of the Imperial House (Neill 1966, 138).[34]

---

[33]"Face," in an honor/shame culture affects all social interaction. To "lose face" or to cause someone to "lose face" is one of the most grievous offenses.

[34]The destruction of the Summer Palace was in retaliation for the torture and death of several British officers. It was intended to embarrass and punish the Imperial family who were viewed as responsible for the British deaths. This event has not been forgotten,

Terms of the second set of treaties included the immediate opening of six additional port cities for foreign residence, allowance of foreigners to travel anywhere in China provided they carried appropriate documentation, agreement that the Christian religion would be tolerated, and profession and propagation of the Christian faith would be protected by law (J. Spence 1990, 180). Christianity had gained permission to legally exist in China—at the barrel of a gun. Another provision of the treaty, which had extensive ramifications, was protection for Chinese Christians. In effect, it removed Chinese Christians from the authority of Chinese law. Many Chinese abused this provision by professing conversion in order to secure the help of the missionary in legal cases (Silbey 2012, 43). Lord Elgin (Neill 1966, 140) cautioned the missionaries that "extending . . . special protection to Chinese converts would invite hypocritical professions of Christianity," but the missionaries discounted Elgin's warnings. Christians in the West, although not favoring war to achieve spiritual ends nor approving of the sale of opium to the Chinese, could not help but interpret the Western victory and ensuing treaty arrangements as being God's way of opening China to the gospel (Covell 1986, 82).

Nothing appeared to matter except achieving the goal of getting into China. Failure to realize what was happening may have doomed the modern missionary enterprise from the very beginning. No realistic alternatives may have existed for them; however, this was not the most significant issue. The key issue was a failure to see what this kind of forced entry did to them and their mission long term. This short-sighted thinking created many consequences for their message, the huge non-Christian society, and the few brave converts. From then until 1949, the gospel in China was proclaimed in the context of power (Covell 1986, 83).

After signing the treaties that ended the Second Opium War, it appeared missionaries had an open door for evangelizing China. They were permitted to travel anywhere, purchase

---

as evidenced by a comment I heard while visiting the rebuilt Summer Palace in Beijing a few years ago. A Chinese mother pointed at me and turning to her daughter, said, "His ancestors burned this place."

property, build churches, and preach openly. Even their converts enjoyed protection. No political obstacles hindered the work. Yet anti-foreign and anti-Christian sentiments were growing. It had become impossible to divorce Christian missionaries and imperialism in the hearts of most Chinese. One leading Chinese official summarized the thoughts of many Chinese people: "Take away your opium and your missionaries, and all will be well" (Silbey 2012, 40).

The anti-Christian missionary feelings, however, were not limited to the Chinese. Rutherford Alcock stated: "It would be decidedly for the peace of China if Christianity and its emissaries were, for the present at least, excluded altogether" (Neill 1966, 147). Although not directly hostile to the missionaries, the British government had to acknowledge that trouble in China arose primarily due to connection with the missionaries. The missionaries, rather than the traders, were more likely to venture farther inland and served as the "point on the edge of the spear" in relationships with the local Chinese" (Neill 1966, 147).[35]

Hong Xiuquan and the Taiping Rebellion

Too little attention has been given to the Chinese Civil War of the mid-nineteenth century. This war, known as the Taiping Rebellion, engulfed China from 1851 to 1864. According to Platt (2012, xxiii), this was "the most destructive war of the nineteenth century." It surpassed the devastation of the American Civil War by thirty times. Half of the provinces of China were affected, and

[35]In 1868, a major incident occurred involving James Hudson Taylor and the China Inland Mission (CIM). The whole purpose of the mission was to place missionaries in all the inland provinces of China. All CIM missionaries were expected to wear Chinese clothes and identify with the local people as much as possible. Also, they were to avoid asking European consular officials to intervene in matters on their behalf. However, circumstances sometimes became quite volatile. In August 1868, rioting broke out in Yangzhou. Although no one was killed, British gunboats sailed up the Yangtze River intent on protecting the British citizens. In the late fall of that same year, CIM missionaries were able to return to Yangzhou however only under British protection. Public opinion in Britain was divided, but some felt "the missionaries were a . . . great deal more trouble than they were worth" (Neill 1966, 144, 145).

more than twenty million Chinese died in the conflict (Platt 2012, xxiii). The effects of the Taiping Rebellion reverberated across nineteenth-century China. Some regretted the fact that Christianity had missed an opportunity for the conversion of a nation. Others bemoaned the reality that the opposition of scholars and officials to the Christian faith had solidified.

The Taiping Rebellion and the life of Hong Xiuquan are inseparably intertwined. Hong was born to a poor Hakka family in southern China in 1814, the fourth of five children (J. Spence 1990, 170). Like thousands of young scholars of his generation, he studied and applied for the Civil Service Examination, the passing of which would qualify him for a position in the government. This challenging ordeal required years of preparation and a thorough knowledge of the Confucian classics. Hong failed the exam three times (Covell 1986, 151). These failures were particularly humiliating for him (J. Spence 1990, 170).

During his 1836 attempt to pass the exam, a Protestant missionary[36] gave Hong a tract written by Liang A-fa, an early Chinese convert.[37] Hong's failures in the exams left him confined to bed due to emotional exhaustion. During that time, he had multiple visions in which he was carried to heaven and conversed with an old man who claimed to be the creator. Hong saw this old man reprimanding Confucius for not keeping China's masses from worshiping demons. The old man and another person in his vision,

---

[36]Jonathan Spence claims that the Protestant missionary was Edwin Stevens, who had recently arrived from the United States (Spence 1990, 170).

[37]The tract was "Good Words for Exhorting the Age" and consisted of nine chapters. Some of the main themes covered included: (1) Adam and Eve's sin and expulsion from the Garden of Eden, (2) Noah's ark and the flood that destroyed the earth, (3) the destruction of Sodom and Gomorrah as judgment for their sin, (4) the prophetic warnings of Isaiah and Jeremiah, (5) Psalm 19 and 33, (6) the Sermon on the Mount, and (7) some comments on the last chapter of Revelation.

Liang A-fa also shared his spiritual testimony. A missionary (according to Spence, it was possibly Edwin Stevens) gave Hong this tract before the civil service examination in Guangzhou (1836). Spence also speculates that a cursory glance at the tract's contents would have shown Hong God's judgment through both flood and fire upon the sinfulness of Noah's age as well as the citizens of Sodom and Gomorrah. He may also have noticed that the Chinese word for "flood" which had destroyed every living thing on earth, was the same as his family name Hong (洪). Hong failed the exam but kept the tract (Spence 1996, 17, 32-33).

referred to as the Elder Brother, gave him a sword and instructed him to kill all the demons (Covell 1986, 151).

Following his recovery in 1837, Hong spent the next six years teaching and preparing for another attempt to pass the exam. The tracts he had received earlier lay forgotten until he failed the exam again in 1843. Afterward, as he examined the tracts more closely, he began to interpret his earlier visions in light of what he was reading. Could the old man be Jehovah? Surely the Elder Brother was Jesus. Hearing that a Christian missionary, Issachar Roberts, lived in Guangzhou, he traveled to see him, seeking a better understanding of the Christian message. Communication between the two men was difficult because Hong's primary language was Hakka, while Roberts ministered in Cantonese. Hong intended to ask Roberts for baptism, but one of Roberts' national helpers facilitated the meeting. He became jealous of Hong's unusual experience and, wanting to protect his position in Roberts' camp, effectively sabotaged the meeting. He suggested that Hong, in addition to asking Roberts for baptism, also request financial help, knowing this would prejudice Roberts against Hong. Hong's interview with Roberts resulted in a refusal to baptize him because he was judged and found insufficiently mature in the faith (Moffett 2005, 298).[38]

Although Hong was not pleased with the outcome of the meeting, he was still convinced that his visions constituted a call of God to deal with unrighteous people, denounce the errors of both Confucianism and Buddhism, and overthrow the emperor in Beijing, establishing the Heavenly Kingdom. Hong organized an army and captured the city of Nanjing (1853), making it his New Jerusalem. He commanded everyone to worship God and destroy their idols. Presses printed the entirety of the New Testament and portions of the Old (Moffett 2005, 298).

Opinions among the Christian community regarding the Taiping Rebellion were divided. Some thought this could be God's way of converting the entire nation. Hong declared that clearing the land of idolatry and leading the Chinese to believe

---

[38]Also, see Covell (1986), 152.

and accept Jesus was his life mission. The hope created by such a declaration soon gave way to concerns about the odd teachings of the Taipings. Hong proclaimed himself as Jesus' younger brother[39] and this report dampened the enthusiasm of those who had been inclined to support the rebellion. Taiping excesses in other areas also caused concern. Hong's followers were to destroy all vestiges of idolatry. "Kill the fiends!" became their battle cry (Covell 1986, 150).

In addition, excessive disciplinary measures were stipulated for followers who did not meet Hong's strict requirements. For instance, he commanded that they must memorize the Ten Commandments; if they failed to do so within three weeks, "cut off their heads." If they are noisy during worship, "cut off their heads." If any are caught in adultery, "cut off their heads." If any smoke tobacco or fail to attend the preaching service, on the first violation, the punishment would be 100 lashes, on the second, 1,000 lashes, and on the third, "cut off their heads" (Moffett 2005, 299).

It was not until the mid-1860s that loyalists to the emperor finally defeated the Taiping rebels. The Taipings' unsuccessful rebellion owes much to its failure to enlist the support of both indigenous anti-Qing dynasty societies[40] and the inability to gain the foreign community's acceptance. The treaties of 1858 and 1860 resulted in Qing concessions that favored the Western powers. These countries knew what they had received from the Qing, but there was no guarantee that the Taipings would honor these agreements.

Platt has elaborated on another related reason as to why the British decided to aid the Qing officials in suppressing the rebellion. The Taiping Rebellion and the American Civil War overlapped from 1861-1864. Both the United States and China served as two of Britain's primary economic markets. Fearing the loss of both

---

[39]Jonathan Spence's (1995) book, *God's Chinese Son*, provides a thorough description of the Taiping Rebellion.

[40]A number of these groups were unwilling to join the Taipings due to their stance on idol worship as well as their perception of the Taipings' move to start a completely new dynasty rather than to restore the previous Ming rule.

markets, Britain chose to intervene in China, while remaining relatively neutral in the American conflict (Platt 2012, xxiv).

Opinions about the Taipings divided the missionary community. Those who viewed the movement favorably were led by W. A. P. Martin[41] who defended the Taipings against charges of unbiblical teachings by asking, "When has Christianity in its incipient stages not presented the appearance of being spurious? The process with both nations and individuals is purgative. Was not the religion of the Middle Ages exceedingly crude and imperfect? And yet light was made to shine out of darkness" (Covell 1986, 175). James Legge (1854, 223), favorably focused on three pillars of the Taiping faith: (1) their stand against idolatry, (2) their desire to serve the one true God, and (3) a belief in the Bible (Covell 1986, 175).

Missionaries who, at least temporarily, supported Hong and his followers saw this as an example of a people movement that sought to make the gospel Chinese. Even though many of their beliefs were substandard still they believed in God, the Bible, Christ, and the atonement, and all of these served as suitable starting points. Covell questions that perhaps all the Taipings needed were "missionaries to make longer commitments to the movement" (Covell 1986, 180).

However, the deeper issue was how Chinese officialdom viewed the rebellion and its future effect on the way the Chinese government viewed Christianity. This remains the critical question in all China-Christian church relationships. How does

---

[41]Martin was an American Presbyterian missionary in China from 1850-1916. He served as an interpreter during the negotiations on the Treaty of Tianjin (1858). He presented a controversial paper on the issue of Chinese ancestral rites during the 1890 Missionary Conference in Shanghai where he contended that kneeling and bowing before ancestors were not idolatrous acts. His evangelistic strategy called for mass conversions and the baptism of new converts as soon as possible after they decided to follow Jesus, regardless of how much they understood Christian doctrine. Missionaries should seek the conversion of people of influence as that could lead to many conversions and the baptisms of large groups of people at one time. Martin also strove to gain support from Western nations for the Taiping movement, believing that they should not be expected to have "mature" beliefs at the "beginning" of their spiritual journey. Solid teaching would correct the erroneous beliefs (Sunquist 2001). Ralph Covell's (1978) book, *W. A. P. Martin, Pioneer of Progress in China*, provides a biography of Martin's life and work.

each perceive the other? Daniel Bays (2012, 61) believes that the perceptions of Christianity by the Chinese government and the Confucian elite were significantly influenced by the Taiping Rebellion for decades past the actual event.

The ensuing four decades (1860-1902) witnessed the intensification of violence against both missionaries and Christians. Why was there such opposition to Christianity? First, in reviewing over one thousand years of Chinese history, the relationship between the state and religion had remained the same. That relationship can be succinctly expressed as 'loyalty to the emperor trumps loyalty to all others' (Kindopp and Hamrin 2004). Civic loyalty outweighs religious loyalty. The Chinese imperial system and its attitude toward religion displayed similarities to what the Early Church faced during the time of the Roman Empire. Any religion would be tolerated by the government if it were not viewed as a threat to the state. In the Roman Empire, toleration existed as long as emperor worship continued. In the Chinese imperial system, as long as religion could be monitored and controlled and loyalty to that religion was not viewed as taking precedence over loyalty to the state, then religious freedom existed.[42] The signing of the unequal treaties brought attention to Christianity by "giving it a unique immunity from the Chinese state, a special protected status that no other religion had" (Kindopp and Hamrin 2004, 29). Chinese Christians also received protection under these treaties, in effect removing them from the "full authority and jurisdiction of their own government" (Kindopp and Hamrin 2004, 29).

The second major opposing force was the Confucian elite. Although Western missionaries viewed the Taipings as being a heretical cult, the elite classes of China did not share that view. The Taipings claimed to be Christians, and the educated elite accepted

---

[42]Jason Kindopp and Carol Lee Hamrin (2004) edited a book entitled, *God and Caesar in China: Policy Implications of Church-State Tensions.* The very title invites the comparison between the Roman Empire and the Chinese imperial system. Although most contributors focus attention on church-state relations in modern-day China, Daniel Bays' (2004) chapter entitled, "A Tradition of State Dominance," explores the historical background. I have also drafted an unpublished paper entitled, "Challenges of Accommodation in an Imperial System: Applications from Revelation 2 for the Chinese Christian Community," which also addresses this issue.

that assertion. It confirmed their suspicions of Christianity as a subversive sect intent on provoking rebellion (Kindopp and Hamrin 2004, 30).

Missionaries threatened the *status quo*. The extraterritoriality clauses in the treaties provided them with an exemption from Chinese law. They had access to government officials. Life in local communities was disrupted. "Rice Christians"[43] would claim that their acceptance of Christ protected them from lawsuits and, in some cases, exempted them from financial obligations at village festivals.[44]

The government viewed Christianity as a threat to its power. Christians threatened the elites' position and status, while the commoners saw them as disrupting community harmony. A sense of powerlessness enveloped all Chinese people, as this "foreign sect" had been given special protection by the new treaties that were forced upon China. Christianity was now irrevocably linked with Western imperialism (Kindopp and Hamrin 2004, 30).[45] The seeds of anti-foreignism had been planted and grew rapidly.

Anti-Foreignism and the Boxer Rebellion

A summary of the nineteenth century notes that various people came to China. Traders came to make money. Diplomats came to gain concessions and privileges. Soldiers came to enforce

[43]"Rice Christians" was a term used to describe Chinese who professed to be Christians in order to enjoy the material benefits that came with their association with the missionaries and the church.

[44]For example, when all members of the community were expected to make contributions for special festivities in honor of local gods, Christians would claim that they were not required to pay because it violated their spiritual beliefs. The Christians' failure to contribute increased the financial load for other members of the community. From the viewpoint of the community, Christianity caused disruption and disunity. In one case, however, the local official rejected the claim of one such "rice Christian" by noting that he still smoked and drank and did not display a Christian lifestyle. He was forced to "pay up."

[45]This linkage comes through as one reads all the documents related to the Three-Self Patriotic Movement and current government regulations governing freedom of religious belief in China. Repeatedly these documents reference that the Chinese church must be independent of all foreign influence.

the agreements. All of these came to take something or gain from the exchange. Cohen (1978, 543) makes an interesting observation: "Alone among foreigners, Christian missionaries came not to take but to give . . . to serve the interests of the Chinese." In that case, "why was it the missionary who inspired the greatest fear and hatred" (Cohen 1978, 543)? He contends that the missionaries' intolerance of Chinese culture combined with an insistence on the Chinese re-ordering their way of life to accommodate the Christian message provoked the opposition (Cohen 1978, 543). Perhaps more accommodating methods could have been adopted. Nevertheless, the key issue remained—Christianity's claim that "Jesus is Lord" contrasted with the state's demands for absolute loyalty.

By the latter half of the nineteenth century, an impartial observer would have to admit that the Qing dynasty was failing. Called by some 'the Sick Man in Asia' China had been mired in the past. Many young intellectuals called for significant reforms while those already positioned in power resisted any change in the *status quo.*[46] Japan's victory over China in 1895 humiliated the country. The Chinese had considered the Japanese to be inferior to the Middle Kingdom in every way. The Japanese victory completed a long series of Chinese defeats on the international scene in the 1800s (Fenby 2008, 3-16).

Meanwhile, domestically, infrastructure was decaying while opponents of change feared that modernization would displace millions of manual laborers. Peasants, overburdened by taxation and the "squeeze" exacted by local officials, struggled to survive (Fenby 2008).

---

[46]Fairbank (1986, 134) reports a conversation between K'ang Yu-wei, one of the main proponents of reform, and a more conservative group of high officials in 1898. The conservative stance was: "The institutions inherited from our ancestors cannot be changed." K'ang replied, "We cannot preserve the realm of the ancestors. What is the use of their institutions?" In separate conversations, K'ang is reported to have said, "The governmental system has made China weak and will ruin her. . . . China will soon perish." In an audience with the emperor, he cautioned against the folly of relying on the high officials for reform. "It will be like climbing a tree to seek for fish."

A deterioration of law and order contributed to an increase in banditry. Opium smoking continued to spread through both urban centers and the rural countryside. Domestic crops that could have been used to feed the populace were replaced by the growing of poppies that competed with the British opium imports (Fenby 2008).

Confucian tradition undergirded the imperial system, emphasizing filial piety and loyalty to the state. Yet, the system had consistently called for benevolent leadership that cared for the welfare of its citizens. As the twentieth century approached, the Mandate of Heaven would soon be revoked.[47] Those changes and the transition years would provide Christian missionaries with a brief window of opportunity to prepare the Chinese church for the storm brewing on China's horizon (Fenby 2008).

The last years of the nineteenth century culminated with a series of natural disasters accentuating the growing domestic dissatisfaction. Foreigners in China became the scapegoats for all that was bad. Missionaries scattered throughout China were easily visible and targeted as one of the reasons behind China's ills. For decades, missionaries were drawn to the country's hinterlands in a desire to fulfill Christ's Great Commission. When the Boxer Rebellion began, these missionaries withstood the worst of the attack.

The Boxers became a popular movement in northern China at the close of the century. They sought to harmonize mind and body for combat using Taoist practices and other magical rituals. After these rituals, the Boxers would go into a trance, foam at the mouth, and arise prepared for battle. Supposedly, spirits now possessed their bodies, making them impervious to foreign bullets or swords (Esherick 1987). Economic and political conditions aided Boxer popularity. The flooding of the Yellow River had brought widespread famine to Shandong province. Plans for a new railroad threatened the livelihood of carters and bargemen (Fairbank and Reischaeuer 1989, 376-377).

---

[47]Changes in dynastic rule were attributed to the imperial family's loss of Heaven's Mandate to rule.

The Empress Dowager Cixi held the real power behind the throne. Favoring the more conservative elements in her court, she decided to support the Boxers to deal with the foreigners and restore China's honor. The rebellion combined both anti-foreign and anti-Christian sentiments. Rumors spread that Christians were responsible for the natural disasters in northern China (Bays 2012, 85).

A couple of wall posters circulating in northern China summarized the Boxer propaganda:

No rain comes from Heaven.
The earth is parched and dry.
And all because the churches
Have bottled up the sky (Fenby 2008, 82).

Pull down the telegraph lines!
Quickly! Hurry up! Smash them . . .
When at last all the Foreign Devils
Are expelled to the very last man,
The Great Qing, united, together,
Will bring peace to this our land (Fenby 2008, 79).

On June 24, 1900, Cixi decreed that all foreigners should be killed. With this encouragement, Boxer gangs moved throughout northern China, killing all foreigners they could find. However, foreigners were not the only ones to fill the cup of the Boxers' wrath. Chinese Christians were slaughtered by the thousands. When the dust settled, about 250 foreigners, almost all of whom were missionaries, had died. But approximately 30,000 Chinese Christians has also been killed (Bays 2012, 85).

The casualty list could have been greater. Some provincial governors refused to publish Cixi's orders. While missionaries and Christians in Shanxi province suffered significant losses,[48]

---

[48]Shanxi province became known as "The Martyr Province," and Yu Xian, its governor, as "The Butcher of Shanxi." On July 9, 1900, forty-six missionaries were herded into the governor's courtyard to be executed. Hattaway (2007, 226) tells the story of one 13-year-old girl's testimony before the governor that day: "Why are you planning to kill us? Haven't our doctors come from far-off lands to give their lives to your people?

neighboring Shaanxi[49] and Gansu provinces enjoyed the protection of their respective provincial governors. Farther south in Nanjing, two telegraph officers changed the empress's words from "Kill all the Christians" to "Protect the Christians" (Hattaway 2007, 114).

Paul Hattaway's book, *China's Book of Martyrs*, takes nearly 600 pages to discuss the martyrs of the past 1,200 years of China's history. One-third of the book covers the martyrs of the two years of the Boxer Rebellion (Hattaway 2007). Samuel Moffett (2005, 487) reports that the number of Protestant martyrs during the Boxer Rebellion exceeded the total number of Protestant martyrs during all previous decades of Christianity's existence in China.

The tremendous loss of 30,000 Christian lives, however, permanently put to rest the thought that Christianity was only a foreign religion. The willingness of Chinese people to lay down their lives for their faith proved that Christianity was much more than a Western religion and that the faith was planted deeply in China's soil.

At the start of the twentieth century, China anticipated monumental changes and challenges for the country. The Qing dynasty was on the verge of collapse. Republican China would struggle to survive. Ultimately, China succumbed to political turmoil. Warlords gave way as the Nationalists and the Communists fought for control of the country. Young people became disillusioned with China's role in the world and lamented their country's weakness. Nationalism began to extend its influence across the country. Famines and displaced refugees left millions struggling to survive. The Japanese replaced the Western powers in

---

Many with hopeless diseases have been healed; some who were blind have received their sight, and health and happiness have been brought into thousands of your homes because of what our doctors have done. Is it because of this good that you are going to kill us? Governor, you talk a lot about filial piety. It is your claim, is it not, that among the hundred virtues filial piety takes the highest place? But you have hundreds of young men in the province who are opium sots and gamblers. Can they exercise filial piety? Can they love their parents and obey their will? Our missionaries have come from foreign lands and have preached Jesus to them, and He has saved them and has given them power to live rightly and to love and obey their parents. Is it then, perhaps, because of this good that has been done that we are to be killed?"

[49]Shanxi and Shaanxi provinces are separate provinces.

their imperialist push into the country. In 1949, the Communists finally claimed victory and announced to the world that "China had stood up" (Brown 1983, 59).

Despite the country's upheaval, God was moving. New groups joined traditional missionary societies. Christian and Missionary Alliance missionaries entered China as early as the last decades of the nineteenth century with a fourfold emphasis: proclaim Christ the Savior, Christ the Sanctifier, Christ the Healer, and Christ the Soon-Coming King (Nienkirchen 1992, 3-25). They were later joined by those who claimed an apostolic experience that looked back to an Acts 2 style baptism in the Holy Spirit that would propel them into the future with empowerment to proclaim the gospel with signs following.

The Communist government that assumed power in 1949 became one of the greatest challenges for the Christian Church. An atheistic regime tightened its control over all religions, confiscating Bibles, imprisoning pastors, and closing churches. By God's grace, that period was preceded by the golden age of Christian missions in China (1900-1925).

The Assemblies of God was one of the new groups to join the societies already working in China. Born in the Pentecostal fires of the 1906 Azusa Street outpouring and officially organized in 1914 in Hot Springs, Arkansas, these new missionaries entered China with an eschatological urgency, expecting the second coming of Jesus Christ at any moment. Many missionaries, based on their interpretation of Matt 24:14, felt that their obedience to the Great Commission could hasten the coming of the Lord.[50] All AG missionaries expected an empowerment of the Holy Spirit with evidence of signs following.[51]

---

[50]"And this gospel of the kingdom will be proclaimed throughout the whole world as a testimony to all nations, and then the end will come" (Matt 24:14).

[51]"But you will receive power when the Holy Spirit has come upon you, and you will be my witnesses . . ." (Acts 1:8). "And these signs will accompany those who believe: in my name they will cast out demons; they will speak in new tongues; they will pick up serpents with their hands; and if they drink any deadly poison, it will not hurt them; they will lay their hands on the sick, and they will recover" (Mark 16:17-18).

The next chapters contain brief biographical sketches of six of these Assemblies of God missionaries to China, whose lives and ministries summarize the methodology and ecclesiology of the entire group. They will focus on how the work of these missionaries during the first half of the twentieth century helped establish the Chinese Church.

Chapter Four

HAROLD ARMSTRONG BAKER: TO THE LEAST OF THESE

Early Life and Preparation

In his autobiography, *Under His Wings,* H. A. Baker (2008a) frequently alludes to the lessons he learned growing up on a farm in Ohio. At the age of ten, his father assigned him the job of plowing the family fields. Grasping the plow handles that came up to his shoulders, he resolved not to turn loose. From early morning until sunset, young Baker plowed. On several occasions, to complete the job, he continued plowing past the time when most of the neighbors had already quit for the day. This "never let go" and "finish the job" mentality followed him throughout his life (H. Baker 2008a, 21).[52]

In reminiscing about his childhood on the farm, Baker outlined the lessons he learned. First, tackle the impossible. A child of ten would not normally plow a ten-acre stone-filled field. Second, expect bumps and rough places. The plow frequently struck hidden rocks that would drag him along for several feet. Third, hang on. Once you take hold, do not turn loose. Do not quit. Do not give

[52]Baker was a prolific writer. However, most of his books have little or no publishing data or copyright dates. The above autobiography, *Under His Wings*, is listed as the 2008a Iris Edition. Iris Ministries is a ministry of Baker's grandson and wife, Roland and Heidi Baker.

up. Fourth, expect the greatest victories and accomplishments to come in the last hour of the day. Everyone else may have turned in for the night, but perseverance brings victory. Finally, finish the job. Do not aim for anything less than 100 percent. Love God with *all* your heart and *all* your strength. Ninety-nine percent is not good enough (H. A. Baker 2008a, 23-24). Years later, before being expelled from China, and after having walked almost 20,000 miles over the mountains and valleys of southwest China, H. A. Baker (2008a, 21) reminisced how his all-day-long walks plowing a ten-acre field had prepared him for his missionary work.

Following high school, Baker enrolled at Ohio's Hiram College. He stayed busy with student activities that included serving as president of a Student Volunteer Movement chapter, leading the Young Men's Christian Association branch at the college, participating in debate competitions, acting in the school play, singing in the church choir on Sundays, joining in college athletics programs, and presidency of the school's literary society. Despite all these activities, H. A. Baker (2008a, 29-45) was able to keep his academics above the 90 percent bar and earn academic scholarships. He graduated as one of the top students of his class. Baker stands out as an exception to many early Pentecostals who considered academic attainment and spiritual anointing to be incompatible (McGee 2004, 95).

H. A. Baker (2008a, 40) was instrumental in choosing his class motto: "*Perseverantia Omnia Vincit* (perseverance overcomes all things)." Lessons from his early childhood on the farm, the discipline and time management required for both his academic studies and extra-curricular activities, and his summer work as a door-to-door salesman earning money for college tuition, all drilled deep into his heart the importance of staying with the task and plowing until the job was done.

During his senior year, he entered an essay writing contest to fulfill the requirements for that year's scholarship application. He chose to write about the change in mission philosophy in India. He explored the history and results of transitioning from an evangelistic focus to a strategy emphasizing education (H. Baker 2008a, 55).

Having proven himself as a successful debater, Baker began to sense that he should use his speaking ability to preach. As he considered the question of where to preach, he felt that preaching at the place of greatest need would honor God most. He described his conclusion by saying, "Going to the foreign mission field was not a matter of sentiment. It was a matter of common sense directed by wisdom from the Lord" (H. Baker 2008a, 40).

Baker married Josephine Witherspoon, a college classmate, in 1909. Both felt called to missionary service in Tibet. They began their preparation by accepting a pastorate in Buffalo where they served for two years (McGee 2004, 97).

First Term in Tibet

The Disciples of Christ commissioned the Bakers for their first term of missionary service. They spent five of the seven years of their first term on the Chinese-Tibetan border. The cultural adjustment proved difficult. Normal response time for a letter sent to the United States was one year. In their Tibetan post, very few people understood either English or Chinese. Baker found that the only people for Mandarin conversations were Chinese merchants, Chinese soldiers, or a few children. H. A. Baker (2008a, 110) described those early days on the Tibetan border as "lost in stagnant inactivity."

Their initial residence was an upstairs floor shared with a Tibetan family. Entrance to their home required passage through a manure-filled downstairs area swarming with flies among the cows and yak. A brief time later, when they could find a more suitable place to live, their cultural adjustment became easier. The Bakers thrived in their new location where they were able to experience the beauty of God's creation through flowers, grass, and trees. Their new home was next to three walnut trees with the possibility of growing some of their fruit, which greatly contributed to their cultural acclimation (H. Baker 2008a, 110). Service during this first term, however, cost the Bakers dearly. Two graves for a son and a daughter on the Tibetan border testify to the price they paid to share the gospel message (H. Baker 2008a, 112-121).

This first term exposed them to teaching about the baptism of the Holy Spirit. Baker had embarked on a six-month journey through the entirety of Yunnan province to meet new missionaries. Travel one-way required two months. Then there was a wait of two additional months for the recruits to arrive, and another two months going back to their station. During this trip, Baker met people who had received the baptism of the Holy Spirit and spoke in tongues. Baker described them as people who "had much of what I had [in] a smaller amount." He spent the return trip to his station reading a book that explained the scriptural basis for the Pentecostal experience. Baker became convinced of the reality of Spirit baptism and speaking in tongues (H. Baker 2008a, 121).

Following their first term, the Bakers returned to the United States for furlough. They resigned from their mission organization and temporarily went into business. Throughout his lifetime, Baker expressed a preference for operating independently of any organizational control. He commented that interpersonal relationships frequently troubled mission organizations, and his opinion was "that wherever it can be done, missionaries had better work independently, each family in full control of its own work" (H. Baker 2008a, 108).[53] But even though Baker refrained from close partnerships with other missionaries, remaining an independent missionary for most of his career, he had no qualms or reservations about working with national or tribal workers. Training of national workers became a key component of Baker's mission strategy.[54]

---

[53]Baker began his missionary ministry with the Disciples of Christ. After resigning and a period in the United States working in business, he and Josephine reapplied for a mission appointment with the China Inland Mission (CIM). They were accepted although Baker made it clear in his autobiography that he disagreed with the CIM's policy concerning children's education. The CIM had a school set up in northeastern China and required all missionary children six years of age and above to attend that school. The Bakers did not wish to send their son, James, away from home. This problem was resolved when both H. A. and Josephine received the baptism of the Holy Spirit and spoke in tongues. This led to their resignation from the CIM and their preparation to return to China as independent Pentecostal missionaries.

[54]The question must be asked as to whether Baker was guilty of the paternalism that so dominated much of the mission work of this time, especially since the sources of information on Baker are primarily from his personal writings.

Personal Pentecost

The Bakers successfully completed their first term of missionary service. However, upon returning to the United States, they resigned their missionary appointment and credentials with the Disciples of Christ. Finding secular employment, they utilized this time to take care of several personal family matters (McGee 2004, 97).

Baker's spiritual search weighed heavily upon his heart during this season. He described this period as a journey through a spiritual wilderness. Despite the spiritual low, Baker hungered deeply to know more about the things of God and, particularly, about the ministry of the Holy Spirit. Poring over books by F. B. Myers, Andrew Murray, and R. A. Torrey, among others, he would study the Scripture references on the Holy Spirit repeatedly. Initially, he resisted the thought of going to the "tongues people" themselves for instruction. He wanted to search things out for himself. The crucial question for H. A. Baker (2008a, 158) concerned the question of speaking in tongues as evidence for Spirit baptism. Was this necessary for all or available only to some?

During this time of searching for direction, H. A. Baker (2008a, 160) received a short letter from an old China missionary friend with the postscript: "Now that you are free and endeavoring to follow the Bible, why do you not seek the baptism of the Holy Spirit as on the day of Pentecost. You will never regret it. I never did."[55]

Having also resisted the thought of attending a Pentecostal meeting, Baker later suggested to his wife, Josephine, that they seek out a group and request the Pentecostals to pray for them as they committed themselves to seeking the baptism of the Holy Spirit—regardless of consequences. The Pentecostals were the specialists. Who would know better than they about this subject? (H. Baker [2008a], 160).

---

[55]Even though Baker, at this point in his autobiography, does not reveal the identity of this missionary friend, it appears from other references that it was Allan Swift, who had earlier experienced Pentecost and had ties with the Pentecostal Missionary Union.

Baker had reconciled himself to seeking the baptism of the Holy Spirit with the accompanying evidence of tongues speech, or he would never return to China. Even after coming to this decision, it was almost three years before he received that baptism and spoke in tongues. Toward the end of those three years, once again desperate, he finally said to God:

> I have been for almost three years seeking you but could not find you as I hoped. I've stopped hunting. Now you hunt me. . . . You know, Lord, that I am a candidate for the fullness of the baptism of the Holy Spirit, for I have put in my application these hundreds of times. Now, Lord, you hunt me. You know where I will be at any particular day or night (H. Baker [2008a?], 166).

Then one day, on a street in Warren, Ohio, on their way to a church meeting, Baker received the infilling of the Spirit, speaking in tongues.[56] Two days later, Josephine received her baptism while alone in their home (H. Baker [2008a?], 167-170).

After receiving their Pentecostal experience, the Bakers felt they should return to China as missionaries but did not know how they would be able to do this without organizational affiliation. Baker's earlier experiences with the Disciples of Christ had left him skeptical of joining any organization where he would be subject to their regulations.

Allan Swift, a missionary with the Pentecostal Missionary Union, invited the Bakers to work with him in China. A $1,000 offering from a Pentecostal congregation provided the needed funding. Within two months of receiving the baptism of the Holy Spirit, they were on their way back to China as independent missionaries (McGee 2004, 97).

---

[56]Baker was stopped on the street twice and asked if he needed help. He received some rather strange looks when he responded by saying he had been praying for the Spirit baptism and was now receiving it. He was finally able to reach the church gathering where he remained until almost two in the morning, speaking in tongues.

The Adullam Mission

The Bakers' ministry in China centered on two primary works. First, they opened an orphanage that became famous because of a revival among the boys there in the 1930s. Many of the boys in the orphanage received visions of heaven and hell. Baker's book, *Visions Beyond the Veil*, documented these events. It was published in thirteen languages and sold tens of thousands of copies (McGee 2004, 97).[57]

Baker's encounter with a boy crying in the streets catalyzed the orphan work. Baker had already experienced a crisis event in his career. After assessing the meager results of his preaching and experiencing rejection by many of the more well-to-do who referred to him mockingly as the "foreign devil," Baker decided to follow Luke 4:18-19 pursuing preaching to the poor, sick, captives, and oppressed.

Following this decision, Baker met a young boy who had been working in the tin mines and had just recently been thrown out on the streets because he was too sick to work. His parents were deceased, and he had no money, so he was begging for food. Baker invited him to go home with him and promised to provide him with clothes to wear and food to eat (H. Baker 1940, 46-47).[58] The Adullam Mission launched that day. Baker took the name "Adullam" from 1 Sam 22:1-2, which describes the distressed, poor, and disconsolate joining David.

In the beginning, the orphanage focused on rescuing boys who had been put to work in the tin mines. Lured by the promise of good jobs or captured by agents who then sold them

---

[57]Baker's books, *Heaven and the Angels* ([1950?]), as well as *Plains of Glory and Gloom* ([1950?]), and *The Three Worlds* (1937), undoubtedly were influenced by what occurred at the Adullam Orphanage during this revival. These books contain repeated references to those who have been raised from the dead and what they saw during the time they were absent from the body. Baker also developed an unusual eschatology that differed in many points from what was generally accepted among rank-and-file Pentecostals. More will be said about that later in this paper.

[58]H. A. Baker (1940), *Seeking and Saving*, was a publication of the Adullam Reading Campaign. The *Adullam News* became a regular publication of the Bakers' ministry.

to mine owners, these trafficked victims labored under desperate conditions. Many of the holes through which the boys crawled extended for up to a mile into the mountains and, in some places, were no more than three feet high. Mine owners frequently forced the boys to descend three and four times a day. Many were beaten for substandard work. Their diet consisted of little more than rice with a small vegetable. Many of the boys became sick after months of hard labor. When they were unable to continue working, they were cast aside and left to fend for themselves (H. Baker 2008a, 180-181).

At one point, more than one hundred children lived at Adullam; during the last two years of operation, it ministered to approximately eighty children. Every day, the residents studied the Bible as well as contributed to the support of the orphanage through such chores as gardening, carpentry, and other tasks.[59]

Later, it became increasingly difficult to find beggar boys on the streets. The Bakers began to sense that God was using this to signal a change in their ministry focus, especially as doors began to open to travel more among the mountain tribes of southern Yunnan province (H. Baker 2008a, 231).

Work among the Mountain Tribes

The Bakers' second primary work was directed toward minority people groups scattered throughout the mountains of southern Yunnan province. Baker referred to these people as the Ka Do.[60]

---

[59]In comparing this work with that of the Anglins in Tai-an, I note that the work in Tai-an was more developed and served as a better model for community development. Also, the Bakers' work with the Adullam Orphanage was temporary and was phased back significantly once he began to travel on evangelistic tours throughout the mountains. However, the Bakers' orphanage included both academic education as well as vocational training. It also maintained long-range goals for the orphans assisted there.

[60]Even though Ka Do is the name Baker used to refer to these tribes, there were other subgroups and tribes that received his ministry. The modern name for the Ka Do is the Hani. A separate section of this paper will discuss the work by the Boltons, Morrisons, and Lewers among the Lisu, another minority group in this part of China.

The Bakers' ministry among the minority tribes began in earnest with an invitation by two Presbyterian missionaries who needed help following up on a people movement among the Ka Do tribe. The Calenders, along with their associate missionary family, the Parks, had been impressed by the move of the Holy Spirit that they had observed in the Adullam Orphanage. Their receptivity to Pentecostal manifestations cannot be overlooked in what happened through the Bakers' work among the mountain tribes (H. Baker 2008a, 275-276).

Calender prepared to accompany Baker on the first trip to introduce him to their contacts but could not complete the trip due to illness. He sent one of his workers to accompany Baker on the last miles of that first journey along with these prophetic words: "Do as you please. Who knows? Perhaps the Lord might want you to do the tribal work. Our mission may be leaving it" (H. Baker 2008a, 277).

Baker's burden increased as he observed the endless number of villages to be visited. Visits rarely lasted more than a couple of days but included the ministry activities of preaching, teaching people how to pray, baptizing converts, removing idols from homes, and praying for the sick. Baker realized his inability to continue in one location for any length of time due to the cries of neighboring villages that wanted him to come and share the gospel with them.[61]

He pondered how he could establish leaders for these fledgling congregations, as he knew his next visit would probably be a year in the future. He expressed concern about how the church would survive and grow. These issues facilitated the development of Baker's methodology of developing indigenous leadership. Although Baker did not preach in the tribal languages, he turned this negative factor into a positive one by focusing on the leadership development of the men who traveled with him as his interpreters.[62]

---

[61]Similar accounts of this ministry occur in both Baker (1940) *Seeking and Saving* and Baker (2008a) *Under His Wings*.

[62]Although Baker did not speak the various tribal dialects, he did speak Mandarin

His methodology was simple. First, keep money out of sight. Build self-supporting, self-governing, and self-propagating churches. He used foreign contributions to support the orphanage work as well as in the seminars, conventions, and short-term schools for training national workers, as he placed a premium on the training of national workers. He viewed this as critical for reaching the villages scattered throughout the mountains. Despite his frequent travels, he was only able to personally visit each location for a few days in the calendar year. Trained workers were essential to conserve the harvest. However, he did not put the native evangelists and pastors on a salary but rather insisted on them being supported by the nationals. Furthermore, he did not embark on building churches in the various villages. Each local group determined its own "where" of worship (H. Baker 1940).

Second, travel simple. "It is not so much a question of getting to the [lost]. It is more a question of how we come" (H. Baker 1940, 119). Traveling simple meant that he adopted the clothing, the food, and the lodging of the villagers. This example of incarnational ministry allowed him to become one with his target people group.

> I might have come to Ka Do Land carried in a chair. I might have come riding on a horse. All these people to whom Jesus sent me walk. The old and the young, the rich and the poor, the men and the women, and the children walk. Why should not I? Paul, the ideal missionary, walked from place to place, walked thousands of miles. Jesus walked from village to village throughout Judea and all Galilee. I walked because I thought it would be most Christlike and would win the most people for Him (H. Baker 1940, 117-118).

Chinese. In later years, when he moved to Taiwan for ministry among the Hakka Chinese, he also studied the Hakka dialect. He began his study of Hakka when he was over seventy years old, well past the age when new languages are usually studied.

When he wrote his book *Seeking and Saving*, H. A. Baker (1940, 118) estimated that he had already walked over 9,000 miles in ministry to the Ka Do people.[63]

Upon arrival in Ka Do villages, he shared meals with them at their tables and slept on their beds.[64] Trudging along mountain trails, he shared Christ and taught biblical principles to his guides and translators: "We walk and we work together. We sweat and we talk together as we climb over the mountains. I get to know the men, and they get to know me. . . . At the conclusion of the day we sleep in the same room or on the same floor" (H. Baker 1940, 153).

Third, preaching and teaching could be scheduled anywhere. He preached in kitchens, courtyards, underneath trees, along the mountain trails, wherever it proved convenient for the listeners. He believed that training national workers and appointing local leadership for each newly established church was critical and non-negotiable. There were no other options. Since Baker operated from a base 200 miles away, follow-up visits for discipleship and training proved extremely difficult.

Baker followed a set routine in his mountain itineraries. He began with one hour of prayer before he got out of bed. He discovered that if he did not pray as soon as he awakened, the affairs of the day would crowd out any chance of personal communion with God. Rising, he would prepare his outfit for travel and eat breakfast. After breakfast, the group would go to a nearby river to baptize new converts. Then they commenced the journey to the next preaching site. If the trip was long, they would walk the entire day without stopping for lunch. As soon as they reached the village, they would begin personal house-to-house visits to talk with the people who had not yet been baptized. A meal preceded the night

---

[63]Before leaving China in 1952, Baker had revised this figure upward to over 20,000 miles.

[64]Baker, upon his first return to the United States after twenty-seven years of ministry in southwest China, noted that he had to readjust to using knives, forks, and spoons with his meals, even to the point of watching others to make sure he was following proper dining etiquette.

meeting where Baker preached to those who were assembling after their day of work in the fields (H. Baker 2008b, 69-70).

Hymn singing played a prominent part in the service and included an explanation of the meaning of the hymn. Every aspect of the service included explanation and biblical teaching. Baker did not preach sermons but rather talked about Jesus—the central theme of every meeting. Jesus, his cross, and the Christian way of life, which consisted of coming to Jesus to make him Lord of all, dominated his messages. The meetings closed with an invitation for people to confess their sins followed by a time of prayer for the Holy Spirit to move among them as he so chose. Baker always included a time of prayer for the sick (H. Baker 2008b, 69-70).

Fourth, Baker believed in the power of the Holy Spirit. He was thoroughly Pentecostal. Miracles of healing, casting out demons, speaking in tongues as villagers were baptized in the Spirit, prophecies, visions—all of these followed his ministry as the Lord confirmed his message with signs following.

Pentecostal Practice

Healing of the sick and power over demons figured prominently in the revival of the mountain tribes. Prayer for the sick became a normal expectation, and such prayer by the Christian community quickly replaced the former calls to sorcerers. In passing from village to village, Baker and native traveling evangelists would frequently find the sick coming to wait for them on the mountain trails requesting prayer for their illnesses (H. Baker 2008b, 7).

Baker consistently refrained from seeking to control manifestations of the Holy Spirit during his meetings with the Ka Do. Speaking in tongues, dancing in the Spirit, dreams and visions, and other physical manifestations were common. If there were any errors in judgment, they would be made on the side of permissiveness rather than control: "We interfered with none of His manifestations, although some of them were such as we had never seen before" (H. Baker 2008b, 18). Commenting on these physical manifestations among the Ka Do, H. A. Baker said:

> But in their simple minds they just expect that if the devil can shake a man, then the Lord is enough bigger than the devil to shake him more and shake the devil, too. They suppose that if their people can become demon possessed, as they have sometimes from days of yore, and under demoniacal power they can and do perform some strange supernatural things, that if God is as mighty as is claimed, he can fill a man with the Holy Spirit so that he may have manifestations of super-human power with supernatural evidence of God (H. Baker 2008b, 18).

Many Ka Dos began to receive the baptism of the Holy Spirit. On one occasion, messengers came to Baker asking about a woman who had received the Spirit's infilling and spoke in tongues while working in the field. They wanted to know if it was possible to receive the Holy Spirit in such a setting. Perhaps remembering the way he received Spirit baptism, H. A. Baker (2008b, 21) responded: "Yes, if you ask the Lord for the Holy Spirit, He will give Him any time and place He sees best."

Baker's Eschatology

Baker's eschatology differed significantly from most of the other Pentecostal missionaries of his era. First, he believed that the church would go through the tribulation. His books *Tribulation to Glory* (1931) and *Through Tribulation* [1950d?] outline his arguments for a post-tribulation rapture of the church (H. Baker [1950a?], 124).

Baker's ideas were even more unusual concerning the fate of those who had never had an adequate witness of Jesus. He concluded that those who had not heard of Jesus did die in their sins and, therefore, could not go to heaven. However, he believed that the sin that sent people to hell was the rejection of salvation through faith in Jesus. Those who had not heard of Jesus could not be guilty of having rejected the gospel message (H. Baker [1950b?], 25).

Baker believed that those who had never heard of Jesus, as well as those who had never had a clear presentation of the gospel message would, upon dying, go to an intermediate state. At that time, they would have the opportunity to accept or reject Christ. He further believed that an individual's actions on earth would predispose one either toward heaven or hell. In the intermediate state, Baker thought angels and demons actively sought to influence these people in their decision. No one could enter heaven without consciously choosing Jesus. Conversely, each person who entered hell had chosen to reject Christ (H. Baker [1950b?], 25-28).

Pentecostals would argue that such a belief would militate against missionary service. A clear presentation of the gospel, if not accepted, would have prevented the individual from having a chance after death to choose Christ (Heb 9:27). However, this never hindered Baker from aggressively preaching to as many people as possible, even to those who were located in remote and almost inaccessible areas, as noted in his statement:

> To the unsaved I have nothing to say about a later chance. So far as I know, when I am talking to him, I am telling him about a present and only chance. Neither he nor I have any reason to suppose that he will ever get a better chance to forsake sin than right now. Whenever I talk to the unsaved about the Lord, I think it may be the last and only real chance they will ever have to be saved for if they turn down the light and the present opportunity to come to Christ, they will be more likely to neglect the second appeal. I know they will become increasingly indifferent to the gospel (H. Baker [1950b?], 40).

Final Years in China and Subsequent Ministry

Baker spent twenty-seven years working in China without a furlough. He felt that he would serve in China until his death. At one point, he had selected a spot and dug his own grave. After filling it back in with dirt, he marked it and left instructions to be buried there when he died. The only thing that prevented that pre-selected grave from being his body's final resting place was his expulsion from China following the Communist takeover (Baker 2008a, 290-291).

Josephine Baker returned to the United States after seventeen years of service. The upheavals caused by Japan's invasion of China influenced her decision to leave. She returned to China in 1949.[65] The Bakers were based out of Kunming while Harold continued to travel throughout the mountains. Finally, in 1952, the Communists refused Baker permission to continue traveling among the mountain tribes, which led to their decision to exit China and return to the U.S. via Hong Kong (H. Baker 2008a, 414-415).

Baker was seventy-one years old when forced to leave China. The Bakers spent their closing years of ministry among the Navajo Indians in New Mexico for two years followed by additional missionary service among the Hakka Chinese in Miaoli, Taiwan (H. Baker 2008a, 453-454).

Summary

Baker's ministry produced lasting results. Hogan stated that one can measure his or her success by the churches planted (Klaus and Petersen 2006, 113). Baker counted forty churches planted during his ministry among the minority tribes in southwest China. Despite his frequent references to the Ka Dos and Ka Do Land, his ministry extended beyond that one tribe. Baker estimated that he baptized six thousand people during his eighteen years of ministry there (Baker 2008a, 393).

Joshua Project states that, as of 1986, there were 40,000 followers of Christ among the Ka Do, with more than 150 full-time Christian workers. In Mojiang County, one-third of the 5,200 believers were teenagers and 35 percent of all Ka Do today are Christians (Joshua Project 2019).

---

[65]Precise dating is difficult, as Baker rarely included dates in his autobiography. It is probable that Josephine returned to the USA in July 1941. She remained in the U.S. for eight years and then returned to Kunming. That dates her return to China in 1949. She remained in Kunming for three years because it was deemed impractical for her to move to the mountains. Baker continued to travel through the Ka Do region while Josephine remained in Kunming. After three years, Baker was denied permission to continue traveling in the mountain regions and other doors of ministry appeared to be closing, prompting them to leave China for Hong Kong in 1952.

Chapter Five

VICTOR PLYMIRE: ACROSS THE TIBETAN PLATEAU

Early Life

Victor Plymire was born in Loganville, Pennsylvania, on January 10, 1881. At the age of two, he became deathly ill, and doctors held out no hope for him to live. His mother refused to accept the doctor's diagnosis. She dedicated her son to God and carried him into another room where she prayed for and received his healing (Plymire 1931b, 1).

At the age of sixteen, Plymire committed his life to Christ during a street meeting. He joined the Mennonite Brethren. Less than two years later, he asked about the possibility of becoming a missionary. Since no one acted on his comments, Plymire assumed that mission work was not for him and even stopped praying about it. However, sometime later he received a telegram asking him to meet with the foreign mission board. Following that meeting, he received a missionary appointment.

Although going out under the Christian and Missionary Alliance (CMA) banner, most of his support came from the Mennonites. He remained affiliated with the CMA until 1919 when he received the baptism of the Holy Spirit in Lancaster, Pennsylvania, while on furlough (Plymire 1931b, 1).

Description of Tibetan Religion and Challenges

Plymire felt called to work among the Tibetans. He authored a report to Noel Perkin, the executive director of the Assemblies of God foreign mission program, entitled "Synopsis of Missionary Efforts in Tibet by V. G. Plymire Covering Years 1908-1931." This document describes the challenges of work among this people group.

First, access into Tibet presented geographical challenges. Tibet is ringed on three sides by either high mountain ranges or deserts and swamps. The only easy means of access was from the east, which meant that Tibet's primary invasions had all come from China (Plymire 1931a, 1-5).

The earliest form of worship in Tibet was the primarily shamanistic Bon religion. Even though Buddhism has been the primary religion of Tibet since the eighth century, it continues to show a distinctive Bon influence. Tibetans have traditionally ascribed sickness and natural disasters, including storms, blizzards, and avalanches to the influence of evil spirits. Shamans, through magic, incantations, and sacrifices, sought to appease demons and spirits and bring relief to the sufferers. They primarily offered animal sacrifices, but Plymire mentioned reports of human sacrifices. Bon worship frequently included private priests who accompanied families as they moved across the Tibetan plateau. Oracles were frequently consulted for guidance. Many of the Bon ceremonies took place at night (Plymire 1931a, 12-14).

Buddhism, introduced to Tibet around 650 CE, became the state religion and incorporated many syncretistic elements, as the average Tibetan still preferred the old ways to the new teachings. The Buddha seemed cold and distant, whereas the destruction of crops, hailstorms, blizzards, and sickness were close and real.

When Padma Sambhava came to Tibet, he firmly established Buddhism within the Tibetan culture and lifestyle, utilizing magic and incantations that seemingly controlled the Bon spirits. Sambhava successfully incorporated Bon beliefs and rituals into the Buddhist system, forming a new branch of Buddhism alternately termed Vajrayana, Tibetan Buddhism, or Lamaism (Plymire 1931a, 13-14). Plymire used the latter term more frequently.

Plymire viewed the monasteries as the strongholds of Lamaism as it was not uncommon to find thousands of lamas residing in the monasteries. He discovered three primary lamaseries near Lhasa: (1) Drepung, the largest in the world, with approximately 8,000 resident lamas; (2) Sera, the second largest in Tibet; and (3) Ganden. The three monasteries, combined, contained almost 20,000 lamas.[66] Farther north and west, in what at Plymire's time was still considered to be Tibet proper, were two other prominent lamaseries: Kumbum and Labrang. The former is located in Qinghai province and not far from Tangar (Huangyuan), where Plymire was based. The latter is located in Gansu Province, close to the Tibetan border, and was near where W. W. Simpson and his son, Willie, were based for their ministries (Plymire 1931a, 14).

Due to the nomadic nature of the Tibetan culture, Plymire was forced to carry everything needed on each evangelistic trip. He prepared cooking utensils, bedding, food supplies, tents, and a few miscellaneous items such as tea for bartering purposes. He also needed equipment to repair shoes as well as tools for horseshoeing and mending clothes. In addition, Plymire would carry large quantities of New Testament Bible portions and tracts to leave with those he visited. The number of tents at each encampment determined the length of his stay. On several occasions, he would find special religious gatherings, where all the households would be in attendance, around sites of religious significance. Whether many or few, Plymire would always make sure that every tent was visited and presented with the claims of Christ and where the people could read, he would also leave gospel literature (Plymire 1931a, 15-16).

Initially, conversions were scarce. Plymire labored sixteen years before he baptized his first convert (Blumhofer 1989b,

---

[66]These figures were contained in Plymire's report to Perkin and reflect the statistics as Plymire knew them in 1931. Additionally, during this period, Tibet encompassed a larger area than it does today and extended into parts of neighboring Chinese provinces. Tangar (or Huangyuan, as it is known today), where Plymire was based for much of his China and Tibetan ministry, is now part of Qinghai Province.

248). The enmity of local priests hindered Plymire in developing relationships. In Tangar, only ten Tibetans attended his first meeting. These ten did not continue attending because local priests had warned them to pay no attention to anything Plymire said. However, the warnings of the priests served to arouse the curiosity of several local Tibetans who wanted to learn more about Plymire's message. Plymire's low-key approach emphasized developing personal relationships rather than holding formal meetings. By playing an organ, singing songs in the Tibetan language, and playing records on a phonograph, the Plymires were able to attract people to their home with ease (Plymire 1931b, 1).

On one occasion, Plymire slyly enticed a visiting Tibetan priest into his home. The priest had been warned that he would die if he went inside the Plymire home. Plymire stood at the entrance talking with the priest and gradually, step by step, moved backward into the reception room. The priest, without realizing what was happening, slowly followed him to continue the conversation. Once inside, Plymire took a picture of the priest and later presented it to him as a gift. This broke the ice and he, as well as others, became more willing to sit in the Plymire home for conversations (Plymire 1931b, 13).

Plymire's Pre-Assemblies of God Missions Work (1908-1919)

Victor Plymire sailed for China from Seattle, Washington, on February 4, 1908, and was affiliated with the CMA. Arriving in Shanghai, he still had several months before he would reach his destination at Taochow on the Gansu-Tibetan border.[67] Along the way, Plymire asked the Lord for a special Scripture promise to

[67]This was the same area where W. W. Simpson, Grace Agar, and other CMA missionaries such as the Ekvalls and Christies served. Plymire traveled with another CMA missionary, Ivan Kauffman, who also later joined the AG. The travel from Shanghai to Gansu province included a three-month long journey up the Han River by boat followed with travel by mule, horse, and finally walking for another 300 plus miles. Victor and David Plymire (1983), as well as Edith Blumhofer (1989b) and Charles Greenaway (1986) have each written about the journey.

claim for his missionary career. He felt impressed to adopt Isaiah 41:10: "Fear thou not; for I am with thee: be not dismayed for I am thy God. I will strengthen thee, yea, I will help thee; yea, I will uphold thee by the right hand of my righteousness" (Plymire 1983, 19-20).[68]

Upon arrival in Gansu, Plymire's first goal was to learn the Tibetan language. Whereas other CMA missionaries who wanted to reach the Tibetans had decided to settle on the Gansu side of the Tibetan border, Plymire maintained the hope of establishing residency on the Tibetan side (Blumhofer 1989b, 247). Learning Tibetan was essential for Plymire to achieve that goal, but finding a teacher proved difficult as Tibetan leaders had threatened the local people with severe punishment for teaching a Westerner their language (Plymire 1983, 23).

The man Plymire chose to teach him the language took his job seriously and included lessons on culture and etiquette as well. On one occasion, his teacher placed a dish of spoiled meat in front of Plymire and told him to eat it. Plymire refused, and the teacher put the dish aside. For three days, the teacher repeated this, each time telling Plymire to eat it. Finally, on the third day, Plymire ate. His teacher told him that he had learned a valuable lesson that day—always to eat what the Tibetans put before him. Refusal would greatly insult his host (Plymire 1983, 24).

At the time, Plymire did not realize that his teacher had ties to a band of robbers, but Plymire had impressed his teacher with his sincerity. On one occasion, when Plymire had planned a trip to a nearby Tibetan village, this teacher advised him to delay a day so that he could notify his bandit friends and ensure safe passage for Plymire (Greenaway 1987, 21).

The relationships Plymire was building with local Tibetans stood him in good stead. On one occasion, angry priests drove him away from the Labrang monastery. Plymire attempted a second visit, and this time he was met by a young Buddhist priest he had befriended at another location. This Buddhist priest vouched for Plymire in an audience with the Grand Lama, resulting in Plymire

---

[68]This verse is quoted from the KJV, which was the version used by Victor Plymire.

receiving permission to hand out his tracts and gospels for ten days at Labrang without interference (Greenaway 1987, 22).

The Assemblies of God Years (1919-1949)

Victor Plymire and Grace Harkless were married on January 1, 1919, following a five-year engagement. The wedding took place in Minchow, Gansu, a short distance from the Tibetan border (Plymire 1983, 59). Shortly after the wedding, they returned to the United States, where they were destined to experience significant changes in their lives and ministry.

Plymire, during the latter part of his second term, had begun to sense the need for greater power in ministry among the Tibetans. This hunger for greater spiritual power to combat the satanic spiritual forces arrayed against him drove him to search for a closer walk with God. While he and his young bride were traveling across the United States, they met some Pentecostal believers who encouraged them to seek the baptism in the Holy Spirit (Plymire 1983, 53, 59).

Following their baptism in the Spirit, the Plymires joined the young Assemblies of God organization and subsequently received ordination in 1920. They went on to pastor a church in Lancaster, Pennsylvania, for a short season, and it was there that their first son, John David, was born. Victor and Grace could not shake the conviction of a missionary call to Tibet, so in February 1922, they set out once again to work among the Tibetans (Plymire 1983, 60).

This time they settled in Tangar, which served as an important trade center on the caravan route from China to Lhasa. Located about twenty-seven miles west of Kumbum, the most famous lamasery in northeastern Tibet, it placed the Plymires in both a propitious religious and economic center. A representative from the Dalai Lama himself lived only two doors down from where Victor and Grace settled (Victor Plymire n.d., 17).

Large caravans of Tibetan traders traveled from Lhasa to Tangar twice each year, with at least one caravan returning to Lhasa, usually in May or June. Ministry in Tangar gave the Plymires access to Tibetans, Chinese residents doing business with Tibetans, as well as the occasional Mongolian and Muslim travelers. Traders coming from Lhasa could not immediately return, as the lengthy journey required them to stay in Tangar for several months to prepare their animals for the return trip (Plymire 1931b, 1).

In addition to the primary lamasery of Kumbum with over 3,600 lamas, there were twenty-two other lamaseries in the province, each with between 200 and 1,000 lamas. Labrang, with over 3,000 lamas, was only a five-day journey southeast of Tangar (Victor Plymire n.d., 3).[69]

Two events in 1925, on the opposite side of the country from the Plymires, led to a wave of nationalistic fervor among the Chinese. First, on May 30 British police killed thirteen Shanghai demonstrators. Second, on June 23 Anglo-French marines killed fifty-two demonstrators in Guangzhou. Consequently, anti-imperialism reached a fever pitch in 1925-26 (Fairbank 1986, 212).

Many foreign governments began advising their citizens to leave the country, as war between China and several major Western powers seemed imminent. The Plymires received this message and prayed about what to do. They felt strongly that the time was ripe for Tibet to hear the gospel, yet, for safety's sake, they decided that Grace and John David would prepare to return to America. Plymire, not knowing if there would be future opportunities for work in Tibet, would attempt to exit by crossing Tibet and sharing the gospel with as many Tibetans as possible as he traveled (Plymire 1983, 69-70).

These plans for Grace and John to return to America and Plymire's evangelistic expedition changed due to an outbreak of smallpox in the Tangar area during the first week of January 1927. Within just a few short days, several residents of the city died. Then, on the night of January 9, young John David became sick. On the third day, it became evident that he had smallpox. Not long after, Grace also came down with the disease; Plymire spent the

[69]I have visited Tangar (known today as Huangyuan) on many occasions. On my first visit to this small town, I questioned why Victor Plymire would have chosen this city as a base of operation. Today it would not qualify as a major commercial center or trade route. However, such was not the case in the 1920s when the Plymires arrived as can be seen from its location along the caravan routes between China and India.

next few days moving from room to room, praying and caring for his family.

On January 20, young John David died. One week later, on January 27, Grace also passed away. Plymire's heart is revealed by his recounting of their last moments:

> On the morning of January 27th, we had our last little talk. We read together from the Word. We sang our last hymn together: "My Anchor Holds." She asked me to help her sit up. . . . then she began to sing in such sweet tones, "Jesus Is Coming for Me." Then her head fell against my right arm (Plymire 1983, 73).

When the local cemetery refused permission for him to bury his loved ones, a Chinese friend came to his assistance by agreeing to sell him a piece of land on the side of the mountain, outside of town. It was the middle of winter, and the ground was frozen solid. Plymire had only enough strength to dig one grave in the frozen ground before placing both coffins inside together (Wood 1993, 4).

Returning to his home in Tangar, he penned these words in a letter to his sister in the United States:

> Why these dear ones were called away I do not know. I do not question. They were so earnest in trying to evangelize this vast unevangelized region. It is so very hard in the natural now entirely alone. For several years we prayed for help. We begged the Lord to send someone to help my dear wife in the work and to be a company while I was itinerating among the nomads, but no one came. Has someone failed God? (Plymire 1983, 74).

George O. Wood's 1993 *Pentecostal Evangel* article, "To Eclipse All Sorrow," contains an interesting aftermath to this story. When Plymire purchased the gravesite for Grace and John, he purchased it in the name of the church. Many years later, that deed in the name of the church enabled the Christians in Huangyuan (formerly known as Tangar) to reclaim property that had been lost to the

Communist Party following 1949. The property and buildings are still used by the church in that city today (Wood 1993, 5).

Plymire continued with his plans to cross Tibet on an evangelistic expedition. The political situation in China at that time was tenuous, with an increasing number of foreigners evacuating each week. He was concerned there might be no way to return once he left, so this might be his last opportunity to evangelize Tibet. He, therefore, made plans to cross the length of Tibet exiting into northern India after undertaking a journey that no other missionary had succeeded in doing.

Such a trip required enormous preparation. He began by purchasing forty-seven yaks. Realizing that there would be only two or three places along the entire journey where necessities could be found, he prepared food for himself, the men who would accompany him, and the animals. He prepared seventy-five pounds of butter, 500 pounds of roasted barley flour, strips of dried raw meat, many pounds of wheat flour for baking bread or making noodles, and several pounds each of salt and tea. He also packed a few delicacies such as dried radishes, onions, and apricots—as well as one pound of American candy (Plymire 1983, 76). However, the most critical item was the gospel literature to distribute along the way. He packed 74,000 gospels and New Testaments, and 40,000 tracts into leather-bound boxes. Almost all the literature was in the Tibetan language (Plymire 1983, 76).

Plymire started the journey at six o'clock in the morning on May 18, 1927, accompanied by two Tibetans and three Chinese. He wrote this prayer in his diary: "Through this trip, O Lord, let me touch as many lives as possible for Thee; and every life I touch do Thou by Thy Spirit quicken—whether through the word I speak, the prayer I breathe, or the life I live" (D. Plymire 1983, 78).

On June 5, 1927, a letter from Plymire was carried back to Tangar by one of the Chinese men accompanying him. It said:

> This will likely be my last letter till I reach India. . . . Thus far the Lord has blessed me. I am troubled some with rheumatism, but God has wonderfully helped me. I expect Him to heal me completely. . . . We have had nice weather now for the past day and a half and I hope it continues

> for some days as we have already been delayed beyond my plans, and our food supplies may run short. … I have tried to give the gospel so that all may hear it at least once (Plymire 1983, 79).

This was the last word received from Plymire for eight months. ". . . So that all may hear it at least once." "Until the farthest nook and corner of Tibet has heard. . . . Until the last man has heard the gospel witness, my work is not done." All of these statements written in Plymire's letters and journal find expression in the current Assemblies of God World Missions' purpose statement: "So *all* can hear" (Mundis 2016, 23).

Difficulties were Plymire's constant companion, as described in the over 300-page journal that he kept of the trip. "Grass almost nonexistent for the animals." "Across the burning, sun-baked desert." "Finding water in stagnant, scum-covered pools." "[Some] yaks died in the sand hills." "I thought of turning back." "Deep snows." "Hunger." "Suffering." "I have never felt so cold in my life." Such descriptions are common throughout his journal.[70]

Since Plymire was unable to communicate with the outside world, many people speculated on whether he was alive or dead. Plymire's brother sent a letter to W. W. Greist in the U.S. House of Representatives requesting information concerning Plymire's status. Greist wrote to the Secretary of State asking about Plymire. Acting Secretary of State, Robert E. Olds, responded with information about a party of three, consisting of a German, a Brit, and an American, who had been murdered in Tibet. They assumed that Victor Plymire was the American, although confirmation was not possible due to the remoteness of the region (Greist, letter to Olds, October 26, 1927).

Convinced that Plymire was dead, the AG Foreign Missions Department stopped sending remittances to his account. When he finally did arrive in India, he wrote to his sister in 1933:

[70] A copy of Victor Plymire's personal journal detailing the events of this expedition can be found in both the FPHC and AGWM Archives in Springfield, Missouri.

> It was very interesting to me, on arrival at Calcutta, to read a press clipping which told how I had been murdered by the Tibetans. Later on, I heard that a few religious papers said a few nice things about me—as is the usual case when one crosses the great divide. Well, praise the Lord, I am still alive and going pretty well at present. I had a very good time among the Tibetans. No trouble anywhere.[71]

Despite the difficulties on this trip, Plymire was able to communicate the gospel throughout the length and breadth of Tibet. Not only did his team take the time on this journey to visit every tent they saw to present the gospel message, but they also spent extended times at various religious fairs, celebrations, and other significant gatherings that often required every family head in the district to attend. At the end of the evangelistic expedition, Victor Plymire (1933a, 4) reported that 73,396 Gospels and Bible portions, as well as 46,542 tracts in the Tibetan language, had been distributed.

Although it had been eight years since Plymire's last furlough and despite the long and challenging expedition across Tibet, he immediately returned to China, arriving in Shanghai on May 11, just a few days shy of one year since his departure. Before returning to Tangar, he married Ruth Weidman on August 8, 1928, in Tianjin, China (Plymire 1983, 133-134).

Upon his return, Plymire renewed his acquaintance with Ga Lo, the chief of the Kantsa tribe. Ga Lo invited Plymire to attend his brother's wedding celebration, and, since the entire tribe was preparing to attend the ceremony, Ga Lo told Plymire to come prepared to tell the tribe about Christianity (Plymire 1983, 174). At the ceremony, Ga Lo told Plymire he believed that this new religion and doctrine was the best he had heard, and he wanted his people to hear more, but "unless you are with us more, this will

---

[71]Plymire's claim in this letter of "no trouble anywhere" does not match up with the accounts of his journal and other brief accounts of the expedition. In fact, he encountered many difficulties, including opposition from various headmen in certain Tibetan regions, one of which occasion nearly ended in all of his company losing their lives. In addition, inclement weather frequently challenged the travelers.

not be possible. Will you come and live with us? If you will, we are prepared to build a house for you and will do our best to take care of your needs" (Plymire 1983, 175-176).

This conversation with Ga Lo revealed a major challenge in Plymire's methodology. Building churches among nomadic people required a different approach. Physical buildings, tied to one geographic location, could not meet the need. Mobile churches under indigenous leadership offered the most suitable solution for planting churches among nomadic tribes. Plymire said as much in his report to Noel Perkin in July 1931: "Personally we do not expect to build any Churches for the people. We are working along the lines of getting them saved and then having them carry on the work, with our oversight. We must have them saved then train them for the work" (Plymire 1931a, 16).

Socio-political turmoil throughout China marked the final decade of the Plymires' missionary ministry among the Tibetans. Attacks came from both inside and outside the country. In 1939, the Plymires again received word that they should evacuate. However, they decided to remain at their post, noting that if it became necessary to flee, they could probably escape through Tibet and find their way out to India. In 1941, at the age of sixty, Plymire once again prepared for another evangelistic expedition into northeastern Tibet (Plymire 1983, 185-186). The remoteness of their station contributed to Plymire's ability to continue conducting evangelistic expeditions throughout the World War II years and the Nationalist-Communist civil war.

The Plymires' final service in China was on Sunday, June 19, 1949, with twenty-five new converts receiving water baptism. The Plymires returned to the United States, where he later died on December 8, 1956. At the beginning of his missionary career, he had claimed Isa 41:10 as God's special promise. Over four decades later, Plymire could look back on a missionary career where he had repeatedly seen God's faithfulness to that promise as he carried the gospel to those who had never heard.

Chapter Six

LESLIE AND AVA ANGLIN: TO THE WIDOWS AND ORPHANS

Early Life

Leslie M. Anglin was born in Stewart County, Georgia, on February 23, 1882. During his childhood, he narrowly escaped death twice. At the age of two, he was rescued from a fiery death, and at eleven, he was saved from drowning. His mother frequently told him that God must have a significant thing for him to do; otherwise, God would not have spared his life (Ketcher 2015, 26). While these near-miraculous escapes from death certainly played an important part in his life, they did not compare to the indelible mark a completely different type of event at the family farm in Georgia made on his life. Three beggars showed up at the family farmhouse, asking for food. Immediately, his mother went into the kitchen and prepared food for them. Anglin later questioned his mother on why she had helped these men who could be lazy or unwilling to work. If so, they were unworthy of assistance. He never forgot his mother's answer. She admitted that perhaps he was right about their unworthiness, but it would be impossible to know their background or life circumstances. Thus, they must give them the benefit of the doubt.

Turning to Scripture, she shared with Anglin the story of the Good Samaritan and how it was easy for people to excuse themselves from helping people in need. True Christians are called to extend mercy, as noted in 1 John 3:17. How can people claim to have the love of God yet refuse to help a person in need, especially if they have the means to assist? Anglin never forgot that experience (Albus 1951, 29-30).

Early on, Anglin showed an interest in mission work. His home church in Georgia frequently hosted missionaries who told stories about people who had never heard about Jesus. Those visits burned deeply into Anglin's heart. One visiting missionary from China was instrumental in turning his attention toward the Far East. Later, Anglin discovered that his local church had supported mission work in the city of Tai-an,[72] where he would later build his ministry. His father had often prayed for Tai-an in northeast China (Albus 1951, 28).

Beginnings in Tai-an

Anglin married Ava Patton on July 18, 1904. Six years later, they left the United States for their first term of missionary service in China, settling in Tai-an. On April 21, 1911, they welcomed Margaret Evelyn into their family. The joy of having a child was fleeting as young Margaret died sixteen months later (Albus 1951, 32-40). The Anglins plunged into evangelistic work, and a busy schedule helped in assuaging the tremendous grief at the loss of their baby.

Anglin, a detailed strategist, would study maps and collect as much information as possible about the target areas. Once he familiarized himself with the area, he would construct an evangelistic plan. As a priority, he would decide on a location for conducting the meetings. Visibility proved critical, as they wanted to attract a crowd when they began to sing. The novelty of seeing and hearing a foreign man and his wife sing would draw crowds, and many people would frequently linger to ask questions. Anglin would often sit for hours talking to groups or individuals (Albus 1951, 44).

Anglin sought to saturate a target area with a gospel witness. He would travel from village to village throughout a region.

[72]When source material is pre-1949 that time period of spelling place names is followed.

Once finished, he would start all over again. These early years of evangelistic work solidified his thinking on effective mission methodology. He concluded that foreign missionaries would never be able to evangelize China effectively. Building a strong national church would require trained and equipped Chinese converts. New believers must be trained and prepared to share the gospel message with their friends and neighbors. The national church must be free from foreign control. This meant that the local church had to be supported by Christian laymen who lived consistent Christian lives in the marketplace and would raise Christian children who would, in turn, continue to pass the Christian message down to subsequent generations (Albus 1951, 45).

Leslie and Ava Anglin proceeded to act on these convictions. In early 1912, they organized their mission in Tai-an. They were committed to continuing the evangelistic outreaches in their area, but they focused attention on training young Chinese Christians who could work more effectively among their people (Albus 1951, 47-48).

About the same time, missionary friends returning to the United States offered to sell the Anglins their home. Even though they did not have the money for the purchase, they could not shake the thought that God was in this offer. Miraculously, God provided the funds, and the home was purchased (Ketcher 2015, 26).

The Home of Onesiphorus

A chance encounter with a beggar boy changed the direction and future of the Anglins' ministry. A young beggar caught their attention while eating lunch during one of their evangelistic campaigns. A few weeks later, when they passed through the same village again, they saw the young boy once more. This time, they saw a large boil disfiguring his face. Anglin later said that it was as if the young beggar's eyes were asking them if they genuinely cared about him and if there was anyone who loved him (Albus 1951, 18-19). The Anglins decided to take the young boy, named Lieu, home with them and assumed responsibility for his care. To some degree, the adoption of this little orphan boy served to fill the vacancy that had been left with the death of their little girl (Albus 1951, 52-53).

Later, this young boy's story appeared in "Repairing the Breach," a testimony written by the Anglins to promote the Home of Onesiphorus. Young Peng Lieu's grandfather and father had lost everything through a combination of bad business decisions, drinking, and gambling. Reduced to poverty, they journeyed to the provincial capital in search of food. Along the way, they met a wealthy lady who bought Lieu's little sister. Later, Lieu's father died, and his mother committed suicide. Young Lieu found an old man who allowed him to sleep in his house, but the young boy had to go out each day and beg for food. His life, as well as the ministry of the Anglins, underwent a significant change as a result of their meeting (Anglin 1933, 5-17).

Approximately four years later, Lieu became a Christian and was baptized. Shortly afterward, the Anglins extended help to a family with a serious need. The husband had died, and the widow and her three sons needed help. Soon, other orphans and a few more needy women joined these. They were given a place to stay in exchange for their help with daily chores on the property (Ketcher 2015, 29).

In a vision one night, Anglin saw a sign over the gate to their house that said, "Home of Onesiphorus." He saw himself standing in front of the gate welcoming boys, girls, men, women, the poor, and the hungry. He discovered the name Onesiphorus mentioned in both 2 Tim 1:16 and 4:19. The former verse says, "May the Lord grant mercy to the household of Onesiphorus, for he often refreshed me and was not ashamed of my chains." Digging deeper, he found the name meant "a bringer of profit" or "one who brings help to a person in need" (Albus 1951, 58).

China's socio-political context of that time, combined with seasons of famine, brought the Anglins into direct confrontation with the tension between compassion and humanitarian work, on the one hand, and preaching the gospel, on the other. Anglin had never given much thought to dedicating his time to working on humanitarian projects. After all, his primary purpose in China was to preach the gospel so that those who had never heard would have the chance to decide to follow Christ. Since that was his true mission, he struggled to decide whether to also invest time in meeting the physical needs of the destitute. Surely helping them spiritually was more important (Albus 1951, 58).

Amid this dilemma, Anglin began to recall familiar Scripture verses, such as: "But if anyone has the world's goods and sees his brother in need, yet closes his heart against him, how does God's love abide in him?" (1 John 3:17). "Religion that is pure and undefiled before God the Father is this: to visit orphans and widows in their affliction, and to keep oneself unstained from the world" (Jas 1:27). "For I was hungry and you gave me food, I was thirsty and you gave me drink, I was a stranger and you welcomed me, I was naked and you clothed me, I was sick and you visited me, I was in prison and you came to me. . . . as you did it to one of the least of these my brothers, you did it to me" (Matt 25:35-40). "Is not this the fast that I choose . . . Is it not to share your bread with the hungry and bring the homeless poor into your house?" (Isa 58:6, 7).

The Anglins began reassessing their priorities and the focus of their work. Anglin envisioned having a home where orphan children as well as other needy people, young and old, could be fed, clothed, housed, and taught the Scriptures. He foresaw that the children who would receive care, when they were grown, would become the foundation for a self-supporting national church. Ultimately, these churches would one day send their own evangelists and missionaries to other parts of China and neighboring countries (Albus 1951, 59).

The following Sunday, Anglin shared this vision with the people at their Tai-an mission. The Holy Spirit moved upon several people in the service that day, and the Anglins sensed that God was confirming what was in their hearts. That night they opened their home to a widow and her three sons. The next day, Anglin made and hung a sign over the gate in front of their home: "Home of Onesiphorus" (Albus 1951, 60).

Not all in the missionary community understood the Anglins' vision. In the initial stages of the work, Anglin frequently heard comments criticizing him for giving up evangelistic work for orphan ministry. Others asked if he had forgotten the importance of preaching the gospel (Albus 1951, 62).

In actuality, evangelism became the centerpiece of the ministry of the Home of Onesiphorus. They had simply adopted a long-range plan, which emphasized planting the gospel message into the lives of young people. They envisioned these young people one day carrying that message to their people and being the heart of Indigenous Chinese churches (Albus 1951, 62-63).

One night, Anglin had a dream of a peanut field. Harvesters had already picked the harvest, except for one small corner area. He lifted the vines and discovered a large number of peanuts waiting to be harvested. In his mind, this symbolized his role in extending ministry to people who had been forgotten or neglected. He continued to dream of the orphans who would leave his home and become Christian laymen as well as pastors and missionaries (Albus 1951, 63).

The Home of Onesiphorus had three primary purposes. First, the Home existed to demonstrate the power and love of God. Anglin believed in ministry to both the physical and spiritual needs of a person. He believed that the things Christians *do* present stronger demonstrations of God's power and love than the things they *say*. Second, the Home provided a means to spread the message of the cross. The Tai-an Home was located in the vicinity of Tai Shan Mountain, an area visited by thousands of Chinese each year for ritual worship of their gods. The Home of Onesiphorus stood as a testimony to streams of men, women, boys, and girls who had been set free to worship the one true God. Finally, the Home was committed to raising up boys and girls who had accepted Christ and training them for roles as either missionaries, evangelists, or Spirit-filled members of a local church (Albus 1951, 109-111).

A natural question arises: Did the Home of Onesiphorus fulfill these three purposes? The Home certainly demonstrated the power and love of God. J. Philip Hogan said that believers practice compassion ministry because Jesus did (Wilson 1997, 143). Anglin shared his personal thoughts regarding the love of Jesus as evidenced in the Home:

> The Home of Onesiphorus was opened in 1916 for the purpose of rescuing the helpless, such as old men and women with no one to care for them, younger women who are left widows with a few children, also boys and girls who are forced by circumstances to beg for a living. The Home has been the means of bringing the Gospel to the destitute in such a practical way they have been convinced that the religion of Jesus is real and they have sought Him and found Him precious to their souls (Anglin 1922, 12).

The Anglins did not stop by simply providing housing, clothing, and food for the destitute. They sought to lift them out of poverty, providing them with education and vocational training. They devised a plan where those being helped also received training that would benefit them in the future, while residents continued to assist with the daily needs of the Home in the meantime.

As the number of residents grew, Leslie and Ava Anglin had to address the issue of education. Therefore, they hired teachers to instruct the children. They wanted to equip the children so that they would fit in with others who were educated in the Chinese schools. They also deemed it essential for everyone in the Home to have the ability to read the Bible (Anglin 1922).

The training did not stop with classroom instruction. Teaching vocational skills was considered every bit as essential. In 1928, Anglin described the orphanage as an "institution where helpless men, women, boys, and girls are cared for, and all who can work are given something to do so that they will not feel that they are merely objects of charity." Every person admitted to the Home was assigned a place and work appropriate to their age, as well as their mental and physical abilities. Anglin said, "Our motto is, 'He that does not work shall not eat'" (Anglin 1928d, 2).[73]

The Home of Onesiphorus became a model of community development, offering a range of vocational training options. Little girls received their first sewing lessons as young as five or six years old. Little boys were employed in carrying water and sweeping

---

[73]Cf. 2 Thess 3:10.

yards. Older girls and women made clothes and engaged in cross-stitching. Older boys and men worked on the farm and in the industrial department (Anglin 1928d, 2).

Girls helped make clothes, shoes, and stockings. Eventually, to save on the cost of purchasing cloth, the Anglins bought a weaving machine and hired a man to teach some of the boys how to operate it. The Home opened a shop to make their furniture, doors, and windows for their buildings. They brought another man in to teach the boys these skills. They later purchased a flour mill for grinding wheat, a major crop in the area (Anglin 1922, 12).

Some of the equipment needed for vocational training required advanced expenditure of money. The needs of the Home were promoted in The *Pentecostal Evangel*, as well as in other publications. In time, the G. A. Lundmark family from Chicago represented the Home to interested partners in the United States (Albus 1951, 90).

Eventually, the industrial department of the school began to generate income. The shoe-making department, for example, made more than enough shoes for the Home's use. Therefore, they decided to sell the excess shoes as a means of supporting the Home. At one point, the Home was selling an average of a hundred pairs of shoes per week (Albus 1951, p. 67).

The flour mill not only paid its way but saved the Home and the city of Tai-an in 1925-26. Two warring armies clashed in combat in the Tai-an area. One of the warring generals came to the city and demanded enough flour to feed all of his soldiers. The city had no way to meet these demands and was faced with the dilemma of surrendering most of the food in the city to feed the soldiers or refusing to comply, which would result in the pillaging and destruction of the town. City leaders came to the Home of Onesiphorus and asked for help. They arranged for the city to provide the grain, and the Home put its flour mill into round-the-clock operation to feed the soldiers (Anglin 1930, 14).

From its humble beginnings in 1916, the Home grew to several hundred residents. By 1927, 500 children and 100 adults lived at the Home of Onesiphorus (Albus 1951, 79). During the 1928 famine, the number swelled to 1,150 residents (Ketcher 2015, 29).

Leslie Anglin was known in the community as "The Onesiphorus Man." People came from great distances to receive help. They believed that if they could somehow reach the Home, they would receive assistance. Anglin determined that he would never turn away anyone in need from his door (Albus 1951, 69-71).

The following excerpts from articles appearing in *The Pentecostal Evangel* convey the magnitude of the need as well as the largeness of the Anglins' hearts:

> We are crowded just now and it doesn't seem possible that we could take in more but when they come and we see their pitiful condition we can't say "no." If a suffering soul is denied help and turned away from the Home and goes out and becomes a victim of death from cold, hunger, or pestilence, somehow I can't stand to think of it, especially when I know that the soul will go into darkness without knowing Christ (Anglin 1924, 11).
>
> We have taken in 30 or more children recently and there are many more waiting to come. The war has left many destitute boys and girls in China. We cannot reach all of them, but many of them have applied to us to take them in. . . . We have over 500 hungry mouths to feed every day. Wheat has to be bought, ground into flour, and bread cooked every day. It requires over 5,600 pounds of bread a week for our home (Anglin 1926a, 10).
>
> There are many old men and women in China who have come down to the evening time of life with no one to care for them. Even though a son in China is very faithful to his mother and father as a rule, there are cases when all the sons have died or perhaps have gone . . . and have never been able to return. The old man or woman is left alone to beg. We have been able to take a few of these into the Home and give them light work to do so that they, too, might be happy (Anglin 1928a, 11).

On one occasion, a family of four walked eighty miles to seek help at the Home. On another day, five boys who had heard about the Home arrived, having walked forty miles. Many of these arrivals came at times when the Home was already overcrowded. Yet Anglin could not say "no" to anyone who asked for help. He would take them in, wash them, feed them, and clothe them, give them a bed to sleep in, and begin the process of teaching them how to make a new life for themselves (Albus 1951, 73).

The second purpose for existence, to spread the message of the cross, was also met. In 1927, Anglin wrote that the typical daily schedule began with a chapel service following breakfast. The service included singing, praying, and reading God's Word, followed by an explanation of its meaning and significance. Ava Anglin had an afternoon Bible lesson for wives and widows of workers. Several separate services were conducted on Sundays, including an afternoon Sunday school and an evening service (Anglin 1927b, 11).

Biblical training held a high priority for the Anglins: "The first important step in the training of all who come into the Home is to lead them to know Jesus as their personal Savior. We have Bible classes, prayer meetings, special meetings, and times of prayer for old and young" (Anglin 1928d, 2).

Anglin's heart was moved during the pilgrim season when hundreds and thousands of Chinese would travel to Tai Shan (Mountain) to worship: "How I long to see a work established here that will show forth to these people the Lord Jesus as Savior of the world" (Anglin 1919, 9). During the 1917 pilgrim season, they sold 5,000 gospel portions, as well as 100 copies of the New Testament, to worshiping pilgrims (Anglin 1917, 11).

Finally, the Home existed to raise up boys and girls who had accepted Christ, and train them for their roles as missionaries, evangelists, and Spirit-filled members of local churches. In 1917, Anglin wrote that every girl in the house and school, except one, had been saved, and nearly all had received the baptism of the Spirit (Anglin 1917, 11). In 1925, he reported that over 200 had received the baptism of the Holy Spirit in the Home and around the city of Tai-an. In 1924, 221 people were baptized in water, and an additional 110 were baptized between January and March of

1925 (Anglin 1925c, 10). In November 1925, Anglin reported that 37 individuals had received the baptism of the Holy Spirit since July 1 of that year (Anglin 1925a, 14). In 1928, he wrote, "Quite a number of our children want to go out as missionaries when they become men and women" (Anglin 1928d, 2).

Perhaps the greatest testimony to the fulfillment of this third purpose for the Home's existence came from the individual stories of changed lives. The first graduating class had three boys and three girls. Two of the boys went out as preachers of the gospel message. The other boy worked as a Christian mechanic. One of the girls married and later, with her husband, engaged in missionary work. The remaining two girls became department leaders at the Home (Albus 1951, 68).

David Chen first entered the Home as a small boy. As an adult, he went to the United States, where he graduated from Moody Bible Institute and later returned for missionary work in China. Samuel Hsiao was rescued from the 1920 famine and graduated from the Home in 1931. After his graduation, he served as an assistant to the Anglins in Tai-an (Albus 1951, 140).

At the beginning of his ministry, Anglin believed that building a strong Chinese national church required trained national believers. In 1933, Anglin again stated that conviction with these prophetic words: "China's great need is self-supporting Chinese Spirit-filled Christian workers who can go out and spread the good news and teach the people the truths of the gospel" (Hurst 2009, 21).

A Lasting Legacy

Leslie Anglin died in 1942. Ava Anglin lived ten years longer. Shortly after her husband's death, she was detained for twenty-nine months in a Japanese concentration camp. However, the ministry of the Home of Onesiphorus continued uninterrupted, led by national Chinese.

Anglin's funeral was one of the largest that the city of Tai-an had witnessed. It seemed the whole city mourned the death of the Onesiphorus Man. One individual following the funeral remarked, "This man's work shall truly live forever" (Albus 1951, 152).

In 2006, the city of Tai-an and the Chinese government held special celebrations to honor the Anglins and the ministry of the Home of Onesiphorus. They extended special invitations for the Assemblies of God to send representatives to join in the commemoration of the 90th anniversary of the Home (Ketcher 2015, 30).

Today, the Home resembles a college campus, featuring several five- and six-story buildings. It continues to minister to the poor, the suffering, and the unwanted. One section of the campus is devoted to caring for severely disabled children and those with special needs. Neither American missionaries nor American finances are allowed at this time. However, the legacy of the Anglins continues to challenge and touch the lives of the Chinese (Hurst 2009, 18).

Chapter Seven

THE WOMEN OF SHANXI: FAITHFULNESS THROUGH THE WAR YEARS

In 1900, Shanxi province became the scene of one of the worst bloodlettings of Christian martyrs for the entire Christian era. The Boxer Rebellion claimed the lives of both foreign missionaries and Chinese Christians throughout large parts of China, but this province was particularly hard hit. The provincial governor, Yu Xian, encouraged the killings which resulted in the martyrdom of more than 150 Protestant missionaries. In addition, hundreds of Chinese believers throughout the province were also hunted down and murdered by authorities because of their Christian testimony (Hattaway 2007, 2110).

Prior to these tragic events; however, God had already begun preparing new missionaries who would come to serve in this key north central province. In Austria-Hungary, 500 miles from Budapest, Marie Stephany was born to a Catholic family on December 9, 1878—the seventh of twelve children (I. Spence, n.d. a, 2). God's call and plan for her life would take her to the United States and then on to China where she would head a team of women missionaries who would make their mark in Shanxi through their exemplary missionary work.

Although the Bard family also conducted significant ministry in the province, most of the Assemblies of God mission work in Shanxi was carried out by four single women. Henrietta Tieleman and Alice Stewart later joined Stephany. The three of them were based in Ta Ch'ang where they planted a church with over 900 people, established an orphanage ministry and a drug addiction deliverance center, held tent meetings in the surrounding villages, and conducted short-term Bible school training. One other single woman, Anna Ziese, made her mark in the provincial capital of Taiyuan through her work in the prisons. Ziese was born in East Germany, which allowed her to remain in China post-1949. She reportedly died from natural causes in 1969.[74]

Single women missionaries played important roles in Assemblies of God missions worldwide. Gary McGee notes that by 1925, 95 of the 250 U.S. AG missionaries were single women. By the mid-1940s, 329 of the 503 American Assemblies of God missionaries serving worldwide were women (McGee 1986, 91-92).[75] This section on Stephany and the women of Shanxi province represents the larger number of missionary women whose devotion challenges believers of the twenty-first century in their commitment to obey the Great Commission.[76]

Ministry of Marie Stephany

Early Life of Marie Stephany

Marie Stephany's early childhood in Austria-Hungary prepared her for future work in Shanxi province. In her autobiographical sketch, *The Dragon Defeated* (n.d.), she describes her stubbornness as a child and her unwillingness to back down or give in to outside pressures. What was viewed as "naughtiness" when she was young later matured and developed into a persistence that served her well as a single woman in war-torn China.

At the age of ten, she worked in wheat fields. When she was eleven, she overheard some women discussing an Austrian family that wanted to hire a Hungarian speaking playmate for their son. On her own, without seeking her parents' approval, she applied for

---

[74]Much of the source material for this section comes from Stephany's (n.d.) *The Dragon Defeated*; Stephany (1939) *The Power of the Gospel in Shansi Province*; Alice Stewart (n.d.) *Like Zion's Mount in China*; David Bundy (2000) "Anna Ziese: For God and China," as well as several articles published in *The Pentecostal Evangel.*

[75]This number includes both the missionary wives and the single women.

[76]See Appendix A, "American Assemblies of God China Missionaries, 1914-1952."

and was accepted into the position. When her mother objected to her leaving home, Stephany explained that she had already made a promise to the family and that they were expecting her, so she had to go (Stephany n.d., 15).

When Stephany was twelve, her father immigrated to the United States. To take advantage of the half-price ticket for minors, he sent word for Marie to join him in Cleveland, Ohio. He planned for the remaining family members to join later (Dalton 1987, 3).

In Cleveland, Stephany found a job working as a housekeeper. She spoke little English, but after scalding her foot while doing housework and being hospitalized for several weeks, she learned English well enough to be understood. The extra care of a German physician in the hospital saved her from having her foot amputated (I. Spence, n.d. a, 3).

At this time, Stephany struggled with the sin of lying. Feeling guilty afterward, she would confess these sins to the local Catholic priest. One day while she was cleaning the house, she looked up to heaven and cried out that she wished her heart was as clean as the floor she was scrubbing. Stephany's heart was filled with unspeakable joy as she became a follower of Jesus that day. Later, when she went to the Catholic Church, the priest asked her what she needed to confess. She replied that she could not remember any of her sins since Jesus had taken them all away (Dalton 1987, 3).

When Stephany left the Catholic Church, she received much criticism and opposition from her family.[77] While attending a CMA church, she heard of the Pentecostal outpouring in Los Angeles. She attended one of R. A. Torrey's meetings in Cleveland, where he proclaimed that every child of God should wait on the Lord for the baptism of the Holy Spirit (Stephany n.d., 47). Deciding that this

---

[77]Marie's forgiveness and deliverance from telling lies left her with strong convictions concerning both telling the truth and living truthfully. If someone came to see her and she was not happy to see them she should not say, "I'm glad to see you." If she was glad to see them leave, she should not encourage them to stay since that would be a lie. She took notice to see if Christian's lives matched their words and if they did not, she lost confidence in them. In her autobiography she reflected that "by telling the truth from my heart, I lost many of my friends" (Stephany n.d., 34).

experience was what she needed, she fasted, prayed, and received Spirit baptism in 1906. At this same time, God began to speak to her about missionary service in China (Dalton 1987, 3-4).

Stephany's Preparation for Missionary Service

Stephany enrolled at Beulah Heights Bible School in North Bergen, New Jersey, for the 1914 fall semester. She was thirty-five years old and experienced difficulty in her studies due to her limited educational background and having received her schooling in a different language (Dalton 1987, 4). Her two years of study at Beulah Heights included practical lessons in adaptation and learning to trust God. Lodging at the school was spartan, but when complaining to God about it, she felt him speaking to her that this was in preparation for worse accommodations that would be awaiting her in China (I. Spence, n.d. a, 6).

Perhaps Stephany's greatest struggles came through her own questions about her worthiness and suitability for missionary service. Her limited educational background, combined with her age, made the prospect of learning Chinese seem impossible.[78] In addition, she worried about the care of her adopted daughter, Gloria,[79] and her mother.

Concerning Stephany's doubts about her aptitude for learning Chinese, God reminded her that through Christ she could do all things (Phil 4:13). As for the care of Gloria and her mother, God told Stephany to simply trust him and leave their care in his hands. Later, God used Marie's pet canary to build up her faith in trusting him to provide for financial and other needs: "Would you

---

[78]Stephany, at thirty-seven, had been told Chinese was one of the most difficult languages in the world to learn; for someone older than thirty, it would be impossible.

[79]Several years earlier, Stephany was approached about caring for an abandoned baby girl. At the time, this brought a lot of criticism and misunderstandings for her. Some thought the baby was hers through an illicit affair. Marie later formalized Gloria's adoption and cared for her until she reached adulthood. Gloria died a few years after her marriage (I. Spence, n. d.). Stephany had led her father to Christ shortly before his death. Her mother was still an unbeliever. The combination of concern for the financial care of both Gloria and her mother weighed heavily on her. In addition, her mother's spiritual well-being weighed on her.

let the little canary you have in a cage starve to death?" Stephany answered, "Of course not. I put the bird there, and I must take care of it (Stephany n.d, 62)."[80] Then she felt the Holy Spirit reminding her that God had called her and placed her in China, therefore he would take care of all aspects of her life (Booze 2001, 4-5).

Yet faith and confidence came slowly and not without battles to overcome the doubts. At one point, Stephany became so discouraged about the prospect of going to China that she prepared to donate the cash raised for her outfit to someone else who would go in her place. As she started with this plan, she noticed an absence of God's presence in her life:

> This time the Lord withdrew His presence from me for three days. When I prayed, it seemed as if God had shut the door against me and would not listen to my cry. The third day as I was standing combing my hair, the Lord spoke to me, saying that if I continually resisted His will, He would withdraw His Holy Spirit from me as He did from King Saul with the result that I would be the most miserable creature on earth, even as Saul was (Stephany n.d., 56).

Stephany's response: "I will go simply to obey Thee, even if I can't do one thing after I get there. I am willing to go as a failure and die there. Anything, Lord, so that You don't withdraw Your Holy Spirit from me" (Stephany n.d., 56).

Marie graduated from Bible School in May of 1916 and received missionary ordination from the Assemblies of God that same year (McGee 2004, 255). By the end of October, she had secured all the necessary funds for her travel to China. However, her send-off was a lonely one as no one came to the station to bid her farewell. Due to some miscommunication, her family and friends showed up at the wrong railway station. As Stephany began her journey, she held

---

[80]This story also appeared in an article by Joyce Booze in 2001, entitled, "Starve a Little Bird?" that appeared in the Fall issue of *Club Connection*, 4-5.

on to God's promise that he would never leave or forsake her (I. Spence, n.d.a, 7).

Stephany's Missionary Service and Methodology

Stephany arrived in Tianjin, North China, on Thanksgiving Day, 1916. After a brief Thanksgiving celebration, she continued on to Taiyuan, the capital of Shanxi province, where she devoted two years to full-time language study. Language learning proved difficult for her. She discovered that her first instructor was addicted to opium and allowed her to get by with wrong pronunciation of words. She replaced him with a teacher from the northern section of Shanxi province whose dialect differed from that used in the provincial capital. However, due to the lack of availability of any other teacher, she hired him with the hope that he would later help her with evangelistic work when she eventually opened her own mission station. Her hopes were realized when he was saved and baptized in the Holy Spirit (Stephany n.d., 61).

Stephany opened her first mission station in the town of Huei Ren, approximately seventy-five miles outside of the provincial capital. After two years, she moved to Ta Ch'ang, which became her permanent mission station (Stephany 1939, 14-18).

Stephany prioritized evangelism.

> One day while I was praying that the Lord would send someone to preach the gospel to the village people, the Lord definitely spoke to me that I should answer my own prayer. In obedience therefore to this call, a mission station was opened about eight years ago in the village of Ta Ch'ang, China. . . . To the north, the east, the south, and the west of us are many other villages with thousands of people sitting in heathen darkness, knowing nothing of the love of God and His power to save. Our aim is to give the gospel not only to the people of this village, but also to the people in the surrounding villages. (Stephany 1928a, 10)

Stephany followed a simple method. Realizing the difficulty of getting people to enter buildings, she purchased a tent for her evangelistic meetings. Her team devoted seven months of every year to this ministry throughout the neighboring villages. Once people responded to invitations to accept Christ, she started holding meetings in their homes. As these grew, they would open a station under local leadership and support. Follow-up meetings helped establish the new disciples and their young church (Stephany 1928c, 11). Later, with the help of three other missionaries, Marie was able to carry on the work of fifteen outstations. Many of these stations were indigenous with local leadership (Stephany 1940a).

Most of the early Assemblies of God missionaries prioritized evangelism, but when confronted with the dire needs of hurting people, they responded with compassion and efforts to alleviate their suffering. Such was the case with Stephany in Shanxi in the early 1920s (McGee 2004, 255-256).

Government officials in Shanxi had struggled to deal with the opium problem for many years. Initial plans called for preparing a place for addicts to live for one year while trying to kick the habit. Success rates were extremely low, as the majority of residents would return to opium use immediately after leaving the facility. Realizing that the situation called for more drastic solutions, officials ordered the beheading of anyone who trafficked opium. In fact, the opium dealers' heads were displayed in public locations to warn others of the severe punishment for selling the drug. However, this did little to alleviate the problem. A later law decreed that officials would execute those who sold *and* used the drug. Hundreds were killed, yet the power of addiction continued to ruin lives (Stephany 1939, 23).

The craving of opium was so strong that men would sell everything they owned, including members of their own families, to buy the drug. Stephany reached out to individuals bound by the "devil's smoke" and proclaimed the power of God to deliver from the addiction. Her approach foreshadowed that of the still decades distant Teen Challenge (McGee 2004, 256). Testimonies of lives set free were abundant.

> Another rich man, because of opium mortgaged his wife and sold his little boy to a temple to become a priest, and finally became a beggar himself, but through the power of the gospel he was completely changed, cleansed, and filled with the Holy Spirit. He remarried the wife he had mortgaged and now both he and his wife are preaching the gospel, and his boy is here with us. (Stephany 1928a, 10)

> A young man named Mr. Yieh had been a drug addict for many years. He pawned everything he possibly could and when he had nothing more of his own to pawn, he stole his mother's grain and exchanged that for drugs. Nothing she or the relatives did could change him. When visiting his mother-in-law's home, he saw how the Lord had wonderfully changed her who had been a drug addict for over twenty years. He went to one of our outstations where we have rooms where these dope addicts may come to live for at least a month to learn about Jesus and to give up the drug habit. Many come but some do not accept the Lord. This young man, however, was saved even before the month was up and was baptized in water (Stephany 1939, 32-33).

Mrs. Kuo had attended the mission station as a young girl and learned the song, "Jesus Loves Me, This I Know." When she was in her early teens, her family gave her in marriage to a non-Christian family and her mother-in-law cruelly mistreated her. When her husband became sick, he became addicted to opium while using it to ease the pain. The Kuo family eventually impoverished themselves trying to satisfy his drug cravings. During those dark days, Mrs. Kuo recalled the words of the song she had learned as a child and wondered if she would ever again feel the same sense of joy she had experienced while singing it years before.

One day, some folks came to her village and pitched a big tent, advertising that meetings would be held there later that day. The whole village turned out to see the big tent and the "foreign devils." As Mrs. Kuo listened, she realized they were talking about the same Jesus she had sung about as a little girl. She heard that drug addicts had been helped by the people conducting these meetings and persuaded her husband to go seeking deliverance. Impressed by the life of the Bible woman at the gospel hall, the husband cried out to God for help and was set free from his addiction. When he returned home a new man in Christ, his wife also opened her heart to Jesus. Soon their home became a site for Bible studies and home meetings (Stewart 1946, 10-11).

The many ministries of Stephany's Ta Ch'ang station required many national workers. Within a few years, more than thirty of the forty national workers who worked with Stephany were former addicts who had been delivered and discipled under her ministry (Hurst 2001, 14).

The famine of 1920 demanded changes in the direction of Stephany's ministry. She had already become aware of the needs of small children because of the prevalent opium addiction in the area. Many addicts had already become too poor to support their children. Baby boys were quickly sold to families who wanted a male heir. However, people did not want baby girls. Some poor families would take in a little girl for the purpose of raising her to be a future daughter-in-law, but most baby girls were either drowned at birth or discarded in barren fields (Stephany 1939, 40).

One day a man found a baby crying in a field and brought the baby to Stephany. The baby, wrapped in straw, was surrounded by three dogs waiting for the baby to die. Stephany accepted the child who weighed slightly over three pounds. A few weeks later, they gave her the name "Hope," symbolizing that there was hope for her to live (Stephany 1939, 40-42).

Hearing that Stephany received babies, beggars would make arrangements to bring unwanted children to her. She would give them ten to twenty cents for each child (Stephany 1939, 42). Eventually, Stephany was caring for thirty children in her home (Dalton 1993a, 4). Later, in her book, *The Power of the Gospel in Shansi Province* (1939), she said a few things about her orphanage: "Although I am not called to this kind of work, I am praying that the Lord will definitely call a missionary to take it upon her heart so that we may be able to take in more children" (Stephany 1939, 40).

Stephany arrived back in the United States in August 1923 for her first furlough and remained there for almost three full years. This three-year respite from her work provided her with the opportunity to personally acquaint supporters with the ministry, enlist prayer support, and raise additional funds for her work. She seized the opportunity to recruit helpers to join her team, and by the time she returned to China in December 1926, two additional missionaries had joined her team.

Miss Henrietta Tieleman (1896-1962) dedicated her life to missionary service at the age of nineteen. She received the baptism of the Holy Spirit at the age of twenty-five; in 1921, she enrolled at Bethel Bible Institute in Newark, New Jersey. She traveled to China in 1926 with the support of Mr. Frank Casley of Turtle Creek, Pennsylvania. She applied for and received appointment with the Assemblies of God in 1931.

Miss Alice Stewart (1902-1993) was born in New York City and graduated from Beulah Bible School in North Bergen, New Jersey. She and Henrietta Tieleman served in China until 1952 when they transferred to Taiwan.

Stewart attended the annual Bible school mission convention when Marie Stephany, James Taylor, and James Salter presented the needs of their respective fields. Stewart became alarmed when she felt that God wanted her to go to China. She had heard of the many missionaries martyred during the Boxer Rebellion, so her first response to the Spirit's promptings was: "Africa, India, the Islands of the Sea, but not China" (Stewart n.d., 9).

At once the Spirit directed her to go and tell Stephany that she was called to China. For two days, Stewart disobeyed this word from God. She was afraid that Stephany, who seemed a stern person, might strictly interrogate her as to why she felt called to China. But each night Stewart noted that Stephany was eyeing her intently. During the third night of the convention, the Spirit spoke again to Alice that this was her last chance to obey his leading. That evening, Stewart told Stephany that God had called her to go to China. Stephany amazed Stewart by embracing her and telling her that she had known for two weeks that God would deal with her about China (Stewart, n.d. 9).

The trio of Stephany, Tieleman, and Stewart served under extremely stressful conditions. Early on, God had given them Ps 91:5-7 as his promise of protection: "Thou shalt not be afraid for the terror by night; nor for the arrow *that* flieth by day; *Nor* for the pestilence *that* walketh in darkness; *nor* for the destruction *that* wasteth at noonday. A thousand shall fall at thy side, and ten thousand at thy right hand; *but* it shall not come nigh thee" (KJV).

Despite the outbreak of the Sino-Japanese war in June of 1937, they stayed and opened up their mission as a refuge station. Even though communication and aid from supporters in the United States was sporadic, God provided for their needs. Turbulent times produced soft and receptive hearts in individuals who were displaced and living in uncertain times. Many were saved and filled with the Holy Spirit, as God turned calamity into blessing.

This team of missionary women, together with their national co-workers, had built a church in Ta Ch'ang that could accommodate approximately a thousand people. The Ta Ch'ang mission, which had begun in a rented house with only one Chinese evangelist to help Stephany, had grown to include several buildings used for an orphanage, an addiction deliverance center, a Bible school, and a church. More than thirty workers assisted the work there and in the various outstations set up from the tent evangelism program. At least two-thirds of these workers had been delivered from addiction to opium. Additionally, twelve students from Ta Ch'ang enrolled in the Truth Bible Institute in Beijing, with twenty more students studying at the local four-month Bible school (Dalton 1987, 5).

Ministry of Anna Ziese (1895-1969)

At the same time as Stephany's team was ministering in Ta Ch'ang, another single woman served in Taiyuan. Anna Ziese, born in East Germany in 1895, traveled to China in 1920 and, with the exception of a brief furlough from 1928 to 1930, remained there until her death in 1969. Although she was sent out as a US Assemblies of God missionary, she never became an American citizen. This enabled her to remain in China post-1949.

She worked primarily with women and prisoners. Many of her letters, published in *The Pentecostal Evangel,* reported results from her prison ministry:

- July 1933: "Please pray for the prisoners. We have three jail meetings a week and they are so open to listen but we long to see them get really saved."
- February 1934: "The work in the prison is very encouraging. We go to the big prison every week where there are 800 men and also many women."
- January 1935a: "We had another baptismal service in the prison, when five women and eighty-one men followed the Lord in water baptism."
- August 1935b: "While Brother Hansen was with us, we had another baptismal service in the prison. Thirty-eight men and nine women were baptized."

Japanese aggression in China, combined with the civil war between the Nationalists and the Communists, made the 1930s a decade of unceasing political turmoil.[81] The Communists had ended their Long March in Yan'an, located in the neighboring Shaanxi province. They planned to expand their influence in Shanxi, the province just east of their base camp. Japanese aggression was moving both westward and southward. The people of Shanxi found themselves caught in the middle.

One of Ziese's letters, written in 1936, reveals the conditions under which she and Stephany's team were laboring:

> Conditions are very bad here now, and the war clouds are hanging low, so we never know what another day may bring forth. People's hearts are failing them for fear and they don't know which way to turn. They are afraid of the

---

[81] Japanese encroachment had begun following the signing of the Treaty of Versailles ending World War I. Japan had signed secret agreements with several of the Allied powers to receive Germany's territory in Shandong province. Later, Japan eyed Manchuria (northeast China) for the next step of its military expansion into China. The "Mukden Incident" of 1931 led to Japan's occupation of Manchuria. Full scale aggression by the Japanese began in 1937 and continued until the end of World War II.

> enemy's airplanes, and, of course, one cannot blame them. . . . I am glad that we, as children of God, know and feel that He is our refuge and strength (Bundy 2000, 16).

Despite the difficult conditions, Ziese never considered evacuation to the United States or out of the danger zone as a serious option. Ruth Melching, who also served in northern China during this time, remembered that Bard, thinking to send her to the United States on furlough, was able to get Ziese as far as Beijing in 1940. She became suspicious of his intentions and excused herself to return to Taiyuan under the pretext of picking up some forgotten items. She refused to return to Beijing (Bundy 2000, 17).

Similarly, when Ziese was told she needed to leave China in 1949, she traveled as far as Shanghai and had her trunks put on a ship. However, at the last moment, she felt she should not leave and, getting off the boat, she returned to Taiyuan. Her trunks arrived in the United States without her (Dalton 1993b, 5).

Ruth Melching, in an oral interview with Adele Flower Dalton, remembered that even though Ziese had good relationships with other missionaries, she chose to work independently in Taiyuan. She had a large church in Taiyuan as well as a smaller church and several outstations for which she was responsible in addition to her extensive prison ministry. Many Chinese co-workers helped her with these ministries. Missionary children, as well as their parents, referred to her as "Auntie Anna." When visitors came, she would stop what she was doing to talk with them. She completely identified with the Chinese (Bundy 2000, 19).

Ziese's unique situation as a missionary with a [East] German passport served her well. After the bombing of Pearl Harbor, most American missionaries still in China were either repatriated to the United States or confined to concentration camps. Germany and Japan, however, were allies in the war, which allowed her some degree of freedom. There were, of course, the challenges of living in both a foreign and civil war zone, but she did have limited freedom for ministry (Bundy 2000, 16-17).

The February 11, 1950, *Pentecostal Evangel* printed one of Anna's letters.

> When I was young and in Bible School we used to sing, "If Jesus goes with me I'll go anywhere," but now after these many years I gladly say, "If Jesus stays with me, I'll stay anywhere," for when we are in His will we find His grace ever sufficient. Thus far I am very glad that I remained in China. The Lord gave me the portion of Scripture, "Be thou faithful unto death." By His grace I want to be faithful at any cost. Please pray for me; also, pray for the dear Chinese (Ziese 1950, n.p.).

Harlan Park, missionary in Hong Kong, received one of Ziese's final letters, dated March 22, 1966. Some of her comments implied that she was unable to write extensively due to censorship and security concerns. The letter does, however, convey that she had no regrets in continuing her commitment to her missionary call.

> We used to sing a song at home, "The Lord has done so much for me throughout the passing years, I cannot tell it all, I cannot tell it all" [emphasis mine] and that is the song in my heart today. But you know there are times in life when to speak is silver and to keep silent is gold. I know you are praying for me, and please continue to do so (Ziese 1966).[82]

Few details are available concerning Ziese's last years. The limited information indicates that she lived in a one-room house, raising goats for both her livelihood and food. In addition, she received a monthly stipend of $3.00 from the Chinese government, which was the average monthly wage at that time. She died during the summer of 1969, an example of a woman who gave her all for the people she loved (Bundy 2000, 18).

---

[82]This letter was handwritten by Ziese and dated Taiyuan, March 22, 1966.

Chapter Eight

WILLIAM WALLACE SIMPSON (1869-1961) AND WILLIAM EKVALL SIMPSON (1901-1932)

The Ministry of William Wallace Simpson

The Early CMA Years

William Wallace Simpson was born October 2, 1869, in a one-room log cabin in eastern Tennessee. At twenty-one, he served as a pastor of a small congregation for four months. During the week, he taught in a local school, and on Sundays he preached. On the second Monday after starting his pastoral responsibilities, he opened his Bible at random to find his text for the following Sunday. He read Mark 16:15: "Go into all the world and proclaim the gospel to the whole creation." He thought that would make a good text, but upon reading it again, he felt it would not be honest for him to preach from that text if he was not practicing it himself. Kneeling in his room, he prayed: "Lord, I am only a poor mountain boy with little talent, but I will obey you with all my heart" (Simpson, n.d., 1).

Simpson decided that the Missionary Training Institute run by A. B. Simpson and the CMA was the best place for him to prepare for missionary service. On February 14, 1892, he read Rom 15:20 where the Apostle Paul declared his ambition not to build on another's foundation but to preach the gospel where it had not yet been declared.[83] Simpson decided that verse suited him and that he would attempt to do the same. Hearing that Tibet was closed to missionaries, he thought, "I'll go there." The following day, he went to see Pastor A. B. Simpson (no relation) and informed him of his decision. Simpson took down his personal prayer book and showed William his entry for that day: "Took by faith that the Lord would call some students to Tibet" (Simpson n.d., 6).[84]

Simpson arrived in Shanghai in April 1892. He met with James Hudson Taylor and asked his advice on the feasibility of settling in Tibet for mission work. Taylor shared his personal opinion that Simpson should first situate in China, for it would be at least ten years before he could enter Tibet. He then bluntly laid out several requirements for a successful entrance into Tibet: (1) learn the Chinese language and customs, (2) understand the Mandarin system of government and how to deal with the government officials, and (3) learn the Tibetan language. Finally, they must expect spiritual forces to oppose them at every step (McGee 2004, 48). Simpson interpreted Taylor's cautionary speech as a warning that work in Tibet must not be undertaken in one's own strength, but only in the power of the Holy Spirit. Simpson claimed specific scriptural promises for each of Taylor's requirements.[85] He found his primary promise from God in Rev 3:8: "I have set before you an open door, which no one is able to shut" (Simpson 1949a).

---

[83]Rom 15:20-29 was the basis for Simpson's belief that Paul had missed God's will in traveling to Jerusalem (Acts 21-23) instead of continuing with his stated ambition of preaching the gospel where it had not yet been proclaimed. He mentioned this in his 1950 sermon, "Redeem the Time" as well as his 1952 message, "Why Not Discern This Time?" and a message in 1953, "The Great Final Message of the Lord Jesus." Copies of these sermons can be found in the AGWM Archives in Springfield, MO.

[84]This account is also given in Edward Koetitz's [1980?], compilation on "William W. Simpson: Missionary to Northwest China, 1892-1949," 57.

[85]For the requirement of language, Simpson claimed Mark 16:17 that "they will speak in new tongues." For dealing with government officials he took Mark 13:9-11, ". . . you will stand before governors and kings for my sake, to bear witness before them. And the gospel must first be proclaimed to all nations. And when they bring you to trial and deliver you over, do not be anxious beforehand what you are to say, but say whatever is given you in that hour, for it is not you who speak, but the Holy Spirit." And for the final requirement, Simpson took Luke 10:19 where Jesus promised, "I have given you authority to tread on serpents and scorpions, and over all the power of the enemy, and nothing shall hurt you" (McGee 2004, 48).

Although Simpson wrote that he was willing to study for as long as necessary to master the languages, he also expected that God would give him a supernatural ability to speak Chinese. When he arrived at CMA headquarters in central China, the director told him to begin language study on May 20. Simpson objected saying that he was praying and trusting God to give him the language. The director told him he would wait until noon to see if God had answered his prayers. If, by noon, he could not speak Chinese, he must start his classes. Simpson later wrote: "I prayed the Lord to guide, and He led me to submit" (Simpson 1953a, 1).[86]

Simpson's language study included both Mandarin Chinese and Tibetan. Following language study, he spent several months in central China evangelizing by tract distribution before traveling to Taochow, which was located on the Gansu/Tibetan border. He arrived on April 7, 1895. After establishing a mission station in Taochow, Simpson returned to Shanghai, where he married Otilia Ekvall on December 7. The young couple arrived back in Taochow on April 12, 1896 (Koetitz [1980?], 2).

Simpson records several examples of power encounters from these early years on the Gansu/Tibetan border. Before their 1899 furlough, they traveled a few miles across the Tibetan border and were preparing to set up their tent for the night when several men from the area showed up and told them they had to leave. No rain had fallen for several months, and the foreigner's (a non-Buddhist) arrival would hinder their prayers. Simpson convinced the Tibetans to allow them to stay the night with the promise that they would leave the next day (Simpson 1948).

Early the next morning, Simpson shot a pheasant near his tent. The local Tibetans arrived in time to see Simpson carrying a dead pheasant and, in consternation, insisted that he leave at once.

---

[86]Simpson based his belief that God would supernaturally enable him to speak Chinese without language study on his interpretation of Mark 16:15-20. Simpson arrived in China in 1892, which preceded the outpouring of the Holy Spirit at both Topeka, Kansas and Azusa Street, so the concept of "missionary tongues" had not yet been voiced. Simpson, however, claimed the promise of "they will speak with new tongues" for himself. He said, "I thanked the Lord for His promise and fully expected He, by the Spirit, would enable me to speak the Chinese language on my arrival in China. . . . I know better now" (Simpson 1953a, 1).

"Now we will never get rain. Who knows whose ancestor you have killed in that dead pheasant?" (Simpson 1948, 4). While Simpson expressed his belief that the Christian God could provide rain, they suddenly heard rain falling on the tent. Rain fell for the next two days, and they allowed Simpson to stay (Simpson 1948).

On another occasion (1902), a leading lama pronounced curses that any foreigner passing through the gate on one particular road would immediately be stricken blind. As Simpson rode through the gate, local Tibetans gathered to observe the effects of the lama's curses. Simpson passed through unharmed, leading the lama to predict that many Tibetans would eventually become followers of the foreign religion (Simpson 1948).

By 1908, the CMA missionaries in Gansu province had heard of the speaking in tongues at Azusa Street. Forty local Chinese believers joined the nine missionaries in January for a week of meetings. At that time, no one expected anything unusual to occur, since they all accepted the CMA stance that they had already received the baptism of the Spirit by faith. Nevertheless, on Friday afternoon, one of the Chinese brothers began to shake and started speaking in tongues. While Simpson was praying, "Lord, what does it mean?" he heard the Chinese brother speak in perfect English, "Eternity is nigh" (Simpson, n.d., 1). Returning home from the convention, Simpson announced to his family and Grace Agar, another CMA missionary working with them in Gansu, that he was seeking the baptism of the Spirit as in Acts 2:4 (Simpson, n.d.).

Four years later, on May 5, 1912, Simpson received the baptism of the Spirit with the evidence of speaking in tongues.[87] On that particular evening, Simpson had gathered together with six other missionaries and four of their children for a time of prayer. Simpson sat at the organ singing the song:

> The mistakes of my life have been many,
> The sins of my heart have been more

---

[87]Grace Agar received Spirit baptism, speaking in tongues while on furlough in 1912. Shortly after her baptism, she resigned from the CMA.

But I come as He has bidden,
And I'll knock at the open door.
I know I am weak and sinful,
It comes to me more and more;
But since the dear Savior has bid me come in,
I'll enter the open door.
I am weakest of those who love Him;
I am poorest of those who pray;
And I scarce can see for weeping;
But He will not say me Nay.
I know I am weak and sinful,
It comes to me more and more;
But since the dear Savior has bid me come in,
I'll enter the open door (Simpson n.d., 9).

As he continued singing, a tremendous sense of his personal sinfulness overwhelmed him. Almost simultaneously, he realized all his sins had been nailed to the cross and that he was the object of Christ's great love. Overcome with joy, he opened his mouth to thank and praise God only to discover that his joy was expressing itself in a holy laughter. A few moments later, he realized he was speaking in another language. Simpson lost all track of time as he spoke in tongues, but remembered that while seated on the floor, he stretched out his hands and petitioned God to pour out the Holy Spirit over the entire region. At that moment, his twelve-year-old daughter, Louise, began to speak in tongues to his left while nine-year-old Milton Christie began speaking in tongues to his right (Simpson n.d., 10-11).

The following morning (May 6, 1912), Chow Chao-nan, a Confucian scholar and one of the first converts in that area, visited Simpson and began speaking in tongues. Over the next two days, Simpson's wife and daughter, Margaret, received the Spirit baptism along with their ten-year-old son, Willie. Margaret, who had just received, laid hands on one of her Chinese friends, and she immediately began to speak in tongues. The next day, so many people came that they had to put the men in one room and the women and girls in another. Over the next ten days, more than thirty local believers were filled with the baptism in the Holy Spirit, as in Acts 2:4 (Simpson 1953a, 9-11).

Simpson began preaching among CMA stations along the Tibetan border, testifying of his Pentecostal experience. Between fifty and sixty Chinese Christians in these stations received the Spirit baptism and spoke in tongues. Three China Inland Mission stations in the area issued invitations for Simpson to share his testimony.

In March 1913, Simpson opened a short-term Bible school in Gansu making his teachings on the Holy Spirit a key component of the curriculum. That same year, W. W. Simpson notified A. B. Simpson that virtually the entire work in northwest China was Pentecostal. The CMA China annual convention in August 1913 resulted in a rejection of Simpson's position on tongues as evidence of the Spirit baptism. Furthermore, the CMA required a signed statement from Simpson that he would refrain from teaching that the baptism of the Holy Spirit was always accompanied by speaking in tongues. The following statement summarized the official position of the CMA: "We hold that the consecrated believer may receive the Holy Spirit in His fullness without speaking in tongues or without any supernatural manifestations whatever" (Simpson n.d., 9).[88] Since the Simpsons were

---

[88]Carl Brumback (1977), in *A Sound from Heaven*, lists debts owed by the Pentecostal movement to the CMA. Teachings on salvation, healing, sanctification, the second coming, as well as emphasis on missions served as cornerstones for the Assemblies of God doctrinal position. The one exception was the teaching on tongues being the evidence of the baptism of the Holy Spirit. The CMA position was that tongues could accompany Spirit baptism but that it should not be viewed as *the* evidence of being filled with the Spirit. Other signs were viewed as equally important among which was holiness/sanctification. Donald Gee bemoaned the substitution of baptism of the Holy Spirit for sanctification in revising the CMA "Fourfold Gospel." Gee worried that the substitution would create casual lifestyles that did not emphasize the importance of holy living. Gee suggested that perhaps Pentecostal assemblies should adopt a "Fivefold Gospel" (Gee 1972, 55).

Many of the early leaders of the young Assemblies of God came from the CMA and included J. W. Welch, Frank M. Boyd, D. W. Kerr, William I. Evans, A. G. Ward, Minnie Draper, W. W. Simpson, and Noel Perkin. The Missionary Training Institute at Nyack, NY helped prepare several of the missionaries who joined the AG ranks after 1914. Victor Plymire and Grace Agar began their ministries with the CMA.

unwilling to sign the doctrinal statement, CMA leaders asked them to resign as missionaries.[89]

W. W. Simpson and the Assemblies of God

Before returning to the United States, Simpson began an itinerant ministry that carried him to several locations in China, where he taught and preached about the Holy Spirit. Many believers were filled with the Spirit through his ministry. Simpson received an invitation from the Anglins in Tai-an. Les and Ava Anglin had previously received the Spirit baptism and accepted the Pentecostal teaching. However, many of the Chinese in Tai-an had not yet experienced the outpouring of the Spirit. In Simpson's meetings, so many believers received the infilling of the Spirit that Simpson claimed the entire work in Tai-an became Pentecostal (Simpson 1953a, 30).

Otilia Simpson suggested a return to the United States in the summer of 1915. It had been thirteen years since their last furlough. Children's schooling needs, combined with Otilia's declining health, pressed the Simpson family to return to the States in July 1915. Later that same year, Simpson attended the St. Louis General Council and chose to affiliate with the Assemblies of God (Simpson n.d., 9). He received missionary appointment on December 29, 1916 (Simpson 1953a, 38).

In a spring 1916 camp meeting in New York, Simpson heard a woman speaking in tongues in Chinese with instructions for him to return to Taochow, Gansu province. When Simpson left the CMA, he had been asked not to return to areas of China where he had previously served. Simpson had promised the CMA that he

---

[89]Charles Nienkirchen (1992) presents the CMA side of the dispute with W.W. Simpson. He notes that W. W. viewed the position of A. B. Simpson and many of the other CMA workers on the China field as being hostile to Pentecostal baptism choosing to emphasize the necessity of a "baptism of love" that did not necessarily require speaking in tongues. In a letter to A. B. Simpson dated October 17, 1916, W. W. Simpson challenged the CMA's official position and urged them to stop fighting against God and that if they would only humbly seek the baptism of the Spirit as described in Acts 2 that they would "get it and then . . . know what I am talking about" (Nienkirchen 1992, 111-112).

would not return unless God definitively showed him that this was his will for him to do so. He interpreted this message in tongues as God's revelation that he should return to his old mission station in northwest China (Simpson 1953a, 32-33).

The ill health of his wife and World War I combined to delay Simpson's return to China. During this delay, Simpson joined the faculty of Bethel Bible Institute in Newark, New Jersey. After Otilia passed away, Simpson began to make plans to return to China and arrived back in 1918. Seven years later, Simpson married Martha Merrill, a new missionary who had arrived in China from Glad Tidings Institute in San Francisco.

Simpson ministered through periods of political turmoil as various warlords vied for control of the area. In 1923, the area experienced famine conditions brought on by both civil turmoil and drought. This led Simpson into famine relief work. He established a home for famine orphans, housing and feeding nearly 500 children from 1928-1930 (Simpson 1953a, 68). In addition, Simpson had previously introduced potatoes in northwest China. These potatoes withstood the drought conditions better than other indigenous crops. Later, Simpson estimated that his "Simpson potatoes" possibly saved the lives of multiplied thousands of people. (Koetitz [1980?]).

During the political turmoil of 1928-1930, several churches of Gansu province gave prophetic words that helped Simpson prepare in advance to face several crises. One such prophecy came on November 28, 1929, and warned of approaching armies that would come from three different directions within forty days. Simpson led the churches in prayer and fasting for God's deliverance and wisdom in dealing with the crisis. God intervened and protected in miraculous ways, ranging from hiding the teenage girls in the famine relief home to protecting them from soldiers who were intent on pillaging and raping young women to sagacious wisdom that protected both the Chinese inhabitants from Muslim soldiers and, a few days later, the Muslim population from the Chinese army (Simpson 1953a, 70-74).

The Communists began their "Long March," moving from Jiangxi province to Yan'an in Shaanxi province in 1933-34. Fleeing from the Nationalist Party's armies, the Communists pillaged their way through Hunan, Guizhou, and Sichuan, burning churches, kidnapping missionaries, and persecuting national Christians. The Simpsons and others in northwest China felt they would be safe in the country's hinterlands. However, in January 1935, missionaries in Gansu received word from the U.S. Consul indicating the Communists were headed their way and that they should make preparations to relocate to a safer area. Following the instructions of Rom 13:1-4 regarding being subservient to governmental powers, the Simpsons prepared to leave Gansu (Simpson 1953a, 84).

Even though Simpson had conducted the bulk of his missionary work in the Gansu-Tibetan border area, he had also traveled to other provinces where he frequently evangelized and taught in local Bible schools. Evacuation from Gansu only meant a relocation in their ministry. Simpson, along with Bard, frequently taught at Truth Bible Institute (TBI), which was established in 1936 in Beijing. TBI was one of the earliest Bible schools of the American Assemblies of God.[90] The importance attached to the training of national leaders can be seen by what Bard wrote: "The dying masses of China who are still in utter darkness of sin . . . can only be reached with the assistance of a strong and well-trained corps of native workers" (Bard 1936a, 8).

During the North China District Council meeting, Simpson reminded the participants that the work in Gansu province had been able to continue, despite the absence of missionaries, because they had earlier committed to the priority of training national workers. The Council committed itself to establishing Truth Bible Institute with Bard as the principal and W. W. Simpson as one of the teachers. Simpson worked evangelistic meetings in north and central China into his Bible school teaching schedule (Simpson 1953a, 87).

The Simpsons returned to the United States for furlough in 1940. That fortuitous timing saved them from internment in Japanese camps during World War II. However, it became

---

[90]Prior to the opening of Truth Bible Institute, Marie Stephany, Henrietta Tieleman, and Alice Stewart in Ta Ch'ang had already opened a short-term Bible school for the training of national workers.

impossible for them to return to China until after World War II ended in 1945. Simpson attended the Minneapolis General Council in 1941, where he sang a revised version of his song, "Take Me Back to China." The lyrics indicated that, even at the age of seventy-two, Simpson had no intention of retiring.

> Two precious daughters fair and son I buried there,
> O how my heart did tear
> I have three dear graves in China.
> Those graves I love them so, Lord Jesus, let me go,
> My heart will break I know, If I can't go back to China.
> By sea no steamers ply, Big warplanes dot the sky,
> And passports men deny;
> They won't let me go to China.
> But Lord, Thou hast all power Before Thee despots cower,
> I cry to Thee this hour,
> O Lord, take me back to China!
> Today I seem to see Loved faces turned to me,
> They are calling me to be
> Again with the flocks in China.
> Though I'm no longer young, Youth's song already sung.
> O who will help along?
> For I'm going back to China (Simpson 1953a, 95)!

Simpson arrived in China alone on January 16, 1946, and worked in China until 1949 separated from the other members of his family who had remained in the United States. Traveling by boat to Shanghai, he reflected on ministry priorities for that season of his life. He was already seventy-seven years old. Fighting between the Nationalists and the Communists for control of the country raged in post-World War II China. After days of contemplation and prayer, Simpson felt that focusing on training the national church should be his priority.

> Every believer must be filled with the Spirit; every believer must be fully qualified and really be an active witness for the Lord. I understood that because I was now alone my ministry must not be as formerly among the unevangelized

> but among the believers, preparing them to do the work of evangelizing China. I, one lone man, could make Jesus known as savior to comparatively very few people, but I could train ten thousand Chinese to make Him known to that many more than I could. . . . preparing the believers to do the work of spreading the Gospel instead of depending on missionaries. That requires their being filled with the Spirit and devoted to witnessing to the unevangelized (Koetitz [1080?], 26).

Simpson had been absent from Gansu province for almost eleven years. A high priority on his list was to check on the churches he had established years earlier. Sending financial assistance had been impossible due to the war with the Japanese. Simpson discovered that the Gansu churches had continued in ministry despite the lack of foreign missionaries and financial aid. Believers delighted in sharing with Simpson how God had blessed their work with signs following. They recounted how God had supernaturally sent rain in response to prayer for drought-stricken areas and how God had spoken prophetic warnings to entire communities. When communities heeded the prophetic warnings, God spared them, while those who chose to ignore the words were destroyed. Simpson heard three testimonies of people raised from the dead.

> The ministers in nearly every Assembly, gathered in District Council in August 1946, reported similar or other signs, miracles, wonders and mighty works of the Holy Spirit. How we all rejoiced and praised the Lord for restoring the Faith once delivered to the saints right here in faraway Northwest China even while all missionaries were absent (Koetitz [1980?], 31).

During that same Council meeting, Simpson taught on what was to become his primary emphasis during his last term of service in China: "Every believer filled with the Spirit and thus made an active and fully qualified witness engaged in making the Gospel known to all the world" (Koetitz [1980?], 31). In teaching venues throughout the country, Simpson continued to emphasize Acts 1:8 and the purpose of the Pentecostal promise for empowerment to witness.

A sense of urgency drove Simpson in the early months of 1949 to redouble efforts for the training of national workers. He spent much of his last months in China in Gansu province visiting established churches. In each venue, he continued his emphasis on the need for believers to receive the baptism of the Holy Spirit and to live and work in expectation that signs and wonders would follow the faithful proclamation of the Word of God. The need for travelling by horseback or on foot, despite being almost eighty years old, did not deter him from devoting himself to the task at hand.

Simpson made plans for a new term (May 1 to August 31, 1949) for Truth Bible Institute, which had relocated to Gansu. Prepared to accept thirty-six women and sixty-four men students to the first term, Simpson assembled supplies for building and bought up large supplies of grain and vegetables in preparation for one hundred new students. Simpson had already received word that his family in the United States desired his return. He had been separated from them for three and a half years, and they were concerned about his safety. He let them know that when the term ended on August 31, he would return to the United States.

In early May, however, church leaders began to tell Simpson that they had received prophetic messages indicating he should leave for the United States soon and that this would be their last chance to see him. Based on these messages, Simpson prepared to leave Gansu on May 12, but on May 9 he sensed the urgency to leave immediately. Political turmoil made travel unpredictable and difficult to schedule without weeks of advance preparation. Miraculously, Simpson was able to arrange transportation, first to Lanzhou and then onward to Shanghai. When Simpson arrived in Shanghai, the city's residents could hear the sound of fighting from only a few miles outside of the city. People sought to leave by any means possible. Simpson arranged transport by ship leaving Shanghai on May 26 and arrived in San Francisco on June 9—one month after being prompted to leave Gansu immediately (Simpson 1953a, 121-125).

James Vigna, a missionary who continued ministry in Gansu, later told Simpson of God's miraculous protection and provision. After the Communist Party had taken Gansu, they held a public trial in which Simpson was sentenced to execution for the death of orphans who had died from dengue fever under his care during the famine of 1929. Having been warned by the Spirit, Simpson had escaped before the Communist takeover (Koetitz [1980?], 39-40).

Simpson wrote his autobiography, *Contending for the Faith*, in 1953. At the age of eighty-four, he still held on to the hope of returning to China. He added a paragraph to the original manuscript on March 29, 1956, which appears to indicate that he had finally come to accept that he would not be returning to China. His words cannot hide his passion for obeying the Great Commission in the power of the Holy Spirit: "I am today 86 and a half years of age and still hoping to preach Christ to the 60,000 Chinese in San Francisco. Pray that the Lord will work with me there in signs, wonders, miracles, and gifts of the Spirit" (Simpson 1953a, 125).

Simpson's preaching and teachings were characterized by the Holy Spirit. From the outpouring of the Holy Spirit in northwest China in 1908 until his departure in 1949, Simpson estimated that he had prayed for over 10,000 nationals to receive the baptism of the Holy Spirit (Simpson 1949a).

Ministry of William Ekvall Simpson (1901-1932)

William Ekvall Simpson was born in Old Orchard, Maine, on October 17, 1901. His parents had already served for almost ten years as missionaries with the CMA on the Tibetan border of northwest China. The Boxer Rebellion in China delayed their return from their first furlough until 1902 (Koetitz [1980?], 49).

Before the birth of Willie Simpson, his parents had given him to God for his work. However, as they passed through New York City on their return to the field, they formalized their intentions, three months after Willie's birth. Pastor A. B. Simpson officiated the dedication ceremony (Koetitz [1980?], 49).

Willie accepted Christ just one month before his tenth birthday. The following year, in May 1912, the Holy Spirit fell on the Simpson household. While his parents and older sisters spoke in tongues along with about thirty local Chinese believers in the front of the house, Willie received his personal experience unnoticed in the kitchen (Koetitz [1980?], 51).

Following the family's return to China in 1917, Willie, who grew up surrounded by Tibetans, felt God's leading to immerse himself in Tibetan culture and language study. At the age of nineteen, he secured a few rooms in the Labrang monastery, establishing a mission presence among almost 4,000 Buddhist priests. In 1919, Willie Simpson applied for and received missionary appointment in absentia for an initial term of seven years (Hogan 1983).

The lyrics to Simpson's favorite song epitomized his missionary ministry:

> The seed I have scattered in springtime with weeping
> And watered with tears and with dews from on high,
> Another will shout when the harvesters' reaping
> Shall gather my grain in the sweet by-and-by.
>
> Chorus: Over and over, yes, deeper and deeper,
> My heart is pierced through with life's sorrowing cry;
> But the tears of the sower and the songs of the reaper
> Shall mingle together in joy by-and-by
>
> The thorns will have choked and the summer suns blasted
> The most of the seed which in springtime I've sown,
> But the Lord Who has watched while my weary toil lasted
> Will give me a harvest for what I have done.
> Another will reap what in springtime I've planted,
> Another rejoice in the fruit of my pain;
> Not knowing my tears when in summer I fainted
> While toiling sad-hearted in sunshine and rain.

> Chorus: By-and-by, by-and-by, by-and-by, by-and by;
> Yes, the tears of the sower and the songs of the reaper
> Shall mingle together in joy by-and-by (Spencer 1957).

Simpson and his Chinese companion, Pastor Hsia Wei-hsin, traveled by horseback, braving robber tribes, vicious dogs, and the inhospitable elements as they slowly developed relationships with the head men of various Tibetan tribes. Strong Buddhist control inhibited individuals interested in the gospel message from confessing the faith. To do so, in many cases, would have resulted in death. After fourteen years of toil, Simpson's primary success was measured in time spent with Chinese preachers and companions who accompanied him on his travels (Koetitz [1980?], 53).

While in Gansu, assisting newly arrived missionaries, Simpson was murdered by Muslim bandits on June 20, 1932 (Koetitz [1980?], 54). Many of the Tibetans he had befriended wept for days upon hearing of Simpson's death. The Peikou Assembly Church in Wen County, Gansu province wrote the following eulogy memorializing his sacrifice:

> It is difficult to find anyone in Chinese society who is willing to sacrifice his life for the truth. The Lord Jesus sacrificed himself on the cross to save the world. . . . The Christians in the Western world hold their lives lightly, but they cherish the truth deeply. . . . [Pastor Simpson] from his childhood he was taught by his father to preach the Word in Western China. His personality and dedicated spirit had great influence. In recent years, the people have suffered from bandits and many disasters of nature. They have lost their homes and become nomads, wandering from place to place because of these misfortunes. Pastor Simpson and his father have worked with good Chinese men, distributing clothing and food and doing whatever they could to help the people. . . . Then suddenly, while the thorns have endured, the violets have been destroyed, and this good man has been killed because of the sinful nature of the people. . . . Alas! If he had continued to live in this world, his accomplishments would have been

> immeasurable because of his dedication and great faith in the Lord. But through this tragedy, dying for the truth, he is now with the Lord in heaven. Now that he is there, to whom can we look for help? In burying him, we have all lost a companion in the gospel.... We are all bereaved. We have lost our teacher and friend.... The tears stream down our cheeks like rain (Peikou Assembly Church, 1983).

Simpson demonstrated his passion and commitment in prayer requests he included in a 1927 letter to supporters. In early 1927, almost all the one hundred missionaries working in Gansu province had evacuated due to anti-foreign tensions throughout the country. Willie submitted the following requests:

- Enablement to preach the Word of God with boldness.
- That human opposition will not hinder the work of God.
- That supernatural empowerment would accompany the preaching of the Word
- Protection in dangerous circumstances.
- Tibet to experience a mighty moving of the Holy Spirit (Hogan 1983).

Simpson's evangelistic passion survived his martyrdom through the national workers who had accompanied him and whom he had trained for ministry (Hogan 1983).

Chapter Nine

LEONARD BOLTON (1900-1961)

Introduction and Early Life

Leonard Bolton's ministry links directly with the move of the Holy Spirit among the Lisu in southwest China and northern Myanmar. Bolton's ministry serves as an example of the strength of teamwork that reached across denominational lines as well as incorporated national Christians into key leadership roles. James Fraser, a missionary with the CIM, pioneered that organization's work among the Flowery Lisu. He later loaned some of his native evangelists to the Assemblies of God to help them begin their outreach to the Black Lisu. Bolton's work among the Lisu built upon the work that had been done by Alfred and Mary Lewer, as well as Ada Buchwalter, whom Leonard Bolton later married.[91] Clifford and Lavada Morrison also extended Bolton's work among the Lisu, carrying it into unreached villages as far away as northern Myanmar. Native evangelists and co-workers, such as David and Ruth Ho, proved the effectiveness of training, mentoring, and releasing nationals for evangelism and church planting.

Leonard Bolton was born in January 1900, the third child and first son of William and Ada Bolton in Bournemouth, England.

[91]Leonard's first wife, Olive, died during childbirth along with the baby. Leonard later married Ada Buchwalter, who was Mary Lewer's sister.

The turn of the century brought waves of Pentecostal revival throughout the world. In 1906, William Bolton received healing for a serious lung condition in one such revival sweeping England. Upon relocating the family business to Bournemouth, the Boltons set up one room in their new home for people to seek the baptism in the Holy Spirit (Ezzo n.d.b, 12-15).

The Bolton business assembled, sold, and repaired bicycles and expanded into motorcycles and automobiles as they became more popular. However, William Bolton believed that the importance of winning a soul for Christ surpassed the value of making sales. Devoutly Pentecostal, many of his neighbors misunderstood and ridiculed the Bolton family's Pentecostal experience (Bolton 1984). When William and Ada went to church with their ten children, some neighbors jeered: "There goes William Bolton and his congregation" (Bolton 1984, 16). Leonard recalled that his father often prayed, "Lord, keep us where the fiery fire burns, and in the place where Thou art glorified" (Bolton 1984, 16).

Leonard accepted Christ in 1912 when his older sister decided to lead the Bolton children in their own church service while the parents attended a prayer meeting. The impromptu service resulted in Leonard's salvation (Ezzo, n.d., 16).[92]

Leonard's teenage years were marked by his own Pentecostal experiences and the miraculous. At thirteen, a visiting missionary from Egypt prayed over Leonard, and he began to speak in tongues. At the same time, he received healing from a serious eye condition. Smith Wigglesworth frequently visited the Bolton home and young Leonard frequently accompanied him as he visited and prayed for the sick in the Bournemouth area (Ezzo n.d.b, 16-21).

The infilling of the Holy Spirit gave Leonard a passion for evangelism. Immediately upon receiving the Spirit baptism, he went next door to tell two of his friends of his experience. He hungered to read and understand God's Word. He assisted in a

---

[92]Leonard's older sister, Winnie, suggested that the Bolton children have their own prayer meeting, which included her telling a Bible story. As she shared a Bible story, Leonard began to cry as he thought about Jesus dying for his sins. He said that from that day forward he never doubted his salvation.

mission outreach in Bournemouth by teaching a Sunday school class and engaging in reaching out to gypsies in the area. During the gypsy outreaches, he met and fell in love with Olive. However, when he proposed marriage to her, she refused, indicating that she could not consider marriage to anyone who did not share her missionary call to China (Ezzo n.d.b, 20-21).

Vicky Bolton had already committed to go to China through the challenge brought by Mary Lewer who had been speaking in area churches about the needs among the tribal peoples of southwest China. Mary and Alfred Lewer had met in China and married in 1917.[93] During Mary's 1922 visit to England, she prayed for three new workers to join her and Alfred in their mission work. Although Bolton had devoted his life to following Jesus, he initially resisted the thought of mission work in China.[94] The Holy Spirit's gentle but persistent wooing continued reminding him of promises he had made to God during his service on the World War I battlefield. Finally, Leonard surrendered to God's call to China, completing the three new workers sought by Mary Lewer. Vicky Bolton returned with Mary to China, and Leonard and Olive would follow after their marriage (Ezzo n.d.b).[95]

---

[93]Mary Buchwalter dedicated her life to God at an Alliance Camp Meeting in 1905. She came from a Mennonite background. At an all-night prayer meeting while attending Nyack Bible Institute, she, along with about thirty other students, received the baptism of the Holy Spirit at 4:00 a.m. Shortly thereafter she felt God leading her to China. She finished her studies at Nyack in 1911 and arrived in China October 1914. Although she held credentials with the Assemblies of God, she did not receive official missionary appointment with the AG until 1926. Alfred Lewer received the baptism of the Spirit in September 1913. After completing a training course at the Pentecostal Missionary Training Home in England, Alfred left for China in 1915. He married Mary Buchwalter on December 18, 1917. Alfred served in China until his death in 1924. Mary continued mission work in China until she was forced out in 1949 (Ezzo, n.d.a).

[94]Ezzo lists two reasons for Leonard's hesitancy. First, his uncle had been murdered in China during the Boxer Rebellion. Second, Leonard had served in France during World War I. His outfit had adopted several pet dogs and one of them gave birth to a litter of puppies, which subsequently was stolen and cooked by Chinese workers in the area during their annual moon festival celebration. Leonard confessed to viewing them as "savages" (Ezzo n.d.b, 26).

[95]William Bolton sent two of his ten children to China. He remarked that Vicky was their "tithe" and Leonard was their "offering." Vicky, Leonard, and Olive went out under the Tibetan Border Mission (Bolton 1984, 20, 62).

Journey to Southwest China

Olive and Leonard Bolton sailed for Rangoon, Burma, in 1924. Alfred Lewer was scheduled to meet them and guide them through Burma to southwest China. However, when the Boltons arrived in Rangoon, no one was there to meet them. They secured temporary accommodations at the local YMCA (Ezzo n.d.b, 31-32). After three days with no sign of Alfred Lewer, Bolton decided to check for any news at the local cablegram office. He received the following message from his father in England: "Alfred Lewer drowned on way to meet you. Praying much for you that God will show you what to do" (Ezzo n.d.b, 32).

Bolton initially responded to this news by wondering if perhaps he and Olive had missed God's will. After sharing the news with his wife, they concluded that they must press on. If they were needed in Wei-hsi while Alfred Lewer still lived, then how much more now that he was gone. Luke 9:62 challenged them: "No one who puts his hand to the plow and looks back is fit for the kingdom of God."

After committing to press on, they pondered how to move forward. As newcomers with no language skills or cultural understanding, they would not know how to navigate the jungles, rivers, and mountains between Rangoon and southwest China. An American Baptist missionary lady suggested that they travel with her group up the Irrawaddy River as far as Bhamo, which would put them 400-500 miles closer to their destination.

Arriving in Bhamo, they noticed a man looking intently at all the arriving foreigners. Approaching each one, he called out in broken English, "Bol-ton? Bao Mushi" (Bolton 1984, 27)? He identified himself as David Ho, one of the national workers who had been accompanying Alfred Lewer when he drowned. He brought with him a letter of introduction from Ada Buchwalter, along with a small vocabulary book to assist with communication and a list of supplies for the Wei-hsi mission station (Ezzo n.d.b, 32-34).

The thirty-five horses loaded with approximately 140 pounds of goods, providing an easy target for the many bandit bands roaming the area. Along the way, one band of thirty bandits attacked the group. Bolton, moved by the realization that these bandits were pilfering much-needed supplies for the mission station, felt a sudden quickening of the Holy Spirit. Picking up a nearby stick, he advanced toward the bandits alternately speaking in tongues, pointing with the stick, and returning to speaking in tongues. The bandits dropped their booty and quickly ran away. Both the accompanying travelers as well as the Wei-hsi mission station personnel rejoiced at God's miraculous intervention (Ezzo n.d.b, 37-38).[96]

James O. Fraser and the CIM's Work with the Lisu

James O. Fraser, a missionary with the China Inland Mission, had already pioneered work among the Flowery Lisu. They shared common language, culture, and religious beliefs with the Black Lisu who were the targets of the Lewers and Ada Buchwalter. Ancestor worship played a prominent role in their animistic worldview. The Lisu worshiped spirits thought to reside in nature. Keeping guardian spirits happy would prevent calamities from malevolent spirits who could bring sickness, natural disasters, and other varied and sundry troubles. Rectifying the trouble required sorcerers who could identify the cause of the problem as well as determine how to exorcise or appease the appropriate demons. The Lisu lined the paths leading into the villages to placate the spirits with small altars containing food offerings (Bolton 1984, 108).

An old Lisu tradition spoke of a white man coming bringing a Book with words of life. The coming of CIM missionaries such as James Fraser and John and Isabel Kuhn, along with the Assemblies of God team of Lewer, Buchwalter, and Bolton, evidenced the timing of the Holy Spirit. Fraser devised a phonetic script and initiated translation of the Scriptures into the Lisu language. All

[96]In 1926 when bandits threatened the Wei-hsi mission station, Bolton had received a warning from the bandit leader that if he used his gun in defense of the station, that the station would be burned. Ada Buchwalter remarked, "Perhaps they should be more concerned about a stick in your hand" (Bolton 1984, 73).

the various Lisu subgroups benefitted from Fraser's work (Bolton 1984, 109).

Commitment to intercessory prayer undergirded the work of both the CIM and the AG among the Lisu. Fraser's initial work among the Lisu had produced a scanty return, and CIM leadership asked Fraser to consider relocating to work with another potentially more receptive people group. He persuaded his leaders to let him stay at his station a little longer. Fraser adopted a prayer strategy with the help of his mother in England. She invited a few key people to pray specifically for Lisu needs. Fraser provided them with detailed prayer requests, including the names of specific places and people. As they prayed, the Spirit began to move among the Flowery Lisu (Crossman 1982).

Fraser used World War I imagery to describe the importance of this intercessory prayer. In the later years of the war, several armies had utilized poisonous gas in their attacks. Fraser noted the ineffectiveness of shooting bullets at the poisonous gas. Gusts of wind, however, would disperse the gas. Even so, the Lisu needed the wind of the Holy Spirit to blow across their land, dispelling the numbing, paralyzing, blinding effects of years of satanic oppression (Crossman 1982).

Following Olive's death, Leonard Bolton walked through a dark valley of discouragement.[97] His own words best summarize the depth of his despair and grief:

> Wave after wave of agony poured over me. First Alfred, now Olive! Was there to be no end to the sacrifice? . . . All that day, I lay on my bed unable to move with the suffering of my heart. Why had God done this? Why had he called me to China only to lose my wife? Then I heard from the doctor that the baby expired. . . . One day, I rose from the bed and decided to take a walk for diversion. . . . I walked to the city wall and climbed up the steps to the top . . . as the evening shadows fell, gloom once again encompassed me. I stopped and looked over the outer part of the wall

---

[97]Olive died in childbirth, along with the baby.

> that dropped about thirty feet. Suddenly, the enemy seemed to whisper to me, "Why don't you just end it all? You could throw yourself down over the wall, and that would be the end of your misery." Then I heard another voice, "I'll never leave thee nor forsake thee. Have I not promised? Be strong and of a good courage. I'll possess the land before thee" (Ezzo n.d.b, 63-65).

Later, Leonard received a letter from a Christian woman in England who stated she had spent a sleepless night praying for the Boltons. The time of her prayers coincided with the time of his walk through the valley of despair. From Fraser to the Boltons and their partners in ministry, both in China and the West, the theme of intercessory prayer ran deep through the Lisu story.

The Lewers requested a couple of Fraser's national workers to assist them as they attempted to reach the Black Lisu. Fraser's affirmative response to this invitation provided a positive example of the power of cross-organizational partnership. The magnitude of the success can be seen in one of Lewer's evangelistic trips which resulted in 200 water baptisms, 100 child dedications, eight new churches set in order with presiding elders, and the enrollment of 100 new enquirers into the Christian faith (Ezzo n.d.b).

The Lewers and David and Ruth Ho

Alfred Lewer demonstrated the effectiveness of incarnational ministry with the Lisu. Donald Gee noted that "the one great secret of his success was the way in which he wholeheartedly made himself one of the people" (Ezzo, n.d.a, 6). As Pastor, the Lisu called upon him to mediate disputes, guide, and give counsel on hundreds of matters (Ezzo, n.d.a). Even though Alfred Lewer's drowning cut short his ministry, his decision to mentor a young Naxi man named Ho Tsan-dien was to have a significant impact on the future success of the Bolton's ministry. At the same time, Mary Lewer mentored a young Tibetan girl named Ah Hsi-lan.

Ah Hsi-lan began work for Mary Lewer while they were living in A-teng-tze, a city on the Tibetan border. Mary, who was expecting their first child, needed someone to assist her with housework and with care for the baby. Hsi-lan's mother, having tried Buddhism, Islam, and several other animistic practices, died searching for peace and had told her daughter that there must be light somewhere and for her to keep looking for the Truth. She never forgot her mother's words and found the peace she searched for while working with the Lewers. Upon baptism, she adopted the biblical name Ruth (Bolton 1984, 110).[98]

Ho Tsan-dien's testimony differed greatly. He also was an orphan and had come to Alfred Lewer looking for work. First appearances were not promising, as young Ho used opium. Lewer evidently saw something in the young man and slowly began to pour his life into mentoring him. Tsan-dien accepted Christ and was baptized, taking the biblical name of David. As a gifted teacher and preacher, he became a natural leader. He and Ah Hsi-lan married and became key leaders in the revival movement among the Lisu (Bolton 1984, 111-112).

Revival among the Lisu came at a heavy cost. Alfred and Mary Lewer had buried their first child at A-teng-tze. Then Alfred drowned going to meet the Boltons. Within a year of the Bolton's arrival in Wei-hsi, Olive died in childbirth along with the baby. Katherine Lewer, the Lewer's second child, returned to China following her graduation from Central Bible Institute. She died from a combination of cholera and typhoid in 1948, following an evangelistic tour to a previously unreached village.[99] David Ho was arrested following the Communist takeover and sentenced to hard labor. Later, he was transferred to another prison where he was left to die of starvation. John Ho, David and Ruth's son, was

---

[98]This was a common practice of this time. The question could be asked as to whether the adoption of a biblical name was something imposed upon national Christians or whether the desire originated with the new convert.

[99]Katherine effectively ministered the gospel to children. She adopted a four-day-old baby boy abandoned by his parents. After her death, the boy, Philip, was taken in and cared for by Mary Lewer. Katherine's last evangelistic trip took her to a previously unevangelized village where she and her mother shared the message of Christ. On the last night, Katherine shared Jesus under an especially strong anointing of the Spirit despite being sick. The next day she was carried on a stretcher to the Wei-hsi mission station where, for the next fifty days, she fought the combined diseases of cholera and typhoid. At her funeral, approximately 150 children followed her coffin to her burial site singing "Everybody Ought to Love Jesus" (Ezzo n.d.a, 13-14).

caught by the Communists in a small chapel and commanded to translate their literature into the Lisu language. When he refused, they chopped off his hands and ripped open his stomach (Bolton 1984; Ezzo n.d.a). "Among the Bolton's relatives, nine graves in China and one in Taiwan bear . . . testimony" (Bolton 1984, 220).

Bringing the Lisu to Christ proved costly, but the testimony of changed lives both inspires and challenges others regarding the price that may be required to reach those people groups still unreached and unengaged.

The Developing Methodology

Incarnational identification continues to be pivotal in the ability of missionaries to adequately convey the gospel message. Leonard Bolton was brought up in an English home where the old cliché "cleanliness is next to godliness" was practiced daily. Adjustment to life in the mountains of southwest China presented constant challenges to that upbringing. In one predominantly Tibetan village, David Ho and Leonard were hosted with yak butter tea. The sight of hair and a few lice floating on the surface of the rancid drink led Leonard to ask for grace, to not only drink the tea but also keep it down. That night, Leonard had difficulty sleeping in the filthy inn. His English custom of cleanliness had been challenged by the Lisu, but this Tibetan village was even dirtier. Revulsion grew inside his heart, and he wondered how he could identify and love people so culturally different. Before falling asleep, he cried out, "Lord, help me" (Bolton 1984, 66-67; McGee 2004, 257)!

That night he dreamed about the filthiest person he had ever seen. The dirt, the ragged clothing, and the stench were worse than anything he had ever experienced. Then, the Lord spoke to him in his dream, saying, "Leonard, that is how you appeared in My sight. But I loved you when you were unlovely. I died on the cross for you. . . . Can you not love these less fortunate people for Me" (McGee 2004, 257)?

From that moment forward, God replaced Bolton's revulsion with strong love for the peoples of southwest China. Whether they were Tibetan, Lisu, or other tribal peoples, he could eat with them, sit with them, sleep in their homes, and minister beside them.

In 1926, the Wei-hsi team comprised Mary Lewer, Ada Buchwalter, and Leonard Bolton. Political uncertainty, banditry, and the early stages of civil war that affected other sections of China also touched the country's southwest corner. During this season of almost continuous crises, romance blossomed between Leonard and Ada, and they began to plan a wedding in Hong Kong following her upcoming deputation in the United States. Events in early 1927 changed those plans. Domestic turmoil caused several foreign consuls to order the evacuation of their citizens. More than 2,000 missionaries left China during this time. Many did not return, even after the crisis had eased in late 1927 and early 1928 (Bays 2012, 112).

Leonard and Ada decided that Ada would evacuate first, traveling initially to England to meet Leonard's family. Leonard would join her later in the United States for their wedding scheduled for April 7, 1928. Following the wedding, Leonard met with the Foreign Missions Committee and received missionary appointment with the American Assemblies of God (Bolton 1984, 96-97).

The American AG missionary team working with the Lisu was expanding. The Boltons first son, Robert, was born in Kunming in February 1929. Clifford and Lavada Morrison also joined the Lisu work and were to have significant impact on the work with the Lisu on both sides of the China border (Bolton 1984).

A missionary strategy was evolving. Leonard and Ada traveled with national workers.[100] In the early morning hours, the team taught the youth the choruses and songs from the Lisu hymnals, which they distributed in every location. They planned to stay in each location several days, which provided ample time for holding evangelistic meetings and teaching basic Christian doctrine to the church community. Older men were appointed as elders with responsibility for teaching and oversight of the new converts. They would then leave for another village, promising to return

---

[100]David and Ruth Ho frequently accompanied the Boltons.

the following year for further teaching and to conduct baptismal services (Bolton 1984, 63).

This practical methodology was developing into a Lisu people movement toward Christ. Whole families were coming into the churches. Some villages were almost entirely Christian. As entire communities were being taught God's Word, church leaders examined local customs in the light of biblical truth. Practices that did not conflict with scriptural teaching were not changed. Within fifteen years, over 1,000 Lisu had been baptized in water (Bolton 1984, 155-156).

The strategy of training Lisu for leadership in indigenous churches was bearing fruit. Lisu Christians began traveling to surrounding villages to preach, teach, and pray for the sick. One of these Lisu leaders was a "Bible woman" named Ao Ma; she had a remarkable salvation experience. Even though she could not read, she exchanged some eggs for a gospel booklet and then asked Ruth Ho to read it to her. Listening to the gospel story through the night, she welcomed the dawning of a new day by accepting Jesus as her Savior. She asked Ruth what she could do for Jesus. Ruth gave her three directives, the final one being, "Give yourself. Learn to read the Book, then go to your village and tell your people about Jesus" (Bolton 1984, 118).[101]

Ao Ma obeyed, learning how to read the Book. She experienced the baptism of the Holy Spirit and began to travel throughout the mountains braving ridicule, bandits, and wild dogs to bring the gifts of healing and salvation to benighted villages. Lepers were healed as she prayed for them. One unusual miracle occurred when Ao Ma found a woman weeping over her dying cow. She had been plowing her field when the cow collapsed and could not get up. Ao Ma told the woman to bring her some oil. Pouring the

---

[101]Ruth's first response was, "Get rid of your corn pipe. . . . Our bodies are temples of the Holy Spirit so we must not defile them by smoking." The second response was "Go sell your silver tribal earrings and ornaments and give the money to God." The final response was "Give yourself . . ." (Bolton 1984, 118).

contents over the cow's head, she prayed. The cow shook its head, stood up, and continued plowing the field (Bolton 1984).

The Boltons prepared a simple catechism for teaching new converts. The main points of the catechism covered the subjects of true repentance, tithing, baptism of the Holy Spirit, and healing.[102] Teaching of believers expanded beyond the catechism to include short-term Bible training seminars where several weeks were set aside for concentrated teaching and study. These short-term training seminars led to the formation of the Ling Kuang (Holy Light) Bible Institute in October 1948, under the oversight of James Baker, son of H. A. and Josephine Baker. Ku Kuai-kung served as dean of the school. Twenty-two students enrolled for the first year of study. The imminent threat of a Communist victory in China fueled the urgency for the training of young Christians.

In November 1949, one month following the formal declaration of Communist victory in China, Leonard and Ada Bolton left China. They realized that their continued presence would jeopardize the safety of their national friends. The Boltons had served for more than twenty-five years among the Lisu. Departure from China, however, did not mean the end of their missionary ministry. Their foreign service record includes terms of service in Jamaica, Bangladesh, and Taiwan, serving alongside their son and daughter-in-law, Robert and Evelyn Bolton (Bolton 1984, 196-206).

In 1956, Maynard Ketcham, Field Secretary for the American Assemblies of God, Far East Region, invited Leonard to join him in attending the Lisu Christians Silver Jubilee Convention in northern Burma. The Burmese Assemblies of God numbered over 7,000 believers, most of whom were Lisu. Lisu evangelists from southwestern China had evangelized Lisu tribes across the border,

[102]True repentance included turning from the worship of spirits, drunken reveling, immorality, profanity, dishonesty, and a decision to turn to serve the one true God. Tithing was emphasized, along with the accompanying promise of blessing as they were faithful to give the tithe. It was expected that believers would seek for and receive the baptism of the Holy Spirit and speak in tongues. Furthermore, it was expected that these same believers would go forth to share with family, friends, and neighboring villages expecting that the Lord would confirm their words with signs following (Bolton 1984, 130).

and their ministry had spread to other Burmese tribal peoples such as the Rawang, Maru, and Kanong, as well as the Burmese. Clifford and Lavada Morrison, who had served with the Boltons in Yunnan province, had transferred their ministry to Burma (Bolton 1984, 201-202).

John Fish, a Lisu, served as general superintendent of the Burmese Assemblies of God. His wife had played with the Bolton children in Wei-hsi. Several Lisu recognized Leonard, calling him by name. They told him they remembered him from the times he had visited and preached in their villages in China. They had escaped into Burma following the Communist takeover but reported that thousands of Lisu believers remained in Yunnan still faithfully serving Jesus (Bolton 1984).

In 1966, American missionaries in Burma were also forced to leave. Maynard Ketcham arrived in the country to sign over mission property and equipment to the national church. In a public ceremony, Ketcham presented a commemorative plaque to Superintendent Fish, saying: "Into your hands we give the torch. Hold it high!" Fish replied, "We are going to miss you, your missionaries, your material and spiritual benefits—but you are not going to take the Holy Spirit out of Burma, are you" (Bolton 1984, 215-216)?

In September 1967, Superintendent Fish reported to Ketcham:

> How about it, Pastor Ketcham—when your missionaries left, we had 180 churches, 12,000 believers, and 25 students in the tribal Bible school. Now we have 300 churches in a fellowship of 25,000 believers and 75 students in the Bible school. See what the Holy Spirit can do! (Bolton 1984, 216)[103]

---

[103]In 2023, I visited Asia Pacific Theological Seminary in Baguio City, Philippines. Several students from Myanmar (Burma) have attended this seminary. I asked one of the students if he knew Leonard Bolton. He immediately responded, "Of course, we all know of the Boltons and their work bringing the Christian message to the Lisu."

Joshua Project (2016a) lists almost 916,000 Lisu living in China. It also claims that 80 percent profess to be Christians.

Summary

Five words summarize the Boltons' methodology: prayer, sacrifice, identification, mobility, and training.

Prayer

It is impossible to separate intercessory prayer from the Lisu revival. It had its beginnings when James Fraser started a special prayer band in his mother's home in England. It continued in the lives of the Pentecostal missionaries who committed their lives to serve and included those who undergirded their efforts in prayer from England and the United States. Their prayers were also joined by native Lisu Christians. The intercessory cries of God's people watered the gospel seed that missionaries and indigenous Christians planted.

Sacrifice

Workers among the Lisu paid a heavy price. Inconvenience in travel, long family separations, sickness, and death were constant companions of the messengers.

Identification

Jesus provided the model with his Incarnation, coming to live among people as Immanuel, "God with us." In the same way, successful work among the Lisu required messengers willing to learn the language, translate the Bible into the Lisu language, and culturally acclimate themselves to Lisu life. Walking with them, eating their food, sharing their problems, and doing life together earned the messengers the right to be heard.

Mobility

Short-term seminars and a Bible school could be set up in a centralized location, but if the Lisu were to be reached, willingness to travel to their remote villages was necessary. Frequently, when the Christian witnesses ministered in a village, requests came from villages farther into the mountains or beyond the next mountain range to come and share the message.

Training

The missionaries may have provided the initial spark that flamed the revival. However, that revival could not have continued without the training of local believers who took the baton and continued carrying the message to others. The villages were too widely scattered and also remote. Visiting the churches once a year would not have succeeded in establishing strong churches. Commitment to the principle of teaching and training provided the means for the Lisu movement to continue in both China and Burma, following the later expulsion of foreign missionaries (Bolton 1984).

In 1919, Ada Buchwalter prepared to begin her missionary career in China. She remembered this poem as she began her journey, which epitomized her life and commitment:

> Let me hold lightly to temporal things,
> I, who am deathless, I who have wings!
> Let me hold fast, Lord, to things of the skies!
> Quicken my vision, open my eyes" (Bolton 1984, 82).

Leonard Bolton suffered a heart attack in Taiwan in February 1961. On the evening of February 18, 1961, as Ada sat by his bedside, Leonard opened his eyes and shared these final words with her. "Ada, the record is finished. I will meet you in the morning." He paused briefly before continuing, "I can see them coming . . . the Lisu" (Bolton 1984, 211).

Possibly, Leonard spoke prophetically of the thousands of Lisu who were yet to come to faith in Christ. However, there could be another interpretation of his final words. In traveling through the mountains, Lisu Christians could see the Boltons winding their way up the narrow mountain trails long before they reached the villages. Frequently, several of the Lisu Christians walked down the trail to welcome them and together joyfully return to the village. Maybe Leonard was seeing Lisu Christians who had preceded him to heaven coming to welcome him home. Perhaps both interpretations are accurate.

Conclusion

The young Assemblies of God organization prioritized missions. Its goal was "the greatest evangelism the world has ever seen" (General Council of the Assemblies of God 1914). In the opening decade of existence, the writings of Roland Allen (1912 and 1927, reprinted in 1962 and 1964), Alice Luce (1921 a, b, c), and J. Roswell Flower (1920) influenced the developing mission philosophy of the organization. The AG committed itself to the indigenous church philosophy following the Pauline model (Luce 1921 a, b, c). Flower (1920, 8) described it as "apostolic ministry in apostolic power."

This foundation has resulted in AGWM's current vision and purpose statement: "Christ will be proclaimed, and His Church will be established in all nations through the power of the Spirit. . . . So all can hear" (Mundis 2016, 23).

Assemblies of God World Missions has eight core values:

1. We are committed to a biblical understanding of the mission of the Church.
2. We are committed to fulfilling our mission in the power of the Holy Spirit through Pentecostal practice and teaching.
3. We are committed to the principles of the indigenous church and partnership.
4. We are committed to understanding the culture and worldview of those people with whom we work.
5. We are committed to practicing spiritual disciplines for the development of personal spiritual formation.

6. We are committed to the team concept of working together as missionaries.
7. We are committed to proclaiming the gospel to unreached people.
8. We are committed to holistic missions in word, deed, and spirit (Easter, et al. 2016, 127).

The next chapter will examine the missiological writings of Roland Allen and Alice Luce to determine their consistency with the Pauline model and New Testament principles. It will also survey whether the Assemblies of God missionaries in pre-1952 China followed the Pauline/Allen/Luce missiological model. It will identify ways in which they deviated from that model and whether they made significant adaptations contributing to the evolving AG missiological philosophy.

Chapter Ten

THE DEVELOPMENT OF ASSEMBLIES OF GOD MISSIOLOGY

Foundations for an Assemblies of God Missiology

When the first General Council of the Assemblies of God gathered for business on Monday, April 6, 1914, all delegates knew the primary discussion points. These had been published repeatedly for weeks leading up to the meetings. E. N. Bell, in the December 1913 issue of the *Word and Witness*, listed five primary reasons for meeting: (1) establishing unity in the faith, (2) discussing the work, both at home and abroad, (3) gaining a better understanding of and methods for doing foreign mission work, (4) legalizing the work, and (5) providing for training of future leaders (Bell 1913, 1).[104]

---

[104]In fuller form, the five purposes were: "First—We come together that we may get a better understanding of what God would have us teach, that we may do away with so many divisions, both in doctrines and in the various names under which our Pentecostal people are working and incorporating. Let us come together as in Acts 15, to study the Word, and pray with and for each other—unity our chief aim. Second—Again, we come together that we know how to conserve the work, that we may all build up and not tear down, both in home and foreign lands. Third—we come together for another reason, that we may get a better understanding of the needs of each foreign field and may know how to place our money in such a way that one mission or missionary shall not suffer, while another not any more worthy, lives in luxuries. Also, that we may discourage wasting money on those who are running here and there accomplishing nothing and may concentrate our support on those who mean business for our King. Fourth—Many of the saints have felt the need of chartering the churches of God in Christ, putting them on a legal basis, and thus obeying the laws of the land, as God says. See Rom. 13. We confess

In 1914, in Hot Springs, Arkansas, 314 Pentecostal Christians gathered together and took a great step of faith to make the evangelization of the world one of its priorities. Later that same year, a second council was held at the Stone Church in Chicago, Illinois, where the delegates reaffirmed their priority of world evangelization by committing themselves to the "greatest evangelism the world has ever seen."[105] A casual observer might think this impossible, as they question how such a small group, with limited resources, could ever hope to make any significant contribution to fulfilling the Great Commission.

However, the movement's commitment to missions and apostolic ministry did not diminish. In 1920, in his report as missionary treasurer for the AG, Flower (1920, 8) stated, "We have a distinctive mission in the world. . . . An apostolic ministry in apostolic power, and fullness is the aim of our Pentecostal missionaries."[106] The early church leaders strongly affirmed the conviction that fulfilling the Great Commission was the top priority of the AG. In fact, the missionary vision of the AG defines its history from the very beginning.

Several Scriptures shaped the developing missiology of the young Assemblies of God: "And this gospel of the kingdom will be proclaimed throughout the whole world as a testimony to all nations, and then the end will come" (Matt 24:14). "Go into all the

---

we have been 'slothful in business' on this point, and because of this many assemblies have been chartered under different names as a local work, in both home and foreign lands. Why not charter under one Bible name, 2 Thess. 2:14. Thus eliminating another phase of division in Pentecostal work? For this purpose also, let us come together. Fifth—We may also have a proposition to lay before the body for a general Bible Training School with a literary department for our people."

[105]The Council was held at Stone Church in Chicago. This commitment is quoted from the General Council of the Assemblies of God Minutes from Monday, November 23, 1914.

[106]Blumhofer (1989a, 18), in her work on the history of the Assemblies of God, places the AG's birth during an age of restorationism, or "the attempt to recapture the presumed vitality, message, and form of the Apostolic Church." The many revival movements during the late nineteenth – and early twentieth – centuries reveal a hunger for a return to the "good old days" (18). Flower's description of "apostolic ministry in apostolic power and fullness" built upon a statement of A. J. Gordon in 1882: "It is apostolic men that make an apostolic age, not a certain date of Anno Domini" (Gordon 1882, 75).

world and proclaim the gospel to the whole creation.... And these signs will accompany those who believe" (Mark 16:15, 17). "But you will receive power when the Holy Spirit has come upon you, and you will be my witnesses... to the end of the earth" (Acts 1:8).

The commitment to world evangelism was undergirded by the belief in the imminent return of Jesus Christ, the conviction that world evangelization would hasten that return, and the belief that the Holy Spirit outpouring was empowering the Church for witness with accompanying signs and wonders. The formation of the General Council was rooted in the desire to unify and maximize the effectiveness of the individual churches' mission outreaches. More could be done together as legal recognition and cooperation permitted more consistent financial support and the correction of some questionable overseas practices (McGee 1986, 74). In the months following the AG's organization at the April 2-14, 1914, meetings in Hot Springs, Arkansas, twenty-seven missionaries chose to affiliate with the newly formed General Council (McGee 1986, 13).

As the General Council deliberated on mission philosophy and practice, they were greatly influenced by several earlier missionary thinkers. Over a century before, William Carey operated with a five-pronged missionary strategy: (1) preach the gospel everywhere; (2) provide the Bible in the language of the people; (3) establish a local church; (4) study the local people's culture, language, and religion; and (5) develop indigenous leaders (Neill 1964, 224-225). Carey developed this strategy from his understanding of Paul's methodology.

Henry Venn (1796-1873) in England and Rufus Anderson (1796-1880) in the United States popularized indigenous church principles. These principles, as outlined by Venn and Anderson, emphasized developing self-governing, self-supporting, and self-propagating churches (Anderson et al. 1994).

In 1886, John Nevius published *The Planting and Development of Missionary Churches.*[107] Objecting that too many missionaries

---

[107]John Nevius (1829-1893), despite spending most of his missionary career in China, is credited with the institution of a method that transformed the mission work in

had adopted the mission station approach to their work, he developed a plan of itinerant ministry that included short-term teaching to train new converts how to do basic evangelism (Tucker 2004, 265).

The above mission writers promoted the establishment of indigenous churches and formed the foundation of AG mission practice from the beginning. It was, however, the writings of Roland Allen[108] and Alice Eveline Luce (1921a, b, c)[109] on Paul's missionary methods that proved critical to the evolving missiology of the AG.

This chapter examines several questions arising from the stateside development of an AG missiology and the praxis of AG missionaries in China during this same timeframe. What did the missiological writings of Roland Allen, Alice Luce, and other

---

Korea. The Nevius method can be summed up by nine points: (1) Missionary personal evangelism in as wide an area as possible; (2) Self-propagation where every believer would learn from another believer, and, in turn, would teach someone else; (3) Self-government under the leadership of its own (frequently unpaid) leaders; (4) Self-support where all meeting sites were provided and paid for by local Christians; (5) Systematic Bible study in small groups; (6) Strict discipline practiced by the believers themselves; (7) Cooperation and unity with other groups; (8) Non-interference in lawsuits or related matters; and (9) Help where possible in the economic needs of the people (Tucker 2004, 266).

[108]Roland Allen (1868-1947) served as an Anglican missionary in China with the Society for the Propagation of the Gospel (SPG) from 1893-1903. His grandson, Hubert J. B. Allen (1995), wrote a biography of Roland Allen's life entitled, *Roland Allen: Pioneer, Priest, and Prophet*. Allen is best-known for his two books, *Missionary Methods: St. Paul's or Ours?* ([1912] 1962) and *The Spontaneous Expansion of the Church and the Causes Which Hinder It* ([1927] 1960a). In the foreword to the grandson's biography, Lesslie Newbigin wrote: "At the center of Allen's message was the conviction that the Holy Spirit is the active agent in the Christian mission. For him, Pentecost was the key for the understanding of mission" (H. Allen 1995, xiii).

[109]Alice Eveline Luce (1873-1955) received her first missionary appointment with the Church Missionary Society, arriving in India in 1896. She worked closely with Minnie Abrams and Pandita Ramabai in India. She received the baptism of the Holy Spirit while visiting an orphanage in 1910. She later received appointment through the American Assemblies of God and played an important role in the development of the American organization's Hispanic ministries. She is considered by many to be the first Assemblies of God missiological writer. Her three articles in *The Pentecostal Evangel* in 1921 on "Paul's Missionary Methods" played a pivotal role in the developing AG missions methodology. Mikeuel Eugene Peterson's 2009 dissertation on Alice Luce's missionary career, leadership, thought, and influence provides an in-depth look at her life and work.

writers propose? How did they interpret Paul's missiological model? Did the AG missionaries in China follow the Allen/Luce model? In what ways did they deviate from that model? Were there significant adaptations that contributed to the evolving missiological philosophy of the AG?

Roland Allen's Missiological Principles

No other non-Assemblies of God person has influenced the development of AG mission strategy more than Roland Allen. Allen, an Anglican, served in northern China until 1903, when ill health forced his return to England (Schnabel 2008, 11).

He later served in Kenya, where he died in 1947. Noted for his teachings on the apostolic paradigm, indigenous churches, and spontaneous expansion of the church, he was quick to critique missionary practices of his age for not following the Pauline model (Plummer and Terry 2012, 236-238). He attended the Edinburgh World Mission Conference in 1910. While many praised the conference, Allen viewed it as confirming his "worst misgivings about the current attitudes of Western missionaries" (Schnabel 2008, 11). Perhaps Allen's concerns can be better interpreted in light of the fact that some people felt that more emphasis should have been given to the authority of the Bible for mission work rather than the large amount of attention given to reports of the various missionary agencies (McGee 1986, 37). Allen would have felt that anything that gave undue attention to Western agencies would cripple the possibility of spontaneous expansion on the mission field. In defense of Allen's position, the years following the Edinburgh Conference saw a "steady decline in evangelistic zeal among many of the mission agencies represented there" (McGee 1986, 37).

Lesslie Newbigin, in his foreword to the 1962 edition of Allen's book, *Missionary Methods: St. Paul's or Ours?* mentions that Allen felt his writings were about fifty years ahead of their time and "would come into their own about the year 1960" (R. Allen

1962, i).[110] Although he spent approximately forty years writing on missiological principles, he is primarily remembered through his books, *Missionary Methods: St. Paul's or Ours?* ([1912] 1962) and *Spontaneous Expansion* ([1927] 1960a).[111]

Luce's three articles in The *Pentecostal Evangel*[112] greatly influenced the discussion of mission practice at the ensuing 1921 General Council. In the first of her articles, she commented:

> When I first went out as a missionary to India 24 years ago, I accepted without hesitation the methods of the Board under which I was working, and went on laboring for many years along these lines. Then a book was written, whose author's name I cannot now recall, entitled "Missionary Methods: Paul's or Ours?" We missionaries all read it, and thought the writer somewhat visionary and unpractical; but that book first opened my eyes to the diametrical distinction between our methods of working and those of the New Testament (Luce 1921a, 6).

Luce, Hodges, and other Assemblies of God practitioners read Allen critically, rejecting his strong episcopal leanings and noting his lack of pneumatological emphases. Luce, although endorsing Allen's primary thesis, asked, "Shall we look for signs to follow?" (Dempster, Klaus, and Petersen, 1991, 212).[113] During his tenure as Executive Director of the AG mission program, Noel Perkin strongly recommended that candidates read Allen's books (McGee 1986, 138).

---

[110]Allen's grandson, aged twelve at the time, asked his grandfather if he could read his books. Roland replied, "Oh, yes, you can read them by all means—but you won't understand them; I don't think anyone is going to understand them until I've been dead ten years" (H. Allen 1995, vii).

[111]Two books contain excerpts of other writings by Allen, including "Pentecost and the World" (1960b) and "The Case for Voluntary Clergy" (1960b). See Paton (2011) and Paton and Long (1983). J. D. Payne (2017) has also edited some of Allen's writings.

[112]The articles were published on January 8, January 22, and February 5, 1921.

[113]Perhaps Allen's neglect of writing on tongues as initial evidence and signs and wonders as accompanying gifts of the Holy Spirit were reasons for this critique. Allen frequently references the Holy Spirit and the missionary's need to depend on the leading of the Holy Spirit in his writings.

Allen may not have written endorsing the baptism of the Holy Spirit with the evidence of speaking in tongues or emphasized signs and wonders, but he did frequently reference the role of the Holy Spirit in the Pauline model. In Allen's lesser-known book, *Missionary Principles*, he states that "missionary zeal depends upon knowledge of the Holy Spirit" (R. Allen 1964, 44). The Spirit of Christ cannot allow the knowledge of the lostness of man to be unaccompanied by compassion and a desire to reach out to these lost souls. The need for spiritual renewal exists where there is a lack of missionary zeal (R. Allen 1964, 45).

One cannot escape Allen's emphasis upon the Holy Spirit's role in the spontaneous expansion of the church. In his book, *Pentecost and the World*, he calls attention to the absence of a command by Christ to preach the gospel (R. Allen 1960b).[114] Instead, Allen stresses that the Holy Spirit directs the mission of the church. Allen also emphasized the necessity for the Chinese to do the work of evangelists. "What made him uneasy was a growing conviction that, although foreigners could be very helpful to the Chinese in providing skills, they were *not* well fitted to be evangelists" (H. Allen 2017, 21). At the same time, Allen attributed the missionaries' concern over the national church being ready to assume leadership to a lack of faith on the part of the missionaries" (H. Allen 1997, 34).

Allen noted the presence of the Holy Spirit in Paul's missionary activities. Acts 13 begins with the account of the church at Antioch, while worshiping and fasting, receiving a prophetic word to set apart Barnabas and Paul for missionary work (Acts 13:2-4). In Acts 13:9, Paul, "filled with the Holy Spirit," works a miracle during the presentation of the gospel in Cyprus. Acts 13:52 references the disciples who were "filled with joy and with the Holy Spirit." The Holy Spirit guided the church council at Jerusalem concerning requirements and expectations for Gentile believers (Acts 15:28). The Holy Spirit both restricted and directed their destinations

---

[114]Allen does reference Acts 10:42 where Peter in his sermon to Cornelius' household says, "And he commanded us to preach to the people and to testify that he is the one appointed by God to be the judge of the living and the dead."

during the second missionary journey (Acts 16:7-10). In Acts 19:1-7, the disciples at Ephesus were given instructions concerning the Holy Spirit. Acts 20:22-23 indicates that the Holy Spirit warned Paul of impending hardships and imprisonment. In Paul's final address to the Ephesian elders, he reminds them that they have been appointed as overseers of the church by the Holy Spirit (Acts 20:28). Allen's writings frequently reference Western missionaries lacking sufficient faith to believe that the Holy Spirit can direct the leadership of young churches in their oversight of the believers (Pocock 2012, 149-150). In *Spontaneous Expansion*, Allen devotes two entire chapters to the concerns that giving young leaders too much authority too soon may lead to a compromise in doctrine or to a lapse in the Christian moral standard.[115]

Paul's epistles emphasized both the fruit of the Holy Spirit (Gal 5:22-23) and the gifts of the Spirit (1 Cor 12). In Rom 1:4, Paul states that the gospel has been preached through the power of the Spirit. Victory over the flesh comes through dependence on the Holy Spirit (Rom 8:1-15; Gal 5:16). The gospel's impact is enforced by the demonstration of the Spirit's power (1 Cor 2:4). Timidity and fear are overcome through the Holy Spirit (2 Tim 1:7). Believers conduct spiritual warfare with the sword of the Spirit (Eph 6:17). The Holy Spirit works sanctification in believers' lives (2 Thess 2:13). And whether Paul is present or not, "the Spirit helps young leaders like Timothy to guard the truth" (Pocock 2012, 150-151).

Allen declared that the administration of the Holy Spirit proved pivotal to the apostolic work:

> It alone explains the promise of remission of sins in the preaching of the apostles. It alone explains the assurance

---

[115]Allen stated that the great heresies in the Early Church arose from the churches which had been established longer, such as Ephesus and Alexandria, but had lost the passion for evangelism (R. Allen 1997, 48). H. Allen (1997, 49) contends that whereas the "Church of those ages was afraid of the human speculation of learned men: we are afraid of the ignorance of illiterate men." He feels that a heretical spirit comes more easily from pride in one's own intellectual capabilities and that those who are new to the faith are more open to the teaching of the Holy Spirit (H. Allen 1997, 49). During Allen's time, the emphases may have been upon "three selfs," but his methodology leaves a wide-open door for the local congregation to engage in self-theologizing.

> of forgiveness which filled the hearts of their converts. It alone explains the new power which was manifested in the life of the Christian Church, the new striving after holiness, the new charity in expressed form for the amelioration of the sufferings of the poorer brethren. It alone explains the certainty of the hope of eternal life which filled the souls of the Christians and enabled them to face persecution and martyrdom. It alone explains the new sense of the value and dignity of the body which led to a new enthusiasm for purity of life. . . . It alone explains the zeal for the salvation of men, which carried the gospel of Christ throughout the then known world (Paton 2011, 42-43).

Decades later, Hogan also declared the imperative of the Holy Spirit's administration of the missionary task:

> Make no mistake, the missionary venture of the Church, no matter how well planned, how finely administrated, or how fully supported, would fail like any other vast human enterprise, were it not where human instrumentality leaves off, a blessed ally takes over. It is the Holy Spirit that calls, it is the Holy Spirit that inspires, it is the Holy Spirit that reveals, and it is the Holy Spirit that administers. The promise of the Holy Spirit is connected with worldwide witnessing (Klaus and Petersen 2006, 32).

Roland Allen's ([1912] 1962) *Missionary Methods* was first published only a few short years following the Welsh Revival and the outpouring of the Holy Spirit at Azusa Street. News of the Welsh Revival and the Azusa Street meetings had reached some missionaries in China by 1907. However, for health reasons, Allen had been forced to return to England in 1903 (H. Allen 1995, 74-75). It would appear that Allen was aware of the revivals in both Wales and the United States, although he does not reference them in his writings. As Lamin Sanneh (2011, xv) comments, "He developed his ideas and opinions specifically with China in mind."

Those ideas and opinions can be summarized as his belief that the missionaries' lack of faith in the work of the Holy Spirit resulted in failure to plant indigenous churches (Pocock 2012, 151). Allen's writings on the importance of the Spirit in mission work coincided with the development of an emerging Pentecostal missiology with emphasis on the work of the Holy Spirit.

Alice Luce and Missionary Methods

Alice Luce was strongly influenced by Pandita Ramabai[116] and Minnie Abrams.[117] Her experiences with them and participation in the Holy Spirit revivals in India opened her heart to the reality of "doing apostolic work along apostolic lines" (McGee 2004, 161). Luce had originally viewed Roland Allen's writing as visionary and impractical. However, following her own Spirit baptism in 1910, she began to seriously compare the methods commonly used on the mission field with the Pauline model described in Acts (McGee 2004, 161).

Mikeuel Eugene Peterson's (2009, 143-145) dissertation on Alice Luce notes three major areas where Allen influenced Luce's developing missiology. Peterson (2009, 143) refers to these influences as "spiritual children, evangelistic centers, and ethnicity or nationality."

Luce's third article on Paul's missionary methods focuses on Paul's relationship to his converts. In this article, Luce (1921c, 6-7) mentions eight aspects of this relationship:

- Paul saw himself as a spiritual father or caregiver.
- His goal was to plant indigenous churches.

---

[116]Pandita Ramabai (1858-1922), an Indian evangelist and social reformer, developed an extensive ministry to Indian women. Her Mukti Mission became a major revival center in the early 1900s. In 1905, Ramabai started prayer groups that specifically met to pray for revival in India and for an outpouring of the Holy Spirit. Within the year, over 550 women were meeting to pray. Later that same year, there was a Holy Spirit outpouring with accompanying tongues (Peterson 2009, 73-76). This was one year prior to Azusa Street.

[117]Minnie Abrams (1859-1912) served as a missionary evangelist. She worked closely with Pandita Ramabai. Her 1906 book, *The Baptism in the Holy Ghost and Fire,* and accounts of the Mukti revival sparked similar moves of the Holy Spirit in Valparaiso, Chile, in 1909. Abrams and Luce worked together in India. During their time at Allahabad in 1910, two Spirit-filled Indian women laid their hands on Luce, and she began to speak in tongues (Peterson 2009, 82-84).

- Hardship and persecution did not deter him.
- When persecution and hardship made it impractical for him to continue in an area, he would move to another venue for ministry.
- He targeted large centers of strategic importance.
- He sought to work harmoniously with all, regardless of nationality or ethnicity.
- He made no distinction between believers based on nationality or ethnicity.
- When disputes arose, he appealed to his home church for guidance.

Luce follows Allen's example, arguing that missionaries must trust the work of the Holy Spirit in the maturation of young believers. She emphasized how Paul prayed for young believers and exhorted them to walk in the Spirit (Peterson 2009, 143). Furthermore, Luce promoted the Pauline strategy of establishing evangelistic centers in strategic cities. Luce's (1921c) third article, however, does not go into detail as Allen does in *Missionary Methods.*[118]

Luce's third emphasis, built upon Allen's earlier observations, dealt with the ethnicity of the converts (Peterson 2009, 144). She rejected paternalistic models and the idea that young converts would need long-term foreign supervision. Young converts and churches might require the counsel of those who had more experience in the faith, but such counsel should be given not from a nationalistic superiority but due to the missionaries' longevity and experience with spiritual matters (Luce 1921c, 6). She come to the following conclusion: "When the Lord raises up spiritually qualified leaders in the native churches themselves, what a joy it

---

[118]Allen speaks of Paul's selection of cities under Roman rule that were intellectual and commercial centers (R. Allen [1912] 1962, 12-13). Allen emphasizes that "to seize a strategic center we need not only a man capable of recognizing it, but a man capable of seizing it" (R. Allen [1912] 1962, 16). He furthermore warns that there is a danger in losing strategic focus, i.e., staying too long in a place thus becoming locked in and forgetting that the local believers should assume the responsibility of evangelizing the surrounding communities: "Once they get in they find it hard to get out" (R. Allen [1912]1962, 17).

will be to us to be subject to them, and to let them take the lead as the Spirit Himself shall guide them" (Luce 1921c, 6-7).

From the above, one can easily see that Luce built on the foundation laid by Allen. However, along with other Pentecostals, she went a step further and taught that the adoption and use of the Pauline methods should be accompanied by the "power and demonstration of the Holy Spirit" (McGee 2004, 161). She asked, "When we go forth to preach the Full Gospel, are we going to expect an experience like that of the denominational missionaries, or shall we look for the signs to follow" (Luce 1921b, 6)?

Luce's articles built upon her own Pentecostal experience in India. Her statement, "there is such a thing as doing an apostolic work along apostolic lines" (Luce 1921a, 6), reveals her conviction that Paul's ministry was marked by power. That same Holy Spirit power was still available. "According to Luce, the essence of missionary ministry was to proclaim the Word of God with signs and wonders" (Peterson 2009, 150).

Luce's first article of January 8, 1921, built upon the call of Paul and Barnabas as outlined in the opening verses of Acts 13. The missionaries' calling and commissioning, coupled with the support of the sending assembly, ensured partnership and accountability. This linkage between the sender and those sent, particularly in the area of prayer support, "has everything to do with the quality of their missionary work and witness" (Luce 1921a, 6).

Luce's views of what constitutes acceptable mission ministry gradually changed over the years. In the early years, she viewed pioneer work as determinative of acceptable mission work.[119] As she aged, her work gradually shifted from an emphasis in pioneering to ministry in Bible schools and writing of books and articles in an effort to facilitate the work of training and resourcing national leadership (Peterson 2009, 151).

---

[119]This viewpoint found its basis in Rom 15:20 where Paul stated that he made "it my ambition to preach the gospel, not where Christ has already been named, lest I build on someone else's foundation." This verse was frequently referenced by other AG missionaries of this era.

Luce took a dim view concerning anything that took the missionary away from the primary task of evangelism. In evaluating her own missionary ministry, she wrote, "I mourn to think of how much time I have spent in serving tables, when I might have been preaching the Gospel" (Luce 1921b, 6). Her view matched the common cry of many early Pentecostal and evangelical missionaries. The conviction that Christ could come at any moment fired the urgency of proclamation. Gifts of healings and workings of miracles should accompany the preaching of God's Word. Other compassionate ministries should be relegated to others and not under the direction of the missionary (Peterson 2009, 153-154).[120] In the December 9, 1922, *Pentecostal Evangel*, Luce (1922, 6), stated: "The Lord has given us salvation that we may share it with others. This puts missionary work far above the level of philanthropic work." Peterson (2009, 155-156) notes that Luce's ministry displayed a genuine concern for the physical needs of the lost. He suggests that her strong statements about the primacy of evangelism should be interpreted against the backdrop of the developing social gospel movement of the early twentieth century.[121]

Both Luce and Allen became strong advocates for what became known as the indigenous mission strategy. Their claims that this was Paul's method endeared it to Pentecostals as well as many evangelicals.

---

[120]Earlier in her missionary ministry, Luce had worked among the many *zenanas* in India. The word *zenana* refers to the secluding of women. Peterson refers to these secluded women as "deprived of conversation with others in the community, and without books, amusements, or knowledge of the outside world or even of nature itself" (Peterson 2009, 51). This ministry undoubtedly contained evangelistic and discipleship components, but some would view it as primarily philanthropic.

[121]Peterson (2009, 156) calls attention to the postmillennial eschatology of the social gospel movement, which encouraged the ridding of the world's social evils as the primary mission of the church. Establishing the Kingdom of God on earth would prepare the way for the coming of Christ and his millennial reign.

Chapter Eleven

ANALYSIS OF AMERICAN ASSEMBLIES OF GOD MISSIOLOGY IN CHINA

The third General Council of the Assemblies of God (GC) declared that missionaries should follow the New Testament model in evangelizing the lost (General Council Combined Minutes 1914-1917, 9-10). Flower (1920, 8) reported to the 1920 General Council that "the vision of our Pentecostal missionaries is becoming more clarified, and it is realized we have a distinctive mission in the world, differing from all other people. An apostolic ministry in apostolic power and fullness is the aim of our Pentecostal Missionaries." At the 1921 General Council in St. Louis, the delegates recorded their most detailed mission guidelines to date, which showed the influence of Luce's (1921a, b, c) articles on Paul's missionary methods. The Council committed the AG to follow indigenous church principles in establishing self-supporting, self-propagating, and self-governing churches. To accomplish that purpose, "the Pauline example will be followed so far as possible, by seeking out neglected regions where the gospel has not yet been preached, lest we build upon another's foundation" (GC Minutes 1921, 61-64).

The biographical narratives in chapters 4 to 9 describe the lives and ministries of selected AG missionaries in early twentieth-century China. These serve as exemplars for the entire AG missionary force in China during this period. Five sets of questions will guide the discussion concerning their commitment to the Pauline method, as described by Allen and Luce.

- Did they display signs of a call from God and a commitment to follow that call in spite of persecution and hardship?
- Did they place priority on evangelism? What role, if any, did compassion ministries play in their methodology? How did they select sites of ministry?
- Did they adhere to indigenous church principles? How did they prepare the church to be self-supporting, self-governing, and self-propagating? Did they empower indigenous leadership?
- What role did the Holy Spirit play in their methodology? Did they minister in apostolic power with accompanying signs and wonders?
- Did they follow the Pauline example of working in teams? How did they involve the sending churches in their ministries? How did their methodology cross cultural boundaries as well as generational lines?

H. A. Baker

Baker's call followed a logical progression. His skill in debating, combined with his Christian commitment, led Baker to the decision that he should preach. That decision led to the question of where to preach. Praying over that decision, he felt the place of greatest need would be the best choice. For Baker, going to the mission field was the logical decision (H. Baker 2008a, 40).

From the point of that decision until his death, only one matter deflected him from his commitment to missions. Upon learning and studying about the baptism of the Holy Spirit, he became convinced that he would be unable to serve effectively without that experience. He sought Spirit baptism for approximately three years before receiving (H. Baker 2008a, 166). Being Spirit-filled, neither hardship nor persecution kept him from pursuing the call of God. At the age of seventy-one, the Communists forced him out of China, but Baker continued to serve, first with the Navajo Indians in New Mexico and later among the Hakka in Taiwan (H. Baker 2008a, 453-454).

Baker's Adullam Orphanage did not fit the early Pentecostals' concept of appropriate Pauline ministry. Alice Luce (1921b, 6) advocated "keeping first things first." She questioned: "Shall we not then realize the greatness of our high calling, and leave to others the works of mercy, philanthropy, etc., which would divert our time and our energies from God's best . . .?" (Luce 1921b, 6). Flower (1920, 12), in his "Missionary Report" in the June 12, 1920, *Pentecostal Evangel,* states that the imminent return of Jesus militates against the "building up of charitable institutions, hospitals and schools as do the denominational societies."

Despite his Adullam Orphanage work, Baker continued to place evangelism and discipleship at the forefront of his ministry. Revival broke out in the orphanage and his commitment to that work lasted only while he sensed the Holy Spirit's leading in that direction. When it became increasingly difficult to find abandoned boys on the streets, he felt God directing a change in ministry focus (H. Baker 2008a, 231). His subsequent trips throughout the mountains of southwest China resulted in the establishment of forty churches and the water baptism of approximately 6,000 people (H. Baker 2008a, 393). He emphasized indigenous church principles, insisting that native evangelists and pastors be supported by their converts who were also responsible for arranging meeting sites for the young churches (H. Baker 1940). Foreign contributions were used for the support of the orphanage, conventions, and short-term training seminars (H. Baker 1940). The continued existence, as of 1986, of 40,000 followers of Christ among the Ka Do with over 150 full-time Christian workers testifies to the success of Baker's training of indigenous leaders for the churches.[122]

Baker's ministry demonstrated apostolic power with accompanying signs and wonders. Believers prayed for the sick and exorcised demons. Word of God's power spread, and Baker's teams frequently found the sick waiting for them in villages and

---

[122]Baker left China in 1952. Baker stated that he had planted forty churches and baptized 6,000 believers. Growth to 40,000 believers and 150 full-time workers in 34 years in an environment hostile to Christianity testifies to Baker's success at planting self-supporting, self-governing, and self-propagating churches. Statistics taken from Joshua Project (2019).

along mountain trails (H. Baker 2008b, 7). "If God is as mighty as is claimed, he can fill a man with the Holy Spirit so that he may have manifestations of superhuman power with supernatural evidence of God" (H. Baker 2008b, 18).

One additional aspect of Baker's ministry must be noted. Baker practiced incarnational ministry. He traveled with national believers, ate with them, and slept in their homes: "We walk and we work together. We sweat and we talk together . . . I get to know the men, and they get to know me" (H. Baker 1940, 153).

Victor Plymire

Given up to die at the age of two, Victor Plymire's mother dedicated him to God and prayed for his healing (V. Plymire 1931b). Sketchy details surround Plymire's missionary call. He did inquire about missionary service at the age of eighteen, only two years after accepting Christ. Sometime later, he received appointment to go to China under the Christian and Missionary Alliance (CMA). Plymire served in China with the CMA for almost eleven years, severing his relationship with them only after receiving the baptism of the Holy Spirit in Lancaster, Pennsylvania, in 1919 (V. Plymire 1931b). His call to the Tibetans exposed him to dangers and difficulties. He served in China until the Communists won China's civil war in 1949.[123]

Plymire's commitment to evangelism is well-documented.[124]

- October 1, 1910, to December 19, 1910. Evangelistic trip to Guide, northeast border of Tibet.
- April 1, 1917, to June 26, 1917. Evangelistic trip to Labrang monastery in Gansu.
- August 1924. Evangelistic trip to the Tibetan border.
- November 1924. Evangelistic trip to Gomba Sobo Monastery.

---

[123]The bibliography contains many essays written by Victor Plymire that detail his hardships and persecution. These essays can be found at both the FPHC and AGWM archives in Springfield, Missouri.

[124]Plymire's reports on all of the trips listed can be found in the AGWM archives in Springfield, Missouri.

- June 5, 1926. Went to Kumbun Monastery to preach to Tibetans.
- May 1927 to April 1928. Evangelistic trip across Tibet following the deaths of Grace and John Plymire. People in the United States thought he had died on this trip, which covered 2,437 miles.[125]
- May 7, 1932, to June 1, 1932. Evangelistic trip in northwest China.
- October 1933 to December 4, 1933. Evangelistic trip from Gansu to Gan-tsa in northeast Tibet.
- June 23, 1934. Evangelistic trip to south Tibet.
- 1934 also included an additional evangelistic trip to northeast Tibet.
- July 6, 1934, to September 1934. Evangelistic trip in Tibet.
- June 22, 1940. Summer months evangelizing along the Tibetan border.[126]

Plymire's longest trip from 1927-28 illustrates his passion for evangelism. On that trip, he prepared approximately 74,000 Gospels and New Testaments, and 40,000 tracts to distribute along the way (D. Plymire 1983, 76). At the beginning of his journey, he prayed, "Let me touch as many lives as possible" (D. Plymire 1983, 78). On June 5, 1927, he wrote, "I have tried to give the gospel so that all may hear it at least once" (D. Plymire 1983, 79).

The nomadic nature of the Tibetans made planting churches in a centralized location almost impossible. The challenges Plymire confronted in church planting are exemplified by a conversation between Victor and Ga Lo, the chief of the Kantsa tribe. Ga Lo had invited Plymire to attend the wedding celebration of his brother, noting that the entire tribe would be there. He extended

---

[125]A copy of Plymire's personal diary for this trip can be found in both FPHC and AGWM archives in Springfield, Missouri.

[126]These are only a sample of Plymire's evangelistic trips in northwest China and Tibet. Vast distances to be covered as well as inclement winter weather required Victor to schedule the large majority of his trips in late spring to early fall. These trips usually lasted for several months.

an invitation for Victor to tell as many people as possible about the Christian religion. "Unless you are with us more, this will not be possible. Will you come and live with us" (Plymire 1983, 175-176)?

Building churches among a nomadic people presented a major challenge to Plymire's methodology and ecclesiology. A different approach would be needed because physical buildings, tied to one geographic location, could not meet the need. Plymire wrote to Noel Perkin of the need to strategize and work for mobile churches under indigenous leadership. A key to success was training converts who would travel with the various tribes as a mobile church (Plymire 1931a).

Plymire lived incarnationally among the Tibetans. Relationships he developed with Tibetans later gave him access where others would have been denied. His opportunity to hand out tracts and talk about Christianity in the Labrang Monastery resulted from an earlier friendship with a young Buddhist priest who vouched for Victor (Greenaway 1987, 22). On another occasion, his Tibetan language teacher urged Plymire to delay travel for one day for him to notify his friends in a robber band to give Victor safe passage (Greenaway 1987, 21). An incarnational lifestyle that emphasized developing personal relationships rather than holding formal meetings served Plymire well on evangelistic trips to various Tibetan tribal gatherings. Results came slowly, as work among a nomadic people required patience.[127]

Roland Allen spoke of Paul's selection of strategic centers. Plymire's selection of Tangar followed Allen's model. Located only twenty-seven miles west of Kumbum, a lamasery with over 3,600 lamas, Tangar was also a major city on the caravan route to and from Lhasa. A representative of the Dalai Lama lived two doors down from the Plymires. Large caravans of Tibetan traders traveled between Lhasa and Tangar. The long distances and time required for travel meant that traders would frequently stay in Tangar for months to prepare their animals for the return trip (Plymire 1931b). Tangar gave the Plymires access to Tibetans,

[127]Plymire labored for sixteen years before he baptized his first convert (Blumhofer 1989b, 248).

Chinese residents doing business with Tibetans, as well as some Mongolians and Muslims (Plymire 1931b).

Leslie Anglin and Marie Stephany

McGee (1994, 11) asks a crucial question: "Saving souls or saving lives?" His article addresses the tension between proclamation of the gospel and compassion ministries. Early writers in the Assemblies of God went on record with a commitment to the "priority of proclamation" (General Council of the Assemblies of God, 1914, 9-10). The Social Gospel movement of the early 1900s found support from those who believed in a postmillennial eschatology.[128]

Fundamentalist and revival movements of the late nineteenth- and early twentieth-centuries emphasized a premillennial return of Christ. If the return of Christ was imminent, then little time remained to evangelize. Flower, in the June 12, 1920, *Pentecostal Evangel*, spoke of "eschatological expectancy" (McGee 1994, 11) in Assemblies of God church services:

> Over and over messages were given in the Spirit that the time would not be long and what was done must be done quickly. We were impressed that the time was so short that the heathen in the neglected parts of the earth would scarcely have time to hear before Jesus should come. (Flower 1920, 12)

A commitment to the priority of evangelism, although looking good on paper, complicated ministry on many fields.

McGee notes that the two countries, India and China, where the largest number of AG missionaries worked prior to World War II, saw large numbers of missionaries engaged in institutional

---

[128]A postmillennial eschatology emphasized that the church's mission was to focus work on addressing existing social evils. Establishing the kingdom of God on earth would prepare the way for Christ's return, inaugurating his millennial reign (Peterson 2009, 156).

work.[129] He also notes that 61 percent of the missionaries in China in 1920 were women. Surprisingly, most of the women missionaries chose to devote their time to evangelism (McGee 1994, 12-13).

Early twentieth-century China was mired in conflict. Armies ravaged the countryside, natural disasters left many people facing starvation, and opium addiction continued to impoverish thousands of Chinese. Missionaries arriving in China purposing to devote their attention to evangelism found themselves unable to ignore the suffering masses. Two such missionary teams were Les and Ava Anglin in Tai-an and Marie Stephany and the women who worked closely with her in Shanxi province.

Stephany, in promoting her orphanage in Ta Ch'ang, wrote: "Although I am not called to this kind of work, I am praying that the Lord will definitely call a missionary to take it upon her heart so that we may be able to take in more children" (Stephany 1939, 40). Even when Alice Stewart and Henrietta Tieleman arrived to join Stephany's team, however, the trio divided their time between orphanage work, opium deliverance ministry, tent evangelism, and short-term Bible school ministries.[130]

The Anglins began their ministry in the Tai-an area with itinerant evangelism. Leslie Anglin would select strategic towns and villages, constructing an evangelistic plan for each location. Saturating each location with a gospel witness, he would return repeatedly after completing each circuit. The scarcity of results and the tremendous need convinced Anglin that there must be a better way (Albus 1951, 44-45).

The Anglins' decision to open the Home of Onesiphorus led to criticism from others in the missionary community. Some criticized him for giving up his evangelistic circuits for orphanage work, and others questioned whether he had forgotten the importance of preaching the gospel (Albus 1951, 62).

---

[129]This would include schools, orphanages, and other institutions assisting needy people. India had the largest percentage with 39 percent, but China was not far behind at 25 percent (McGee 1994, 12).

[130]This is described more fully in the chapter on Marie Stephany. See the bibliographical references for Stephany, Stewart, and Tieleman.

Almost a century later, missiologists find themselves in a better position to evaluate these two ministries and assess their conformity and/or deviation from the Allen/Luce model. Despite their heavy involvement in compassion ministries, evangelism remained at the forefront of their endeavors. Furthermore, their commitment to preparing the next generation to serve provided a wonderful means for the continuation and support of indigenous churches.

The Home of Onesiphorus began in 1916 and existed for three purposes. First, it demonstrated the love of Christ through ministry to both physical and spiritual needs. Second, the institution's existence daily gave witness to the message of Christianity. The third purpose, however, looked farther down the road to a time when those who had been served in the orphanage would be adults and go forth as missionaries, evangelists, or Spirit-filled members of local churches (Albus 1951, 109-111).

Anglin's prophetic statement in 1933 indicated that China's greatest need was for self-supporting, Spirit-filled Chinese Christians to evangelize the Chinese and plant churches (Hurst 2009), which echoed Allen's philosophy of spontaneous expansion. Allen constantly stressed the necessity of the Chinese evangelizing their own people. Missionaries could be helpful in training, but foreigners "were not well fitted to be evangelists" (H. Allen 2017, 21).

The Home of Onesiphorus graduated six students in their first class. Two of the three boys became preachers of the gospel; the other worked as a Christian mechanic. One of the girls married, and together with her husband, became missionaries. The remaining two girls became leaders at the Home (Albus 1951, 68).

In 1925, Anglin reported that more than 200 people had received the baptism of the Holy Spirit. From 1924-1925, over 330 had received water baptism (Anglin 1925c). In 1928, he wrote that several of the children wanted to become missionaries when they grew up (Anglin 1928d).

Stephany devoted seven months of the year to tent evangelism. Groups of converts would then begin to meet in homes where discipleship and training took place. Later, with the help of her missionary team, she was able to establish fifteen outstations.

These stations, however, were indigenous with local leadership (Stephany 1940a).

Tent evangelism, outstations, leadership development, opium deliverance centers, orphanages—all of these ministries required large amounts of time and energy. Stephany prepared national workers from her converts. Within a few years, more than thirty of the forty national workers were former addicts who had been delivered and discipled under her team's ministry (Hurst 2001). Adele Dalton reported that twelve students from Ta Ch'ang enrolled in Truth Bible Institute in Beijing, with twenty additional students studying at the local short-term Bible school (Dalton 1987).

Anglin and Stephany followed Allen and Luce's models of indigenous church principles by empowering indigenous leadership. They dug deeper by not only planting indigenous churches but also developing indigenous institutions. Anglin and Stephany both appealed to foreign sources for financial assistance, but they also required the local Chinese to make financial commitments. Everyone at the Home of Onesiphorus was expected to work, and many of its financial needs were met through their assorted work projects. Stephany's group sent out their own missionaries to neighboring areas (Stewart 1945).

The teams that partnered with Anglin and Stephany displayed a healthy blend. On one hand, it could be said that they grew their team through their national converts, but a blended partnership followed. The Holy Spirit began to fall in Tai-an as the Anglins invited W. W. Simpson to preach in their city. Simpson reported that so many believers had received the baptism of the Spirit in Tai-an that the entire work could be considered Pentecostal (Simpson 1953a, 30). Bard and Simpson taught in many of the short-term Bible schools held in the Ta Ch'ang area with Stephany. Anglin and Stephany frequently reported their praise reports, financial needs, and prayer requests in *The Pentecostal Evangel* and other publications.[131]

Both ministries served during turbulent times, proving their commitment to follow God's call despite hardship and

---

[131]See the bibliographical references for Anglin and Stephany.

persecution. Fighting warlords, the civil war between the Communists and Nationalists, and Japanese encroachment and aggression that started in the early 1930s made missionary work in China dangerous. Stephany, Stewart, and Tieleman were confined for periods of time by the Japanese. Both Stewart and Tieleman remained in China following the Communist takeover. They remained until 1952 when they transferred to Taiwan and worked with Chinese there.[132] Leslie Anglin died in 1942. Following his death, his wife Ava was detained for twenty-nine months in a Japanese concentration camp (Albus 1951).

William Wallace Simpson

William Wallace Simpson's commitment to mission service was built primarily upon two passages of Scripture. At the age of twenty-one, he served a small congregation in rural Tennessee. Shortly after assuming his pastoral responsibilities, he randomly selected Mark 16:15 as his text. In preparing the sermon, however, the Holy Spirit convicted him that it was not right for him to preach from that text if he was not prepared to obey it (Simpson n.d.a).

Romans 15:18-21 guided Simpson's missionary career. "Obedience—by word and deed, by the power of signs and wonders, by the power of the Spirit of God . . . and thus I make it my ambition to preach the gospel, not where Christ has already been named, lest I build on someone else's foundation." Simpson's writings and sermons frequently incorporate this passage of Scripture.[133]

Simpson's pursuit of the call of God came at great cost to him and his family. In 1932, his son Willie was martyred, which is well-known, but he also buried two daughters in China.[134] He served in Gansu, northwest China, during the time when Chinese and Muslim warlords vied for control of the area. Simpson frequently

---

[132]See Stewart's (n.d.) autobiographical account in *Like Zion's Mount in China*.

[133]An extensive list of Simpson's personal writings and sermons are included in the bibliography.

[134]See Koetitz [1980?], Simpson (1953a and 1957).

found himself and his converts caught in the middle between these warring factions (Simpson 1953a).

Following World War II, at the age of seventy-seven, Simpson immediately began preparing to return to China. Traveling by ship, he spent several weeks reflecting on his ministry priorities for that season of his life. After much prayer, Simpson concluded that his focus should be "preparing the believers to do the work of spreading the Gospel . . . that requires their being filled with the Spirit and devoted to witnessing to the unevangelized" (Koetitz [1980?], 26). This focus follows Roland Allen's methodology for spontaneous expansion (R. Allen 1960a) and Luce's (1921b, 6) exhortation to look for "signs to follow" when "doing an apostolic work along apostolic lines."

Simpson constantly taught and preached on the necessity of Holy Spirit baptism and speaking in tongues. Both he and his converts expected God to confirm his Word with accompanying signs and wonders. Upon returning to Gansu province in 1946, believers welcomed his return and shared many reports of the supernatural, including rain in response to prayer for drought-stricken areas; prophetic warnings to the church, which when heeded, had preserved the church from physical harm from marauding armies; and healings, including three reports of people being brought back to life (Simpson 1953a).[135]

Simpson believed training a new generation of Chinese believers was essential for the evangelization of China. He taught in many short-term Bible schools as well as Truth Bible Institute (TBI) in Beijing and other extension sites. He spent his last months in China preparing for one-hundred students to attend the new term at the relocated TBI, which was scheduled to meet in Gansu from May 1 to August 31, 1949 (Simpson 1953a).[136] Simpson

---

[135]The churches that Simpson visited at this time had grown during Simpson's absence of almost eleven years (Koetitz [1980?]). Even today, visitors can find churches in southern Gansu province that still identify themselves as Assemblies of God churches. Books of Simpson's sermons and hymnals with songs that Simpson translated and others that he wrote still circulate among the churches.

[136]Even though Simpson left earlier than anticipated, the Bible school term continued.

incorporated compassion ministries into his ministry.[137] From beginning to end, he focused on evangelizing the unreached areas of China and the world, training believers to do that work, and emphasizing the necessity of baptism in the empowering Holy Spirit.

Leonard and Ada Bolton

The Bolton's methodology has already been summarized at the conclusion of Chapter 9 with five words: prayer, sacrifice, identification, mobility, and training. Those five words provide excellent benchmarks for evaluation of all Assemblies of God mission ministry in China during this period.

The Holy Spirit's role in methodology and ecclesiology cannot be minimized. As a child, Leonard Bolton remembered his father's oft-repeated prayer: "Lord, keep us where the fiery fire burns . . ." (Bolton 1984, 16).

Prayer paved the way for revival among the Lisu. The influence of prayer is repeatedly seen in the Bolton's missionary call and service, as the following examples reveal.

- Revival among the Lisu traces its roots back to the prayer ministry of James Fraser (CIM) and his mother's cottage prayer group (Crossman 1982).
- As a teenager, a visiting missionary prayed over Leonard. He received the baptism of the Holy Spirit and began speaking in tongues. At the same time, he received healing from a serious eye condition (Ezzo n.d.b, 16-21).
- Smith Wigglesworth visited the Bolton home on several occasions, modeling prayer before young Leonard (Ezzo n.d.b).

---

[137]During the 1920s, Simpson responded to famine in Gansu by opening a temporary orphanage that housed and fed approximately five-hundred children from 1928-1930 (Simpson 1953a, 68). Earlier he had introduced potatoes to the area, which withstood the drought conditions better than other indigenous crops, saving many lives (Koetitz [1980?]).

- During her 1922 visit to England, Mary Lewer prayed that God would give her three new workers for China (Ezzo n.d.b)
- The telegram bringing news of Alfred Lewer's death also brought assurances that people were "praying much for you that God will show you what to do" (Ezzo n.d.b, 32).
- Following the reception of the news of Alfred's death, Leonard and Olive Bolton prayed for Alfred Lewer's family in southwest China as well as for direction on what to do (Bolton 1984, 26).
- When Olive Bolton and the newborn baby died, a Christian woman in England, unaware of the circumstances, spent a sleepless night in prayer for the Boltons (Bolton 1984, 51).

Prayer and dependence upon the Holy Spirit for guidance and empowerment provided a solid foundation upon which ministry to the Lisu was built. Those prayers enabled Leonard and Ada Bolton to persevere through great hardship. Nine graves in China and one in Taiwan, added to the martyrs' deaths of co-workers, David and John Ho, testify to the cost (Bolton 1984, 220).

The incarnational ministry of the Boltons and their team illustrate a methodology that crossed cultural boundaries. Walking with the Lisu, eating Lisu food, sharing Lisu problems, and doing life together with the Lisu earned them the right to be heard (Bolton 1984, 220).

The large percentage of Lisu Christians in China[138] and the expansion of the work among the Lisu into northern Myanmar (Burma) testifies to the indigenization of the work. Closed doors to foreign missions work in both China and Myanmar have not kept the Lisu churches from growing. Commitment to training national workers and transferring leadership to these young men and women replicates the Pauline model. John Fish, a Lisu and the Burmese AG superintendent, asked Maynard Ketcham, the

---

[138]Joshua Project estimates that 80 percent of the Lisu in China are Christians (Joshua Project, 2016a).

field secretary for the American Assemblies of God work in Asia Pacific, in 1966, "You are not going to take the Holy Spirit out of Burma, are you?" (Bolton 1984, 215-216). He answered his own rhetorical question a year later in a report to Ketcham: "See what the Holy Spirit can do!" (Bolton 1984, 216).

Roland Allen repeatedly emphasized the role of the Holy Spirit in the expansion of the church. He stressed the necessity of dependence on the leading of the Spirit. Allen chided missionaries for lack of faith for the Holy Spirit to mature and empower young leaders.[139]

Luce contended that young converts and churches could benefit from the counsel of those who had more experience in the faith. Such counsel should be given from the position of equals and not as superiors. Luce (1921c, 6-7) concluded that "when the Lord raises up spiritually qualified leaders in the native churches themselves, what a joy it will be . . . to let them take the lead as the Spirit Himself shall guide them."

Summary

Five questions guided this discussion on the methodology of the exemplars of AG mission methodology in China and its conformity or deviation from the Allen/Luce models. Those questions revolve around (1) call and commitment, (2) priority of evangelism, (3) adherence to indigenous church principles, (4) role of the Holy Spirit, and (5) partnership and teams. Not all questions are equally relevant to each narrative, but a close look at the narrative gives clear proof that these early missionaries followed the Allen/Luce methodology.

The major deviation reflects the issue addressed in Gary McGee's (1994) article, "Saving Souls or Saving Lives?" This issue of the role of compassion work and social justice issues continues to be debated. The missionaries selected in this study navigated the two extremes in admirable fashion. They responded to physical

---

[139]A list of Allen's books can be found in the bibliography. All of them represent Allen's beliefs in the necessity of dependence on the Holy Spirit.

and spiritual needs with a holistic approach, realizing that "the spiritual needs of hundreds of millions of people in our world are too great and the cries of the hungry and the oppressed are too loud for Christians to ignore either, even if one's eschatology chimes that midnight has come" (McGee 1994, 21).

An examination of AGWMs *Missionary Manual* through the years illustrates the development of a holistic model of ministry. The *Missionary Manual* of 1977 and 1981 reveal the change in statement of purpose that incorporated inclusion for compassion ministries:

> The Division of Foreign Missions [now AGWM] is committed primarily to the fulfillment of the Great Commission. Its basic policy is to evangelize the world, establish churches after the New Testament pattern, and train national believers to preach the gospel to their own people and in a continuing mission to other nations. We recognize that the only way to evangelize the world is to teach the people of each country to reach their own nation for Christ. (Division of Foreign Missions of the Assemblies of God 1977, 8.)
>
> The Pauline example shall be followed as far as possible by seeking out neglected regions where the gospel has not been preached, as well as by establishing self-supporting, self-governing, self-propagating national churches. (Division of Foreign Missions of the Assemblies of God 1977, 9.)
>
> The mission strategy of the Division of Foreign Missions shall be the widest possible evangelization of the spiritually lost through every available means, the establishment of indigenous churches after the New Testament pattern, the training of national believers to proclaim the gospel to their own people in an expanding mission to other peoples and the showing of compassion for suffering peoples in a manner representing the love of Jesus Christ. (Division of Foreign Missions of the Assemblies of God 1981, 1-4.)

Everett Wilson quotes a statement from Hogan's 1986 annual report: "The Communists may out-think us, out-talk us, out-argue us, out-work us, and out-live us, but they cannot, they must not, they will not, by God's grace, out-love us" (Wilson 1997, 139). The current list of AGWM core values includes the statement "We are committed to holistic mission in word, deed, and spirit" (Easter et al. 2016, 127). The Assemblies of God missionaries in early twentieth-century China made their contribution to this change in stated purpose. They did so without compromising the commitment to follow the Pauline example in evangelizing to the ends of the earth, discipling converts, and planting churches.

Chapter Twelve

THE CHALLENGE OF CHINA TODAY

A new age for Christianity in China began with the Communist Party's victory over the Chinese Nationalists in 1949. Western missionaries either voluntarily left China or were expelled. Some predicted that the small Chinese church would not be able to survive the anticipated persecution. In the 1950s, the China Communist Party (CCP) established the Three Self Patriotic Movement to oversee and control existing churches. Pastors and churches were expected to give primary loyalty to the state. The limited freedom of the 1950s gave way to more aggressive efforts in the 1960s to exterminate Christianity. The persecution of the Cultural Revolution led to the closure of churches, and Christians were forced to worship underground. In 1979, as government policies concerning religious practice began to relax, the world discovered that Christianity had actually grown during the years of persecution (Lambert 1991, 9-10).

Did the methodology employed by the pre-1952 Assemblies of God missionaries impact the growth of the Chinese church, and if so, how did their methodology prepare and equip believers for growth during periods of persecution? To answer this question, the differences between the official state-recognized church and the unofficial family churches must be examined. How were both affected, and in what ways? What challenges confront the Chinese church today, and what can the Church, at large, learn from their current methodology? Finally, Pauline methods influenced the pre-1952 missionaries. In the following chapter, we will examine what the apostle Paul might have done if he had lived in China in the twenty-first century. How might he approach the challenges of mission ministry in the modern Chinese context?

The Three-Self Patriotic Movement

The Three- Self Patriotic Movement (TSPM) officially began in 1954, five years after Mao Zedong and the Communist Party liberated China. However, even before 1949, the Chinese Communists had formed a Religious Affairs Bureau to oversee all religious activities in the country following their successful revolution (Van Houten 1988, iii-iv).

Despite appearing to be new, the Communist Party's policy merely continued the old line, which had been in practice for more than 2,000 years. Religion was subservient to the state and under its control. As long as religion posed no threat to the state, it would be tolerated. It is worth noting that, with the exception of Daoism, all major religions, including Buddhism, were imported from outside countries (Bohr 1983, 322).

When Mao assumed the reins of leadership in China, he promoted the idea of religious toleration as long as it could be controlled by the state. He was influenced by the need to avoid internal dissension between the followers of Islam and Buddhism. Many of these Muslims and Buddhists lived in strategic border areas of the southwest and northwest. Mao used the term "united front" to describe his goal of joining all social groups in building a strong China (Lambert 1991, 29-54).[140]

Mao's united front strategy was based on a system of primary and secondary contradictions. Atheistic Communism was at variance or in contradiction with Islam, Christianity, and many other religious beliefs. China's economic position posed another contradiction. Because Mao viewed China's modernization as of

---

[140]Tony Lambert's (1991, 29-54) *The Resurrection of the Chinese Church* contains an explanation of the "united front" policy of the Chinese Communist Party. The Chinese government sought to achieve two goals: (1) "the correct handling of the beliefs of religious believers in China" (Lambert 1991, 42) and (2) uniting believers to serve the goals for Chinese modernization (1991, 42-43).

higher importance, it was designated a primary contradiction (Chao 1988, x-xiii). The CCP viewed the atheism versus theism conflict as a secondary contradiction. Secondary contradictions could temporarily be set aside to unite the country in pursuit of a higher goal (Chao 1988, x-xiii). This resulted in Christians experiencing a degree of religious toleration provided they severed all foreign ties and remained patriotic. Government officials believed that patriotism required all other existing loyalties to take a subservient place to the state (Bohr 1983, 324).

The Cultural Revolution of 1966-76, where there was a complete absence of religious toleration, came to be seen as an aberration and not reflective of the long-term goals and policies of the Party. Deng Xiaoping, who once said that it did not matter if the cat was white or black as long as it caught mice, adopted a pragmatic approach (Lambert 1991, 4). He said, "If people work hard, the government doesn't care which religion they practice" (Bohr 1983, 326-327).

Requiring everything to come under state control played a pivotal role in the establishment of the TSPM. First, the government embraced Christianity as a necessary part of the united front since all citizens were needed for modernization. Second, organizing a state organization to supervise religious practice allowed for easier control of the Christian religion by the state.

In 1981, K. H. Ting[141] was elected chairperson of the TSPM and president of the China Christian Council (CCC). Ting was born in Shanghai in 1915. In 1949, he resided in Canada. In spite of many warnings about the danger of returning to China, he immediately began preparations to return to China with his family, arriving back in Shanghai in 1951 (Whitehead 1989, 3-7).

---

[141]Ting Kuang-hsun or Ding Guangxun, in Pinyin. I have adopted the Romanized "Ting" or K. H. Ting since that was the way Philip L. Wickeri (2007) referred to him in *Reconstructing Christianity in China: K. H. Ting and the Chinese Church*. Wickeri has written extensively on Ting's life and work. See also Janice and Philip Wickeri (2002), *A Chinese Contribution to Ecumenical Theology: Selected Writings of Bishop K. H. Ting*, and Philip L. Wickeri (1988) *Seeking the Common Ground: Protestant Christianity, the Three-Self Movement, and China's United Front*. Also, Raymond Whitehead (1989) has edited a collection of Ting's sermons in *No Longer Strangers: Selected Writings of K. H. Ting*.

Y. T. Wu, the former secretary of the YMCA publications, had been Ting's mentor. Wu served as the first chairman of the TSPM and had, from the onset, fully cooperated with the Communist Party's efforts to control the church (Lambert 1994, 45).

Article 36 and Document 19

Understanding the official government policies concerning the practice of Christianity in China is essential to recognizing the divide between the government-sanctioned church and the underground church.[142] Article 36 of the 1982 Constitution and Document 19, issued on March 31 of the same year, assert the official religious policies of the Chinese Communist Party.

The Constitution states:

> Citizens of the People's Republic of China enjoy freedom of religious belief. No state organization, public organization or individual may compel citizens to believe in, or not to believe in, any religion; nor may they discriminate against citizens who believe in, or do not believe in, any religion. The state protects normal religious activities. No one may make use of religion to engage in activities that disrupt public order, impair the health of citizens or interfere with the educational system of the state. Religious bodies and religious affairs are not subject to any foreign domination (Lazarotto 1983, 268).

Document 19 addresses restrictions on religious liberty. The Party still must promote atheism. The practice of religion is a *private* affair. Any interference with the "administration of the

---

[142]Differing opinions exist concerning these two branches of the Chinese church. Some contend that the true church in China can only be found in the underground church due to the strong influence of the state on the TSPM churches. The debate between these two poles, at times, has been hot and heavy. In actuality, there are TSPM churches that are extremely evangelistic with a deep love for Christ. There are also those that are spiritually cold and whose doctrine falls woefully short of the New Testament standard. The same can be said of house churches across China.

State, the legal system, education in schools, and all public forms of education" is prohibited (Lambert 1994, 55-56).

How local officials interpret these documents determines the degree of latitude in religious practice in any area. Several important considerations are:

- The Constitution's statement of "freedom of religious belief" does not extend to Party members. They must adhere to the Party's atheistic ideology (Lazzarotto 1983, 272).
- Freedom of religious belief does not include with it the freedom to evangelize or propagate one's faith. "Forcing people to believe in religion is an infringement on the freedom of religious belief of other people and is, therefore, extremely wrong and can never be allowed" (Lazzarotto 1983, 282-283).
- Religious faith may be propagated inside temples, churches, or other legally designated areas. Individuals under the age of eighteen are not to be evangelized (Lazzarotto 1983, 282-283).
- The definition of what fits under the classification of *normal* religious activities depends on the interpretation of the leadership of the government and the TSPM.

Five very *normal*—according to Western viewpoints—activities would be deemed as not *normal*, and, therefore, would be classified as illegal: (1) any religious meeting being conducted in a non-designated site, thus prohibiting itinerant evangelism; (2) evangelization of anyone under the age of eighteen; (3) anyone conducting religious meetings who has not been ordained by the TSPM and China Christian Council (CCC); (4) possession and distribution of any unauthorized Christian literature, whether produced in China or brought in from abroad; and (5) exorcism and prayer for the sick (Lambert 1994, 69-70). The Pauline methodology contradicts all five of these prohibitions.

In China, freedom of religion basically means the right to believe in one's heart. It does not include basic expressions of faith in society, such as marriage and family life. Religion remains a private affair without societal influence (Chao 1988, vii-viii).

The TSPM's origins are rooted in the desire of the Communist Party to control the Protestant Christian Church in China. As long as Christianity remains a secondary contradiction, religious practice enjoys a degree of tolerance. Several factors, however, could lead to a stricter interpretation of existing laws and implementation of tighter controls. Two such factors are: (1) the ability of the TSPM to bring all Christian groups under its umbrella, which would also, by definition, bring foreign interference and involvement with the Chinese church under control; and (2) the perception that the church becomes a rival for the loyalty of Chinese young people (Bohr 1983, 332-333).

The latter factor concerns the Party, presenting an interesting dilemma to the Christian church. The church has a golden opportunity to minister to the needs and problems of China's youth. To do so, however, would send a clear message to the Party that the church is competing for the minds of China's young people. If the Party feels a line has been crossed, it will implement increasingly rigid control mechanisms (Bohr 1983, 338-340).

The TSPM continues to face accusations of theological liberalism and politicization. Whereas Western people have a tendency to separate issues of church and state, such is not the case in China. The government tightly controls religion so that it contributes to ongoing political stability. As such, everything has political ramifications (Chan 2002, 4).

One example strikes at the very definition of the TSPM, which promotes self-government, self-support, and self-propagation. When the Communists first took control in China, many indigenous churches were already in existence, which qualified as three-self by definition. Watchman Nee with the Little Flock, and the independent churches pastored by Wang Ming-dao and Allen Yuan are three examples. These churches were self-governing, self-supporting, strong in evangelistic outreach, and under no foreign control. All three pastors rejected offers to join the TSPM and were imprisoned for several years (Lambert 1994, 13-14).

The TSPM claims that they provide a credible Christian witness in China because they (1) represent the truly patriotic

Christians; (2) remove the stigma of Christianity being a foreign religion; and (3) enable the re-opening of old church buildings as well as the printing of Bibles and other Christian literature (D. Adeney 1985, 168-169). Adeney's research identifies the following reasons for church leaders joining the TSPM: (1) to become legal; (2) to be allowed to witness publicly; (3) to encourage people who are curious about Christianity; (4) to minister to all new Christians; and (5) to connect with other Christian believers (D. Adeney 1985, 180). However, these are only valid if the churches and their leadership adhere strictly to the Party's religious policy. All witnessing, all evangelism, and all ministry must take place in designated areas by designated personnel.

Adeney lists several reasons churches oppose joining the TSPM. They believe that Christ is the head of the church and not the state. They believe that joining the TSPM results in censorship of teaching by the church. The history of the TSPM includes many examples of collaboration with the Religious Affairs Bureau and the Public Security Bureau leading to the imprisonment of many pastors and Christians. They feel that association with the TSPM limits opportunities for evangelism, including those under the age of eighteen. They feel that the TSPM serves as a political platform. Furthermore, they object to the regulation that only those who receive state-approved training and are approved by the Party can conduct religious services (D. Adeney 1985, 181-184).

In 2003, Jonathan Chao related a response from house church leaders to an invitation from the government to join the TSPM. These house church leaders began by emphasizing that they should not be considered revolutionary or unpatriotic. Three major issues divided the TSPM and the house church: (1) who leads the church, (2) the issue of evangelism, and (3) fellowship with the Church-at-large (Chao 2003).

Chao's interviewees claim that the government's religious policies control all church actions. The governmental policy limits preaching to individuals licensed by the Religious Affairs Bureau. These church leaders believe that God calls preachers. The government designates spheres of religious activity for each licensed clergyman and each registered church. These actions contradict the Great Commission, which commands going to the ends of the earth to preach the gospel. Furthermore, they claim that prohibitions against evangelizing and teaching people under the age of eighteen contradict Jesus's practice of welcoming children. These house church leaders also state that government policy strictly limiting foreign ministry prevents them from receiving encouragement and participation with the church abroad and violates scriptural teaching on the universal church. No division exists between Jews and Gentiles, and Chinese and foreigners. Believers should be noted for the love they have for one another. In short, joining the TSPM would compromise their faith and put them at variance with several biblical teachings as they interpreted them (Chao 2003).

A Comparison of the Theology and Teachings of K. H. Ting and the Apostle Paul

In her second article on Paul's missionary methods, Alice Luce addressed the message that Paul preached. She summarized the Apostle's message as "proclaiming Christ first, last and all the time" (Luce 1921b, 6). Paul's powerful message was confirmed by God with accompanying signs and wonders (Luce 1921b, 6). Luce, furthermore, states that Paul "preached the Full Gospel in every place, never compromising nor catering to the prejudices of the people, their customs or their social position" (Luce 1921b, 6). Later in that same article, she summarized the key points in Paul's evangelistic message:

- Repentance from sin and turning toward God
- Faith in Jesus Christ
- Jesus as the only Savior from sin
- Jesus crucified, resurrected, and coming again in glory
- God's wrath poured out against sin
- Salvation by free grace alone
- A life of holiness and baptism of the Holy Spirit
- Healing for the body (Luce 1921b, 6)

Ting's view on original sin differs from that of Paul. Whereas Paul states that "[n]one is righteous, no, not one" (Rom 3:10) and "all have sinned, and come short of the glory of God" (Rom 3:23

KJV), Ting states that one of the problems Christianity has had in China is belief in the innate sinfulness of man. He affirmed that belief in man's basic goodness is inherent in Chinese culture and philosophy. This teaching goes back to Confucius and Mencius who believed that mankind was basically good by nature (Ting 1989, 32). Ting (1989, 127) also hints at a universalist theology that accepts multiple paths to God when he states that "the Christian gospel . . . makes room for multiple manifestations of truth."

Ting's published writings frequently associate missionary work with Western imperialism. Missionaries are not needed or wanted in China. Addressing the Third National Christian Conference in 1980, Ting (2000) stated:

> We want to declare before the whole world: church and evangelistic work inside China is the right and responsibility of our Chinese Church; no people outside China, regardless of their skin, should carry on any activity of a missionary nature inside China or directed at China, without the expressed consent of Chinese Church authorities. If such people were indeed motivated by nothing but their faith, then they would at least stop to consider Paul's statement: "My ambition is to preach the Gospel, not where Christ has already been named, lest I build on another man's foundation" (Rom. 15:20)[143] Once Corinth had a church, Paul said to the Corinthians that he wanted "to preach the Gospel in lands beyond" them, in order to avoid boasting of work already done by others, for he did not want to preach the Gospel "in another's field" (2 Cor. 10:16). Now, outside of China there are those who are trying to mobilize Christians to leave their own places where their preaching is most suitable, and send them into our field, thus destroying the foundation of our

[143]Note the difference in W. W. Simpson's and Ting's use of this text. Ting seems to assume that if the gospel has been preached in one corner of China, that the entire country should be considered as having been evangelized.

> thirty years of Three-Self. We cannot help asking, why would they want to do this? (Ting 2000, 70.)

Ting uses the analogy of international trade and tariffs by comparing the TSPM and China's strict control of all international contacts to protect local churches from non-approved teaching to that of nations levying tariffs on incoming goods to protect local businesses (Ting 2000, 104).

In 1979, Ting (1989, 108) said, "Let us suppose a missionary goes to China and Christians there ask if he or she supports the Three-Self Movement. Now if the answer is yes, then this missionary should not be there; and if the answer is no, Chinese Christians surely cannot accept such a person."

These post-1949 statements by Ting do not match those he made before Communist Liberation. In 1948, Ting (1989, 52) said, "Nothing can really kill the church unless it is induced to forget its missionary task." Such a contrast in statements perhaps reflects one of the major purposes of the Communist Party's use of the TSPM. Denial of the Church's missionary purpose would weaken the Church and speed up its decline. A comparison of several pre-1949 and post-1949 statements by Ting further confirms the politicization of the TSPM.

In 1948, Ting said:

> Missionaries from older churches are certainly needed by younger churches, and for reasons that will largely hold good even when the latter grow strong. Missionaries bring us the experience and heritage of older and stronger traditions;[144] they link us with the reality and the richness of the whole body of Christ; they bring us tried methods useful in our own lands; through their life and deeds they help us gain access to people otherwise difficult to reach; as fellow-students in Christ, they use their learning

---

[144]This sounds remarkably similar to Luce's statements on young converts and churches utilizing the experience of those who had been longer in the faith (Luce 1921c, 6).

> in the teaching and training of youth, preparing us to tackle the big untouched areas. They themselves receive inspiration when they see people accepting Christ for the first time and realize the tremendous impact that the New Testament makes on the life and minds of new converts and their communities. This in itself is an experience that, properly interpreted, spreads out to enrich the spirituality of the universal church. Last but not least, missionaries are important to the mother churches as active communicators keeping the missionary torch burning and invigorating the whole of church life (Ting 1989, 52-53).

In 1948, Ting (1989, 53) also said that the New Testament was written because of the missionary work of the Early Church.

Reconciling Ting's pre-TSPM statements with those he made as a leader of the movement proves difficult. In the 1940s, his statements sound compatible with most Evangelical views of missionary work. They emphasize the importance of missions and evangelism. They stress the partnership of the missionary and the national church. The New Testament is a missionary book.

Similar challenges exist in reconciling Ting's pre-1949 and post-1949 comments about evangelism. In 1948, Ting (1989, 52) said that "evangelism is the lifeblood of the church. It is only in reaching out into the world that the church can keep the gospel vital for itself." In his 1948 message entitled "A Vital Vocation," Ting (1989) said:

> It is most natural for Christians to want to tell others about Christ. . . . If Christ has become anything at all to you, he must be everything to you. And if indeed he is everything to you, how anxious you must be that he should be made to mean everything to all people everywhere. That anxiety in you corresponds in a small way to the eternal divine longing that all humanity return to God. . . . The conquest of the world[145] by God's love allows no alternative (Ting 1989, 52).

---

[145]This phrase, "conquest of the world," is a very interesting imperialist phrase and

By 1983, this drive toward evangelization seems to have been tempered significantly when he wrote that evangelization simply takes place where people live and work. There is no need to go, for "we do not put much emphasis on the Great Commission as given in Matthew 28" (Ting 1983, 312-313). For Christians, the ends of the earth, according to Ting (1983, 317), is where they are: "Thus, transnational evangelism has not risen as a question on our agenda." Ting gives a practical reason for not prioritizing evangelism: the church's current resources are insufficient to provide the training and nurture new converts need (Ting 1983, 316).

The TSPM could invite foreign churches to assist. In actuality, however, that is not a viable option. Ting, in 1979, recognized the shortage of Bibles in China, stating that he knew of some young people who had hand-copied the Bible into notebooks. He felt that such hunger for God's Word necessitated printing Bibles in China. However, he also said, "We certainly do not want to import a Chinese Bible from a foreign country, because that gives no credibility to Chinese Christianity" (Ting 1989, 109).

Coming to simplistic conclusions about the TSPM and the house church movement in China, however, is dangerous. Some TSPM pastors and churches remain evangelistic and outreach oriented. Some TSPM pastors provide an umbrella of protection for house churches meeting in their vicinity. In some locations, church members attend both TSPM gatherings and house groups (Bohr 1983, 335). Genuine believers can be found on both sides. The danger of accepting a simplistic conclusion is that "it encourages foreign efforts to divide Chinese Christians against each other" (Bohr 1983, 335).

Jonathan Chao (1988, xxvi) states that from the viewpoint of some house church leaders three basic issues must be addressed: (1) who leads the church—Christ or the state? (2) the question of whether or not to evangelize, and (3) should the Chinese church be cut off from fellowship with Christians of other nations? Pauline methodology insists that Christ is the head of the Church. Christ

---

definitely not in tune with Ting's post-1949 writings.

commands believers to take the gospel to the ends of the earth, and Christ unites all—Jew and Gentile, male and female, bond and free, rich and poor—as members of God's family.

The Back to Jerusalem Movement

Timothy Tennent mentions C. Peter Wagner's prediction that by the year 2025, China would be sending out more foreign missionaries than any other country (Tennent 2007, 236). Wagner's prediction rested on two facts. First, the Chinese church had grown exponentially. Second, Chinese Christians believed that God had ordained them to play a significant role in end-time evangelism. The Back to Jerusalem Movement (BTJM or B2J) was birthed out of this spiritual setting (Tennent 2007, 236).

Back to Jerusalem does not mean that this missionary movement limits itself to the city of Jerusalem. It refers to a belief in the Chinese Church that God has specifically called them to evangelize the countries, cities, towns, and people groups between China and Jerusalem. It encompasses the worlds of Islam, Buddhism, and Hinduism (Hattaway 2003, x).

Two men—Mark Ma and Simon Zao—rose to leadership positions in this indigenous missionary movement. In November of 1942, Mark Ma felt impressed that "the door to Xinjiang is already open. Enter and preach the gospel" (Hattaway 2003, 29). Xinjiang is located in the far northwest corner of China and remains the homeland of most of the Muslim Uyghurs in China. During the twelfth and thirteenth centuries, most Uyghurs (Keirats) were followers of Jesus (Moffett 1998, 400), but during the fourteenth century, Timur (Tamerlane) either killed the Christians among them or forcibly converted them to Islam (Moffett 1998, 422, 480).

Renewed work among the Uyghurs produced promising results in the early twentieth century. This, however, also passed through the flames of persecution, as noted by Joshua Project:

> The Swedish Missionary Society recommended work among the Uygur in 1902. By the 1930s, more than 300 Uyghurs had been converted, primarily in Kashgar. When Abdullah Khan came to Yarkant in 1933, he expelled the

> missionaries and killed the Uyghur believers in a mass execution, claiming, "It is my duty, according to our law, to put you to death, because by your preaching you destroyed the faith of some of us" (Joshua Project 2016b).

In 2016, Joshua Project (2016b) estimated that fifty known Uyghur Christians lived among a population of almost 12 million.

Mark Ma believed that God had reserved the area of the world from Xinjiang westward back to the Middle East specifically for the Chinese to evangelize. Ma, as well as several of his students, came to sense that Xinjiang was not only a mission field, but also a training ground to prepare them for missionary outreach back across the old Silk Road directly through the heart of the Islamic countries of Central Asia (Tennent 2007, 236).

These early Chinese missionary pioneers started toward Xinjiang. However, the timing of their travel coincided with the Communist rise to power in 1949. When they arrived in Kashgar, authorities arrested many of them and accused them of traitorous activities for attempting to leave the country. Simon Zao, the other key leader of the Back to Jerusalem movement, was imprisoned for forty years. He was released in 1988 (Tennent 2007, 237). Almost seventy years have passed since Ma, Zao, and the other members of the student movement left on that first trip to Xinjiang.[146] Jason Mandryk (2010, 216) states that, between 1975 and 2010, evangelicals in China grew from 2.7 million to over 75 million.[147] Many of these evangelical Chinese Christians feel that their time living in a hostile environment has prepared them for work along the Silk Road back to Jerusalem.

The Back to Jerusalem movement was birthed and spread in Chinese soil. It is impossible to say authoritatively whether the American AG missionaries contributed significantly to the birth of this indigenous missionary movement. One thing can be said: early

---

[146]Paul Hattaway (2003) recounts the story of Ma and Zao (see Chapters 3 and 4, pp. 28-62).

[147]Many different estimates exist for the number of Christians in China. Mandryk qualifies his estimate to Evangelical Christians.

American missionaries believed in the urgency of the time and that preaching the gospel throughout the world for a witness to all nations would precede Christ's return to earth. They demonstrated Pauline methods, expecting the Holy Spirit's empowerment with accompanying signs and wonders. Furthermore, they lived out their witness in hostile environments and remained faithful to their task in spite of hardship and persecution. Their emphasis on training national leadership gave them a platform for communicating their missiology by word and deed.

Mingri Jin (2016) studied the Back to Jerusalem movement from the viewpoint of the Chinese church and emphasizes two main points. First, despite the Chinese Church not having a burden for missions and evangelism for almost 1,400 years, this movement has significantly challenged the Chinese Church to engage in evangelical missions. Second, the Chinese Church's eschatology has contributed greatly to the growth of the movement (Jin 2016, 2). Some Chinese believers feel that God has reserved this particular portion of the spiritual harvest field for the Chinese church (Hattaway 2003, 19).

Jin recognizes several challenges of the movement. The PRC's official policy concerning religion and evangelism makes it impossible for such a movement to be organized within China. Representatives for the movement who live outside of China have promoted and enlisted the support of foreign churches and organizations for financial support of the movement. This contradicts the lifestyles of the original B2J members who supported themselves financially with no foreign subsidies. It places what originally was developing as an indigenous mission movement in danger of being pre-empted by the West. Finally, those who have responded to "go" have oftentimes left unprepared, both culturally and theologically (Jin 2016, 20-21).[148]

---

[148]Jin's (2016) book addresses the issues of the movement from a practical vantage point, sensing the importance of providing a biblical foundation for the vision of Ma and Zao. The title of his book, *Back to Jerusalem with All Nations: A Biblical Foundation,* communicates the ideas of a partnership that builds on a solid foundation.

Current Challenges Facing the Chinese Church

The twenty-first century Chinese Church faces daunting challenges. Effectively confronting these challenges will tax their creativity. The specter of an authoritarian state that does not permit dissent, coupled with massive changes in society, will require the leading of the Holy Spirit to navigate these turbulent times.

First, since the early 1980s, China's urban population has increased by 500 million people (Fulton 2015, 6). Over the next fifteen years, urban migration will continue at a projected rate of 13 million per year (Fulton 2015, 6). Shenzhen serves as an example of this urban movement. In 1980, it was a sleepy fishing village of 30,000 people across the border from Hong Kong. Now more than 10 million people call it home.[149] With this urban migration comes the dissolution of the traditional Chinese family. China's consumerism has transformed society from being export-driven to being consumer-oriented. In addition, China's major cities have become gateways to the world (Fulton 2015, 7).

What does this urban migration and globalization mean for the church? Traditionally, the house church movement was a rural phenomenon. How will these house church members' faith be affected as they transition to city living? Where will they worship? How will they evangelize? What of the Chinese diaspora that has carried Chinese Christians to the far corners of the globe? Will it be said of them that "those who were scattered went about preaching the word" (Acts 8:4)?

Second, China's one-child policy seriously impacts the aged, young adults, and children.[150] How will children handle the stress

---

[149]"Shenzhen, China," *Encyclopaedia Britannica*, updated March 1, 2019 (accessed March 30, 2019 https://britannica.com/place/Shenzhen). As of 2010, Shenzhen's population had reached 10,360,000, qualifying it to be the fifth largest city in China. Four of the ten largest cities in China are located in the Pearl River Delta with a combined population exceeding 36 million. That figure only includes the populations of Guangzhou, Shenzhen, Dongguan, and Foshan (https://www.statista.com).

[150]China's one-child policy is no longer in force. However, the thirty plus years of it being in place has had, and continues to have, a marked impact on China. For example, many young Chinese couples have told me they will not have more than one child, even though policy now allows it, because it is too expensive to care for aging parents and

of carrying all the expectations of parents and grandparents? How will children brought up as little emperors and little empresses develop values like generosity and sacrifice? The one-child policy left China with a gender ratio of 119 boys for every 100 girls (Fulton 2015, 13). In some rural areas, the ratio is as high as 135:100 (Fulton 2015, 13). Where will all the young men reaching marrying age find wives? An estimated 30 million men face the reality of being bare branches (Mandryk 2010, 218).[151] With some areas reporting the disparity between young men and young women approaching 30 to 40 percent, will there be an increase in human trafficking, sexual promiscuity, and homosexuality (Mandryk 2010, 218)? Between 1989 and 2014, cohabitation before marriage increased from 15 percent to 43 percent (Fulton 2015, 12). Will Christian men and women marry outside their faith? What about the care for aging parents? By 2050, the elderly will number 400 million[152] or one-third of China's population (Fulton 2015, 14).[153]

Third, urban migration has created massive challenges for the family. Will the entire family move to the city? China's *hukou* system complicates the problem.[154] This system pegs a child's household registration to that of the mother and determines where he/she can go to school. If the child's parents are migrant workers in the city, and the child's *hukou* is in the rural countryside, then moving with parents to the city means there is little opportunity to go to school. Will the child be left under the care of grandparents, perhaps only seeing their parents once a year (Fulton 2015, 8, 59-60)?

---

finance education costs for children.

[151]Bare branches refers to those who have no children—as if they are a branch with no fruit.

[152]Campbell (2019) estimates that by 2050, there will be 330 million Chinese over the age of 65.

[153]Xinran has written several books that graphically describe several of these societal issues. A member of the Chinese diaspora, Xinran's books include, *The Good Women of China* (2002), *Message from an Unknown Chinese Mother: Stories of Loss and Love* (2010) and *Buy Me the Sky: The Remarkable Truth of China's One-Child Generations* (2015).

[154]The *hukou* system establishes identity, citizenship, and proof of social status. As such, it influences every aspect of daily life, including employment and education opportunities, marriage, and family matters (Cheng and Selden 1994).

Fourth, can the church unify? As presented from the opening pages of this chapter, the Chinese Church has been divided between those attending the legally recognized church and house churches. Recently, a third type of church has been added, which is sometimes dubbed the "emerging church." The emerging church in the city operates in an in-between land. Chinese religious policy has forced churches to remain disconnected—almost like small islands, worlds apart from fellow believers. Trust in leadership becomes an issue. Lack of solid biblical teaching can result in groups devolving into cultic practices or a syncretism that resembles practices in Chinese traditional folk religions (Fulton 2015, 109-125).

These four categories do not exhaust the list of challenges facing the Chinese Church of the twenty-first century. Nevertheless, they point out the tremendous opportunities confronting the Church today.

One hundred years ago, the American Assemblies of God responded to the call of God to preach the gospel to the Chinese. They, too, faced monumental challenges, but they went to China expecting the Holy Spirit to accompany and guide them. Each missionary, seemingly, had a special scriptural promise that encouraged them through difficult times. They anticipated that signs and wonders would accompany their ministry. Gary McGee referred to this as "the radical strategy in modern missions" (McGee 1997, 69). Today's challenges demand a similar response—a cry for a radical strategy, "so all can hear."[155]

[155] "So all can hear" is the current purpose statement of Assemblies of God World Missions (Easter et. al 2016). Individual chapters were written by members of the 2016 AGWM Executive Committee.

Chapter Thirteen

PAUL AS A CHINESE CHRISTIAN IN THE TWENTY-FIRST CENTURY

Chapters 4 to 11 of this book examined Assemblies of God missionaries in China in the first half of the twentieth century, with their challenges and opportunities, held up against the backdrop of the Pauline/Allen/Luce methodology. Having evaluated the above, is it possible to predict how Paul might have lived out his missionary call and work in the twenty-first century? In addition, how might Baker, Plymire, Anglin, Stephany, Simpson, and Bolton have ministered in modern China?

Both Roland Allen and Alice Luce held the Apostle Paul up as a missionary model. They were not the first to do so, and many other individuals have taken a close look at Paul's life and methodology since their time. Paul's missionary passion combined apocalyptic fervor with a mission strategy that took time for discipleship and planting churches. He longed to preach the gospel "where Christ was not known" (Rom 15:20 NIV 2011). Yet, he took time to nurture young believers and newly established churches through pastoral visits, lengthy letters, and sending members of his ministry team to encourage and work with them. His counsel to several of these churches on many practical matters took time, but it also illustrates the importance Paul attached to discipleship (Bosch 1991, 131).

Eckhard Schnabel notes one writer's assessment of how quickly Paul established churches. After a short time, he was already on his way to new fields intending to carry the gospel to the ends of the earth (Schnabel 2008, 196). Schnabel also notes that views such as this fail to take note of the length of time Paul spent in Corinth and Ephesus. Paul's frequency of travel needs some qualification: "Paul's repeated visits to the churches which he had established demonstrates the significance of his anxiety for all the churches" (Schnabel 2008, 196).

A close reading of Acts (notably chapters 16-17) confirms that the Holy Spirit directed Paul. However, at times, one wonders if he was fully aware of how he was being led. Concerning the second missionary journey, Allen suggested that Paul proceeded with several changes to any predetermined plan he might have had. The Spirit did not permit him to preach in Asia at that particular time. Attempting to proceed to Bithynia, the Spirit once again checked him. Lodging overnight at Troas, he dreams of a Macedonian man asking for help. Paul then preaches in Philippi, Thessalonica, and Berea, but then is apparently driven out of Macedonia and goes to Athens. Perhaps he considered Athens a temporary stop until circumstances calmed down in Macedonia. Leaving Athens, he goes to Corinth, but Scripture is unclear whether this was a logical choice or if there was a direct leading of the Holy Spirit to do so. The theme that comes through is that Paul's steps are being guided and directed by the Spirit (R. Allen 1962, 11).

Yet, there seems to have been a strategy. Paul focused on certain strategic centers that became hubs from which the gospel could go into the surrounding environs. The selection of these centers was not sufficient in itself. Allen uses the examples of cities as prisons, safes,[156] and swamps that keep the gospel locked down and contrasts that with cities as railway stations, mints, and springs from which life flows outward. It takes a Spirit-directed person to recognize strategic centers and a Spirit-empowered person to be capable of seizing those places (R. Allen 1962, 16-17).

Hogan, in a 1969 *Pentecostal Evangel* article, asked how the Early Church of the first century produced the greatest evangelism the world has ever seen. The response? They were "daily in the

---

[156]"Safes," in this context, refers to bank safes where money and valuables were stored as compared to being in circulation. Allen contrasts the limitations of "prisons, safes, and swamps" with the openness of railway stations, mints, and springs of water.

temple, and in every house, they ceased not to teach and preach Jesus Christ" (Klaus and Petersen 2006, 95).

Religious tolerance in the Roman world required only a gesture of loyalty to the Empire through token emperor worship. As long as that requirement was met, all religions were tolerated, making dramatic conversions unnecessary. Common practice added new gods to the already existing pantheon. Early Christians, however, insisted on the uniqueness of Jesus and refused to remain silent about accepting the religious pluralism of the era (Green 2003, 21).

The improbability of their mission's success overwhelms the observer. Christians witnessed a crucified criminal, who spoke to the Romans of the weakness of their faith. Greeks mocked the idea of resurrection. The Jews abhorred the thought that Jesus was Lord and the promised Messiah (Green 2003, 50). Nevertheless, Christians talked about Jesus daily in the temple, in their workplaces, and in their homes.

Paul preached to anyone who would listen. In Salamis, he preached to the Jews in the synagogue (Acts 13:5). In Paphos, he shared with the Jewish community and with the provincial governor (Acts 13:6). In Pisidian Antioch, he engaged Jews, God-fearers, and proselytes as well as Gentiles outside the synagogue (Acts 13:14-48). In Iconium, he talked to both Jews and Gentiles (Acts 14:1). In Lystra, he shared the gospel with a priest of Zeus (Acts 14:8-18). In Philippi, he evangelized a jailor while in prison as well as prominent women of the city (Acts 16). In Athens, philosophers and city officials heard his testimony (Acts 17). He preached to the poor and the well-to-do. Powerful officials and slaves were all targets of his ministry (Schnabel 2008, 310-311). Paul's method was "the utilization of all venues that allowed the spreading of the news of Jesus Christ" (Schnabel 2008, 304). His purpose was so all can hear.

How would Paul confront the issues mentioned in the previous chapter: (1) urban migration, (2) the one-child policy and the family in modern China, and (3) division in the church of China? Would he spend time in the resurgent Confucian centers and Buddhist temples? Would he spend time teaching existing groups of believers to ground them in the faith and protect them from the heretical teachings of Eastern Lightning and Falungong? Would he strategically target some of the major university cities to reach out to the more than twenty million university students (Mandryk 2010, 223)? Would he concentrate his time on the Han Chinese, or would he target one or more of the fifty-five official minority groups in the country?

Would he prioritize proclamation, or would he adopt a more holistic approach? Jason Mandryk (2010, 219), in the seventh edition of *Operation World*, reports that 83 million disabled people (one-fifth of the world's total disabled population) live in China. China has the highest number of suicides in the world, numbering at nearly 300,000 per year (2010, 219).[157] HIV/AIDS infection rates are vastly under-reported. With studies projecting 20-30 million men left single by the year 2020 due to the gender imbalance created by the one-child policy, the threat of rape, human trafficking, female slavery, prostitution, and homosexuality loom ominously on the horizon (Mandryk 2010, 218-219).[158]

In the face of the contemporary challenges of modern China, where would a twenty-first century Paul begin? From its humble beginnings, the American Assemblies of God committed itself to following the Pauline methods outlined in the New Testament. The biographical narratives outlined in this book detailed the methodology and praxis of American AG missionaries in early twentieth-century China. Those methods closely followed the Pauline model as understood by Allen/Luce. Have these methods influenced the existing Chinese church? Are they applicable

---

[157]In 2016, the WHO reported the suicide rate as 9.7 per 100,000 of the population. The WHO also estimated there are 54 million people in China suffering from depression and 41 million suffering from some form of anxiety disorder. The desire to seek treatment is largely hindered by China's strict social norms and stigmas as well as religious and cultural beliefs regarding personal reputation and social harmony. The WHO rated China as one of five countries worldwide with the highest rates of depression.

[158]In 2021, China's census report revealed a gender ratio of 112 male to 100 female births compared to the global average of 105-106 males to 100 females. While these figures reflect a decreasing rate in the gender difference, it does mean there are approximately 31 million more men in the country than women. The internet abounds with links about mental health issues and gender imbalance in China. Some of the internet sites for this and the previous footnote are: https://www.who.int; https://insight.kellogg.northwestern.edu; https://www.statista.com; https://www.globaltimes.cn; and https://www.pewresearch.org.

to today's China? In short, if Baker, Plymire, Anglin, Stephany, Simpson, and Bolton worked in contemporary China, could their methodology be successful? The degree of influence upon the existing Chinese church may be inferred from observations of the practice of the growing fellowships in China since 1949. The applicability of century-old practices depends on whether creative methods of use can be discovered and implemented. There is room for optimism, especially as one reviews the narratives of how God has worked in previous generations.

An understanding of the official stance of the TSPM, as described above, creates doubt regarding whether churches can practice the early twentieth-century methodology if they adhere to official government policies. The six missionary narratives studied in this project reveal an absolute commitment to the Lordship of Jesus Christ that would not compromise the message. Such commitment has proved to be crucial to the survival of the Chinese church through the decades of harassment and persecution.

Many house church groups cite the limitation on evangelism as a primary reason for their unwillingness to join the TSPM. Additionally, current government regulations restrict the activities of officially recognized churches to a designated location. Outreach for evangelism and compassionate outreaches to minister to society's needs are difficult in groups adhering closely to the government position.

Government requirements that delineate a separation between clergy and laity, choosing only to recognize those who fulfill government standards as qualified to conduct services, severely limit the number of meeting sites in the country. Refusing to adhere to such regulations allowed the Chinese church to exponentially increase during the second half of the twentieth-century.

Pentecostal ministry, taught and lived out by their mentors, undoubtedly influenced the young Chinese church that found itself forced to stand on its own. As Fish, superintendent of Lisu, said to Maynard Ketchaam in 1966, "You are not going to take the Holy Spirit [with you], are you" (Bolton 1984, 215-216)? One year later, Fish reported dramatic increases in the number of churches, believers, and Bible school students, triumphantly stating, "See what the Holy Spirit can do" (Bolton 1984, 216)!

A commitment to the Pentecostal experience of Spirit baptism marked each of the missionary exemplars. Commitment to evangelism and ministering to physical needs received priority emphases. Training national Chinese believers reflected a belief in the ability of God to use all believers in apostolic gifts.

Baker spent several years in the USA because he felt he dared not return to China without the empowerment of the Holy Spirit. Once baptized in the Spirit, he demonstrated apostolic power. Time spent with those traveling with him allowed him to pour his soul into theirs. His disciples believed deeply that God was mighty; therefore, he could heal the sick and dispose of devils. In the orphanage, along mountain trails, under spreading mango trees, or in kitchens, Baker and his companions went everywhere talking about Jesus.

Plymire built relationships and earned the right to be heard. At times, he adopted low-key methods to bring Tibetans into his home—things as simple as a camera or a phonograph. On many occasions, he went directly to the lamaseries, religious fairs, or even the weddings of clan chiefs. On such trips, he did not rest until every tent and every person had the chance to hear the gospel at least once. He became all things to all people, going to the ends of the earth . . . so all can hear.

Anglin could never say "no" to a person in need. "For I was hungry and you gave me food, I was thirsty and you gave me drink, I was a stranger and you welcomed me, I was naked and you clothed me, I was sick and you visited me, I was in prison and you came to me" (Matt 25:35-36). "If a suffering soul is denied help and turned away and becomes a victim . . . somehow I can't stand to think of it" (Anglin 1924). Such love for people could not be silenced. Such compassion was spoken of everywhere, influencing many people to travel long distances because they had heard they would not be turned away.

Stephany took Jesus to the weak, the despised, the hurting, and the disenfranchised. From the girls in her orphanage to individuals delivered from life threatening addictions, dozens were prepared for ministry to help her in various outreaches. From lives plucked from hopelessness and turmoil came those who referred to her as Mother Peace (McGee 2004).

Simpson began with a conviction that he must take the gospel to the ends of the earth. The magnitude of the need forced him to admit that he himself could never accomplish that dream. He decided, however, that he could train national workers and, empowered by the Holy Spirit, they could change the nation.

Bolton's mentorship that transitioned to partnership with key nationals prepared and equipped them for leadership. Prayer, sacrifice, identification, mobility, and training (Bolton 1984) exemplify key characteristics of the growing Chinese church.

God gave each missionary a special promise or a prayer that would enable them to face seemingly insurmountable obstacles. "Fear thou not; for I am with thee . . . I will strengthen thee; yea, I will help thee; yea, I will uphold thee by the right hand of my righteousness" (Isa 41:10 KJV). ". . . share your bread with the hungry and bring the homeless poor into your house" (Isa 58:7). "Thou shalt not be afraid of the terror by night; nor for the arrow that flieth by day; nor for the pestilence that walketh in darkness; nor for the destruction that wasteth at noonday. A thousand shall fall at thy side, and ten thousand at thy right hand; but it shall not come nigh thee (Ps 91:5-7 KJV). ". . . obedience—by word and deed, by the power of signs and wonders, by the power of the Spirit of God . . . and thus I make it my ambition to preach the gospel" (Rom 15:18-20). "Lord, keep us where the fiery fire burns" (Bolton 1984, 16). "Let me hold fast, Lord, to things of the skies! Quicken my vision, open my eyes" (Bolton 1984, 82).

Certain conclusions can be drawn based on what Paul did during the first century. Paul undoubtedly developed an urban emphasis. Although Paul passionately longed to preach Christ everywhere, he would probably choose a strategic center from which the church, once planted, could expand outward. Economic centers, university centers, major commercial hubs, centers of political power—all would be possibilities. But Paul's dependence upon the leading of the Holy Spirit in the selection of ministry centers must not be overlooked.

Plymire selected Tangar [Huangyuan] as a ministry hub because of its strategic location along the caravan routes from

China to Lhasa (V. Plymire n.d.d). Tangar also placed him within traveling distance of important Tibetan lamaseries (V. Plymire 1931a).

The Anglins' selection of Tai'an for the Home of Onesiphorus placed it close to Tai Shan Mountain, which received thousands of Chinese visitors each year (Albus 1951). The accessibility of such a well-known location undoubtedly contributed to many people being able to reach the Home to receive help.

Some ministry center locations, however, defy reason. Stephany chose Ta Ch'ang as the seat of her ministry. However, the selection of this seemingly obscure village proved advantageous during the 1930s and early 1940s when Shanxi province became a pivotal battleground between the Nationalists, Communists, and Japanese.

Paul obviously would develop a team of partners. Barnabas, Silvanus, Titus, Timothy, Priscilla, Aquila, Epaphroditus, Epaphras, Aristarchus, Gaius, Jason, and several others are mentioned as partnering with Paul in his missionary journeys (Bosch 1991, 332). Wherever Paul went, he would be anticipating individuals prepared by the Holy Spirit to join him.

Baker set up short-term training centers to equip potential pastors and evangelists. He spent time mentoring those who would translate his messages from Mandarin Chinese into the local tribal dialects. The Boltons mentored national believers who later became key leaders of the Lisu church. The Anglins did not stop with ministry to the physical needs of those who came to their Home. Their commitment to the spiritual development of each Home member resulted in many residents leaving to become pastors, evangelists, and key lay leaders of national churches. Stephany also made short-term training centers a key component in her work. The theoretical became practical as many individuals trained later worked in tent evangelism and as house group leaders. Simpson taught at various venues throughout China and marked his last term of service in China with a commitment to train national evangelists and pastors. Plymire's plan for a successful nomadic ministry rested upon the conviction that equipping

Tibetan believers was the key to reaching the various clans among whom they would live.

Paul would constantly be pressing onward. He would do so geographically as well as culturally. He would not be able to rest until Jesus was proclaimed and known among the Naxi, Bai, Bendi, Zhuang, Uyghur, Hui, Dongxiang, Mongol, Tibetan, and other minority groups as well as among the Han. Paul would plant churches, which would be the surest way to reach the unreached. He would train converts theologically, biblically, and practically to reach out beyond their own circles. These churches would be involved holistically with the needs of their communities. He would reach out in compassion to touch the hurting and disenfranchised in their particular locations. Paul would undoubtedly take some of the young people from these churches to travel with him on evangelistic and mission tours and, in some places, would have left them behind to assist in building up a new local community of faith.

Would Paul encounter persecution and opposition in twenty-first-century China? Undoubtedly, he would, but Paul would not be deterred. He would feel an obligation to the lost. "I am obligated both to Greeks and non-Greeks, both to the wise and the foolish" (Rom 1:14 NIV 2011). Paul was also indebted to Christ. An obligation to him who died [Christ] produces obligation to those for whom he died (Bosch 1991, 135). That is why Paul would say, "Woe to me if I do not preach the gospel" (1 Cor 9:16 NIV 2011)!

Finally, Paul would move under the leadership and direction of the Holy Spirit. That makes it difficult to predict specifically how a twenty-first century Paul would work in modern China. The same would be said for the missionaries examined in this project. We can, however, safely say that they would be people of fire and passion, led by the Holy Spirit.

The methodology of the subjects of the above narratives proves sound. In a country where foreign missionaries are not welcomed, the keys to evangelism, discipleship, and church planting rest with national believers. They will face hardship as did Baker, Plymire, Anglin, Stephany, Simpson, and Bolton. Some will pay the ultimate price in their suffering. Their success will depend upon prayer and dependence on the Holy Spirit. These pioneers served as examples, but the torch they were forced to lay down in 1952 has been picked up by Chinese believers who have, in turn, carried it and, through their example, marked the way for a new generation to follow.

Mandryk's *Operation World* (2010) lists several answers to prayer that evidence the impact of former missionaries. The church's survival through intense persecution and growth to over 75 million evangelicals has sprung up from seeds of commitment exemplified in the lives of a former generation (Mandryk 2010, 216). Christians throughout China have engaged in social causes, choosing to respond in compassionate ways touching the lives of millions (Mandryk 2010, 216). The Chinese church's mission vision has thrust many believers to reach out to both ethnic minorities and to neighboring countries. Strategy development, member care, and international partnerships pose significant challenges for the Chinese Christian community in fulfilling that vision (Mandryk 2010, 222).

Passion for the lost is critical for effective ministry. Hogan eloquently affirms this reality: "There is no adequate substitute for persons whose hearts are on fire and who will put forth the effort to learn a language, identify themselves with a foreign culture, and live among the lost to establish a witness for Jesus Christ" (Wilson 1997, 57). Hogan also understood the importance of God's calling: "We still believe there is no substitute for a man [or woman] whose heart is on fire and in whose life the call of God is compelling and real" (Wilson 1997, 93).

Leonard Bolton, on his deathbed, declared: "I can see them coming . . . the Lisu" (Bolton 1984, 211). Perhaps the cloud of witnesses in Heb 12:1, standing on heaven's balcony, can also say that they see a host of Chinese pastors, teachers, evangelists, missionaries, tentmakers, and lay leaders coming forward to take their place in God's harvest field. Perhaps Willie Simpson is singing, "Another will reap what in springtime I've planted. . . . The tears of the sower and the songs of the reaper shall mingle together in joy by-and-by" (Spencer 1957).

The methods of St. Paul, Roland Allen, Alice Luce, H. A. Baker, Victor Plymire, Leslie Anglin, Marie Stephany, W. W. Simpson, and Leonard Bolton are workable in modern China. They do not depend upon favorable governmental regulations, technology, finances, equipment, or institutions. They do depend upon obedience to God's call and his leading, as well as the empowerment of the Holy Spirit.

Chapter Fourteen

CONCLUSION

Further Studies

Chapter 1 refers to the two questions the angel asked Hagar as she was fleeing from Sarai: "[w]here have you come from and where are you going" (Gen 16:8)? This project has included both a look at the past and a glance into the future. The look in both directions, past and future, requires more work to complete the picture.

Where have you come from? This project examined the lives and ministries of a few select American AG missionaries. Further study is needed to examine the lives and ministries of other Assemblies of God missionaries.

To believe that other national church organizations made no meaningful contribution deprives them of recognition due to their call, commitment, and sacrifice. In recent times, missionaries from Asia, Africa, and Latin America have reinforced the contribution of these groups, primarily from the West in the early years.

The emphasis on establishing indigenous churches opens up a new vista for study. The True Jesus Church, Little Flock, and Jesus Family churches were led by national leadership from their beginnings. Their history and contribution to Chinese Christianity must not be overlooked.

Added to this must be the stories of individual believers. This includes not just major leaders such as John Sung, Watchman Nee, or Wang Mingdao, but also the countless nameless leaders, who through their faithful witness and lay ministry, have enabled the spontaneous expansion of the Chinese Church.

Where are you going? Chapter 12 includes a list of some of the major challenges and opportunities confronting Chinese Christians. Will a peaceful coexistence be possible between the TSPM, the house church, and the emerging church in China with the Chinese Communist Party? Will these various branches of the church be able to minister in unity? Will they follow the methodological and ecclesiastical practices exemplified by the missionaries studied in this project? Will they be influenced by Allen, Luce, and others who have emphasized Paul's indigenous church principles? How will they incorporate self-theologizing, self-caring, and self-missionizing with the original "three-self's" mentioned in this study? Will ethnic minorities throughout China make meaningful contributions? What form will partnership between the Chinese church and other foreign organizations take?

Conclusion

This project presents a descriptive study upon which others can build. The narrative history informs both the attempts of contemporary missionaries ministering in China and the Chinese world, as well as the Chinese church. This narrative study reveals at least five key components for effective missiological endeavors around the globe. First, individuals following God's call to fulfill the Great Commission will encounter difficulties and opposition. These unavoidable obstacles could tempt one to quit and pursue an easier lifestyle. These six narratives remind Christians of the cost expended to bring the Church to this point in history. Christians in the twenty-first century can receive encouragement to add their voice and labor to these earlier pioneers. In the face of persecution and hardship, a clear knowledge of God's call and realization that one has been sent by God proves invaluable.

Second, this generation of missionaries must not lose sight of the priority of evangelism. Human needs abound, shouting for attention. Jesus said, "For you always have the poor with you" (Mark 14:7). These narratives address the importance of ministering to human need. Such compassion demonstrates God's love for the world and provides a powerful testimony to the lost. Compassion ministries hold the potential of opening otherwise closed doors, but that should not be the motivation. Everett Wilson, quoting J. Philip Hogan, states: "Demonstrating the truth of Christ's words and sharing the love of God are our intent" (Wilson 1997, 154). Christ consistently demonstrates the importance of addressing deeper spiritual needs. Jesus' first words to the paralytic were, "Son, your sins are forgiven" (Mark 2:5). He admonished his disciples to deny themselves and take up his cross with these words: "For what does it profit a man to gain the whole world and forfeit his soul? For what can a man give in return for his soul" (Mark 8:36, 37). The humanitarian work mentioned in the narratives of this study serves as the backdrop for the overriding theme of the priority of evangelism.

Third, China's history demonstrates that foreign missionaries come and go, and open doors too quickly slam shut. To survive and thrive, the Chinese church must be self-supporting, self-governing, self-propagating, self-theologizing, self-caring, and self-missionizing. China's socio-political context, combined with the developing missiology of the AG organization, compelled these early pioneers to adopt indigenous church principles.

Fourth, the role of the Holy Spirit and prayer cannot be minimized. Current AG workers, influenced by the history and legacy of these pioneers, are encouraged to adopt the mantra of proactive presence, primary partnership, and Pentecostal practice. The survival and growth of the post-1949 Chinese church cannot be explained without the work of the Holy Spirit. Only heaven will reveal the added role that the prayers of Christians, both inside and outside of China, played in this move of the Spirit.

Finally, the role and need for relationships, partnerships, and teams must be acknowledged. The Home of Onesiphorus joined financial contributions of foreign supporters with the work of widows, orphans, and refugees to build a work that continues to the present day. Without the partnership of national Chinese, the women of Shanxi province could never have accomplished their tent evangelism, established outstations, built an orphanage, and conducted deliverance ministries. Churches planted by the Bakers and Boltons would never have survived without ministry teams caring for established works and pushing themselves forward in self-propagation. In the closing years of his ministry, Simpson realized that the magnitude of China's needs was too great for one individual to address. Training national workers who were sent out and empowered by the Holy Spirit would be the only way to successfully grow the Chinese church.

The burden for missions work in China has expanded to include those from Latin America, Africa, and other Asian countries. Chinese laws and regulations make it imperative that those who would seek to bless the Chinese church do so in partnership with the existing Chinese church. Such partnership and team building holds forth the possibility of a synergy that could see "this gospel of the kingdom . . . proclaimed throughout the whole world as a testimony to all nations, and then the end will come" (Matt. 24:14).

May the Chinese church rise up and build upon its legacy and dedicate itself to the greatest evangelism the world has yet seen. May the Chinese church take its place in the harvest field, adopting New Testament methods but with Chinese characteristics, empowered by the Holy Spirit, and accompanied by signs and wonders. May they proclaim the message in word and deed as the Lord of the Harvest adds daily to the Church.

BIBLIOGRAPHY

Abrams, Minnie. 1906. *The Baptism in the Holy Ghost and Fire.* 2nd ed. Kedgaon, India: Mukti Mission Press.

Adeney, David. 1985. *The Church's Long March.* Ventura, CA: Regal Books.

Adeney, Miriam. 1996. "McMissions." *Christianity Today.* November 11, 1996.

Albus, Harry. 1951. *20th Century Onesiphorus: The Life Story of Leslie M. Anglin.* Grand Rapids: Eerdmans.

Allen, Hubert. 2017. "Roland Allen: A Biographical Note." In *The Ministry of Expansion: The Priesthood of the Laity*, edited by J. D. Payne, 19-29. Pasadena, CA: William Carey Library.

Allen, Hubert J. B. 1995. *Roland Allen: Pioneer, Priest, and Prophet.* Grand Rapids: Eerdmans.

Allen, Roland. 1960a. *The Spontaneous Expansion of the Church and the Causes which Hinder It.* London: World Dominion Press (Orig. pub. 1927).

________. 1960b. "Pentecost and the World." In *The Ministry of the Spirit: Selected Writings of Roland Allen.* London: World Dominion Press.

________. 1960c. "The Case for Voluntary Clergy." In *The Ministry of the Spirit: Selected Writings of Roland Allen.* London: World Dominion Press.

________. 1962. *Missionary Methods: St. Paul's or Ours?* Grand Rapids: Eerdmans. (Orig. pub. 1912).

________. 1964. *Missionary Principles.* Grand Rapids: Eerdmans.

Anderson, Allan. 2004. *An Introduction to Pentecostalism.* Cambridge: Cambridge University Press.

Anderson, Gerald, ed. 1998. *Biographical Dictionary of Christian Missions.* Grand Rapids: Eerdmans.

Anderson, Gerald H., Robert T. Coote, Norman A. Horner, and James M. Phillips, eds. 1994. *Mission Legacies*. Maryknoll, NY: Orbis Books.

Anglin, Leslie. 1917. "Amongst China's Millions." *Pentecostal Evangel,* October 6, 1917.

________. 1919. "Taianfu, Shantung, China." *Pentecostal Evangel,* August 23, 1919.

________. 1922. "The Home of Onesiphorus." *Pentecostal Evangel,* September 2, 1922.

________. 1924. "Rescue the Perishing." *Pentecostal Evangel,* May 10, 1924.

________. 1925a. "Distress in China." *Pentecostal Evangel,* November 14, 1925.

________. 1925b. "Great Need at Home of Onesiphorus." *Pentecostal Evangel,* July 18, 1925.

________. 1925c. "Year's Report from the Home of Onesiphorus." *Pentecostal Evangel,* March 21, 1925.

________. 1926a. "Feeding Five Hundred Hungry Mouths." *Pentecostal Evangel,* June 5, 1926.

________. 1926b. "Great Need in Brother Anglin's Work." *Pentecostal Evangel,* January 9, 1926.

________. 1926c. "Needles, Thread, and Yarn Needed." *Pentecostal Evangel,* August 21, 1926.

________. 1927a. "Can You Help?" *Pentecostal Evangel,* September 3, 1927.

________. 1927b. "Home of Onesiphorus News Items." *Pentecostal Evangel,* April 30, 1927.

________. 1928a. "Caring for the Aged of China." *Pentecostal Evangel,* August 4, 1928.

________. 1928b. "Help the Children." *The Latter Rain Evangel,* November 1928.

________. 1928c. "Home of Onesiphorus." *Pentecostal Evangel,* March 24, 1928.

________. 1928d. "Our Mottoes." *Gospel Gleaners,* August 12, 1928.

________. 1930. "How a Flour Mill Saved a Town." *Pentecostal Evangel,* April 5, 1930.

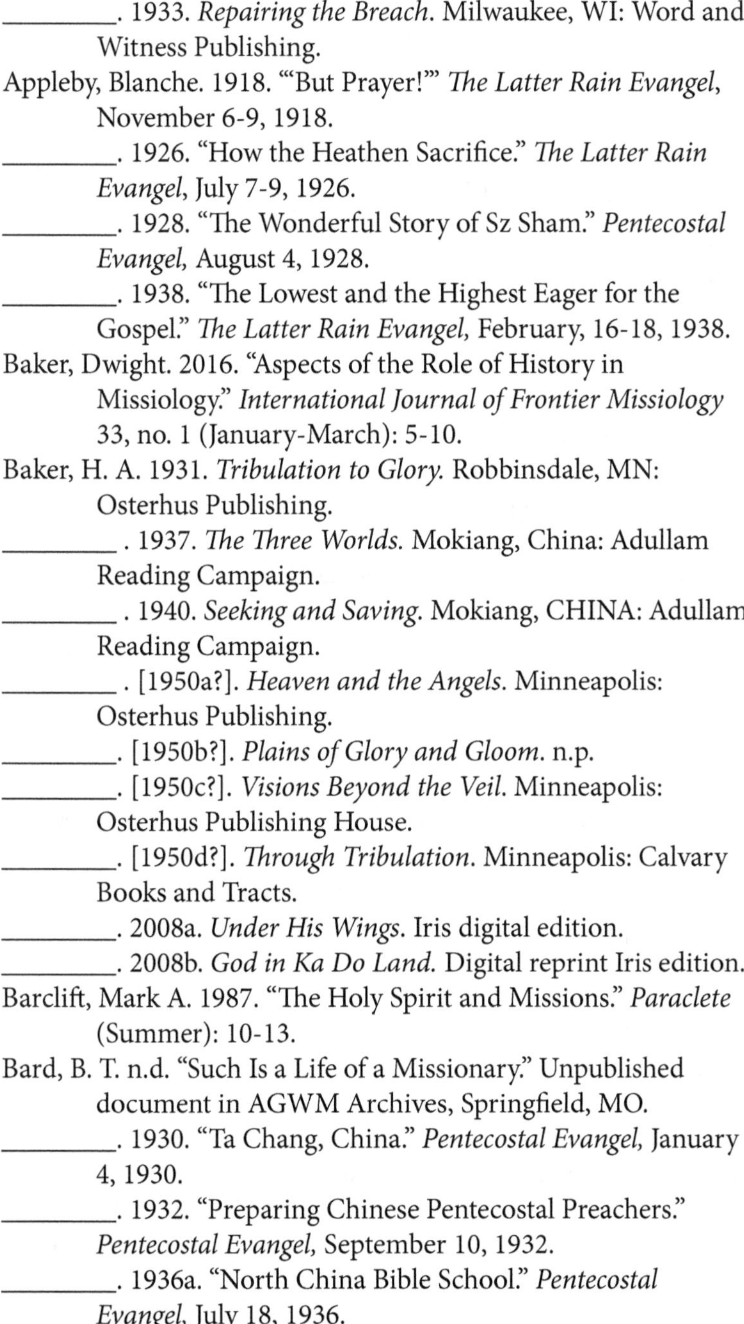

________. 1933. *Repairing the Breach*. Milwaukee, WI: Word and Witness Publishing.

Appleby, Blanche. 1918. "'But Prayer!'" *The Latter Rain Evangel*, November 6-9, 1918.

________. 1926. "How the Heathen Sacrifice." *The Latter Rain Evangel*, July 7-9, 1926.

________. 1928. "The Wonderful Story of Sz Sham." *Pentecostal Evangel*, August 4, 1928.

________. 1938. "The Lowest and the Highest Eager for the Gospel." *The Latter Rain Evangel*, February, 16-18, 1938.

Baker, Dwight. 2016. "Aspects of the Role of History in Missiology." *International Journal of Frontier Missiology* 33, no. 1 (January-March): 5-10.

Baker, H. A. 1931. *Tribulation to Glory*. Robbinsdale, MN: Osterhus Publishing.

________ . 1937. *The Three Worlds*. Mokiang, China: Adullam Reading Campaign.

________ . 1940. *Seeking and Saving*. Mokiang, CHINA: Adullam Reading Campaign.

________ . [1950a?]. *Heaven and the Angels*. Minneapolis: Osterhus Publishing.

________. [1950b?]. *Plains of Glory and Gloom*. n.p.

________. [1950c?]. *Visions Beyond the Veil*. Minneapolis: Osterhus Publishing House.

________. [1950d?]. *Through Tribulation*. Minneapolis: Calvary Books and Tracts.

________. 2008a. *Under His Wings*. Iris digital edition.

________. 2008b. *God in Ka Do Land*. Digital reprint Iris edition.

Barclift, Mark A. 1987. "The Holy Spirit and Missions." *Paraclete* (Summer): 10-13.

Bard, B. T. n.d. "Such Is a Life of a Missionary." Unpublished document in AGWM Archives, Springfield, MO.

________. 1930. "Ta Chang, China." *Pentecostal Evangel*, January 4, 1930.

________. 1932. "Preparing Chinese Pentecostal Preachers." *Pentecostal Evangel*, September 10, 1932.

________. 1936a. "North China Bible School." *Pentecostal Evangel*, July 18, 1936.

________. 1936b. "One Hundred Baptized in Peiping Jail." *Pentecostal Evangel,* November 7, 1936.

________. 1937a. "Bible School in North China." *Pentecostal Evangel,* January 16, 1937.

________. 1937b. "News from the Truth Bible Institute, Peiping, China." *Pentecostal Evangel,* August 14, 1937.

________. 1938a. "Chinese Young People Consecrate for Missionary Work." *Pentecostal Evangel,* October 1, 1938.

________. 1938b. "Truth Bible Institute Expands." *Pentecostal Evangel,* January 24, 1938.

________. 1940. "Joy Unspeakable and Full of Glory." *Pentecostal Evangel,* June 15, 1940.

Bates, M. Searle. 1974. "The Theology of American Missionaries." In *The Missionary Enterprise in China and America,* edited by John King Fairbank. Cambridge: Harvard University Press.

Bays, Daniel. 2004. "A Tradition of State Dominance." In *God and Caesar in China: Policy Implications of Church-State Tensions*, edited by Jason Kindopp and Carol Lee Hamrin. Washington: Brookings Institution Press.

________. 2012. *A New History of Christianity in China*. West Sussex, UK: Wiley-Blackwell.

Bell, E. N. 1913. "General Convention of Pentecostal Saints and Churches of God in Christ, Hot Springs, Arkansas, April 2 to 12, 1914." *Word and Witness*, December, 1, 1913.

Bianco, Lucien. 1971. *Origins of the Chinese Revolution, 1915-1949*. Stanford, CA: Stanford University Press.

Blan, Nora. n.d. "Over Rugged Mountains: W. E. Simpson." Manuscript from AGWM Archives, Springfield, MO: 1-16.

Blumhofer, Edith L. 1985a. "American Pentecostalism in Historical Perspective." *Paraclete* (Winter): 10-14.

________. 1985b. *The Assemblies of God: A Popular History*. Springfield, MO: Gospel Publishing House.

________. 1989a. *The Assemblies of God: A Chapter in the Story of American Pentecostalism, Volume 1-To 1941*. Springfield, MO: Gospel Publishing House.

________. 1989b. *"Pentecost in My Soul."* Springfield, MO: Gospel Publishing House.

Boer, Harry R. 1961. *Pentecost and Missions.* Grand Rapids: Eerdmans.

Bohr, P. Richard. 1983. "State and Religion in China Today: Christianity's Future in a Marxist Setting." *Missiology: An International Review* XI, no. 3 (July): 324-340.

Bolton, Leonard. 1984. *China Call.* Springfield, MO: Gospel Publishing House.

Booze, Joyce. 2001. "Starve a Little Bird?" *Club Connection* (Fall): 4-5.

Bosch, David J. 1980. *Witness to the World: The Christian Mission in Theological Perspective.* Eugene: Wipf and Stock.

________. 1991. *Transforming Mission: Paradigm Shifts in Theology of Mission.* Maryknoll, NY: Orbis Books.

Brooks, M. Paul. 1989. "Bible Colleges and the Expansion of the Pentecostal Movement." *Paraclete* 23, no. 2 (Spring): 9-17.

Brown, G. Thompson. 1983. *Christianity in the People's Republic of China.* Atlanta: John Knox Press.

Brumback, Carl. 1977. *A Sound from Heaven.* Springfield, MO: Gospel Publishing House.

Bundy, David. 2000. "Anna Ziese: For God and China." *AG Heritage* 20, no. 3 (Fall): 12-19.

Burgess, Stanley M., and Eduard M. Van der Maas, eds. 2003. *The New International Dictionary of Pentecostal and Charismatic Movements.* Grand Rapids: Zondervan.

Bush, Richard C., Jr. 1970. *Religion in Communist China.* Nashville: Abingdon Press.

Campbell, Charlie. 2019. "China's Aging Population is a Major Threat to Its Future." *Time.* February 9, 2019.

Cary-Elwes, Columba. 1957. *China and the Cross. Studies in Missionary History.* London: Longmans, Green, and Company.

Chan, Kim-kwong. 2002. "China's WTO Accession—One Year Later." *China Source* 4, no. 4 (Winter): 1-4, 15.

Chan, Kim-kwong, and Eric R. Carlson. 2005. *Religious Freedom in China: Policy, Administration, and Regulation: A*

Research Handbook. Hong Kong: Institute for Culture, Commerce, and Religion.

Chao, Jonathan. 1988. "Church and State in Socialist China, 1949-1988." In *Wise as Serpents, Harmless as Doves*, edited by Richard Van Houten, vii-xxxiv. Pasadena, CA: William Carey Library.

________, trans. 2003. "Attitude of Chinese House Churches towards the Government, Its Religious Policy, and the Three-Self Movement." Accessed October 13, 2003. http://www.ccee.org.tw/cmi/belief23.htm.

Ch'en, Kenneth. 1964. *Buddhism in China: A Historical Survey*. Princeton, NY: Princeton University Press.

Cheng, Tiejun, and Mark Selden. 1994. "The Origins and Social Consequences of China's *Hukou* System." *The China Quarterly* 139 (Sept.): 644-668.

"China: Population of Shenzhen 1995-2035." Accessed March 30, 2019. https.//www.statista.com.

Cohen, Paul A. 1963. *China and Christianity: The Missionary Movement and the Growth of Chinese Antiforeignism, 1860-1870*. Cambridge: Harvard University Press.

________. 1978. "Christian Missions and Their Impact to 1900." In *The Cambridge History of China, Volume 10: Late Ch'ing, 1800-1911, Part 1*, edited by Denis Twitchett and John K. Fairbank, 543-590. Cambridge: Cambridge University Press.

Cook, Richard R., and David W. Pao, eds. 2011. *After Imperialism: Christian Identity in China and the Global Evangelical Movement*. Eugene: Pickwick Publications.

Covell, Ralph R. 1978. *W. A. P. Martin: Pioneer of Progress in China*. Washington: Christian College Consortium.

________. 1986. *Confucius, the Buddha, and Christ: A History of the Gospel in Chinese*. Maryknoll, NY: Orbis Books.

________. 1995. *The Liberating Gospel in China*. Grand Rapids: Baker.

Crossman, Eileen Fraser. 1982. *Mountain Rain: A Biography of James O. Fraser*. Singapore: OMF Books.

Dalton, Adele Flower. 1987. "Mother Peace." *AG Heritage* 7, no. 4 (Winter): 3-5.

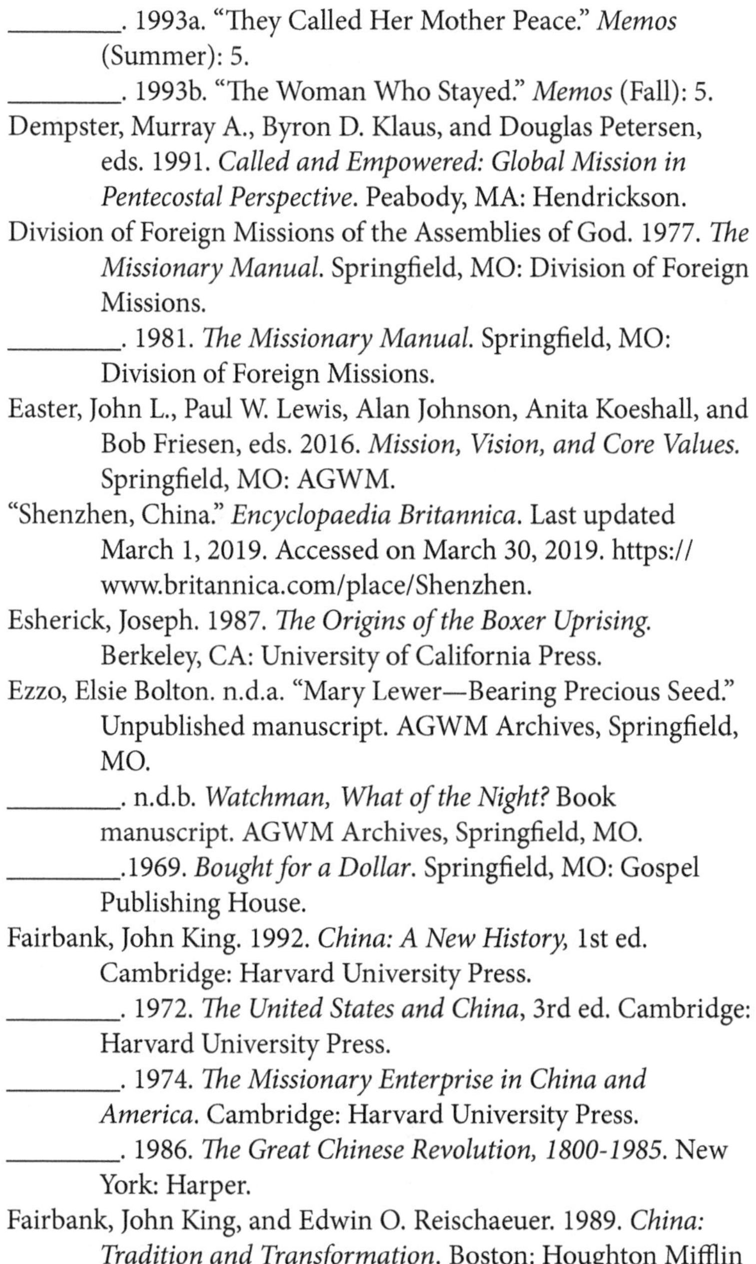

________. 1993a. "They Called Her Mother Peace." *Memos* (Summer): 5.

________. 1993b. "The Woman Who Stayed." *Memos* (Fall): 5.

Dempster, Murray A., Byron D. Klaus, and Douglas Petersen, eds. 1991. *Called and Empowered: Global Mission in Pentecostal Perspective.* Peabody, MA: Hendrickson.

Division of Foreign Missions of the Assemblies of God. 1977. *The Missionary Manual.* Springfield, MO: Division of Foreign Missions.

________. 1981. *The Missionary Manual.* Springfield, MO: Division of Foreign Missions.

Easter, John L., Paul W. Lewis, Alan Johnson, Anita Koeshall, and Bob Friesen, eds. 2016. *Mission, Vision, and Core Values.* Springfield, MO: AGWM.

"Shenzhen, China." *Encyclopaedia Britannica.* Last updated March 1, 2019. Accessed on March 30, 2019. https://www.britannica.com/place/Shenzhen.

Esherick, Joseph. 1987. *The Origins of the Boxer Uprising.* Berkeley, CA: University of California Press.

Ezzo, Elsie Bolton. n.d.a. "Mary Lewer—Bearing Precious Seed." Unpublished manuscript. AGWM Archives, Springfield, MO.

________. n.d.b. *Watchman, What of the Night?* Book manuscript. AGWM Archives, Springfield, MO.

________.1969. *Bought for a Dollar.* Springfield, MO: Gospel Publishing House.

Fairbank, John King. 1992. *China: A New History,* 1st ed. Cambridge: Harvard University Press.

________. 1972. *The United States and China,* 3rd ed. Cambridge: Harvard University Press.

________. 1974. *The Missionary Enterprise in China and America.* Cambridge: Harvard University Press.

________. 1986. *The Great Chinese Revolution, 1800-1985.* New York: Harper.

Fairbank, John King, and Edwin O. Reischaeuer. 1989. *China: Tradition and Transformation.* Boston: Houghton Mifflin Company.

Fairbank, John King, and Merle Goldman. 2006. *China: A New History*, 2nd ed. Cambridge: Harvard University Press.

Fenby, Jonathan. 2008. *The Penguin History of Modern China: The Fall and Rise of a Great Power, 1850-2008*. London: Allen Lane.

Flower, J. Roswell. 1920. "Report of Missionary Treasurer for Year Ending September 1, 1920." *Pentecostal Evangel*, October 16, 1920.

Fulton, Brent. 2015. *China's Urban Christians: A Light that Cannot Be Hidden*. Eugene: Pickwick Publications.

Furth, Charlotte. 1983. "Intellectual Change: From the Reform Movement to the May Fourth Movement, 1895-1920." In *The Cambridge History of China, Volume 12: Republican China, 1912-1949, Part 1*, edited by John K. Fairbank, 322-405. Cambridge: Cambridge University Press.

General Council of the Assemblies of God. 1914. Combined Minutes 1914-1917. November 23, 1914.

Gill, Brad. 2016. "Ralph Winter and the Strategic Use of History." *International Journal of Frontier Missiology* 33, no. 1 (Jan.-Mar.): 3.

Goforth, Rosalind. 1937. *Goforth of China*. Minneapolis: Dimension Books.

Gordon, A. J. 1882. *The Ministry of Healing*. New York: Christian Alliance Publishing.

Green, Michael. 2003. *Evangelism in the Early Church*, revised edition. Grand Rapids: Eerdmans.

Greenaway, Charles E. 1986. "Fenced with Iron, Part I." *The Evangelist* (Dec.): 27.

________. 1987. "Fenced with Iron, Part II." *The Evangelist* (Jan.): 21-22.

Greist, W. W. 1927. Letter to Secretary of State in response to Letter of Inquiry from Victor Plymire's Brother. AGWM Archives, Springfield, MO.

Harrison, John A. 1967. *China Since 1800*. New York: Harcourt Brace and World.

Hartley, L. P. 1953. *The Go-Between*. New York: New York Review of Books.

Harvey, Thomas Alan. 2002. *Acquainted with Grief: Wang*

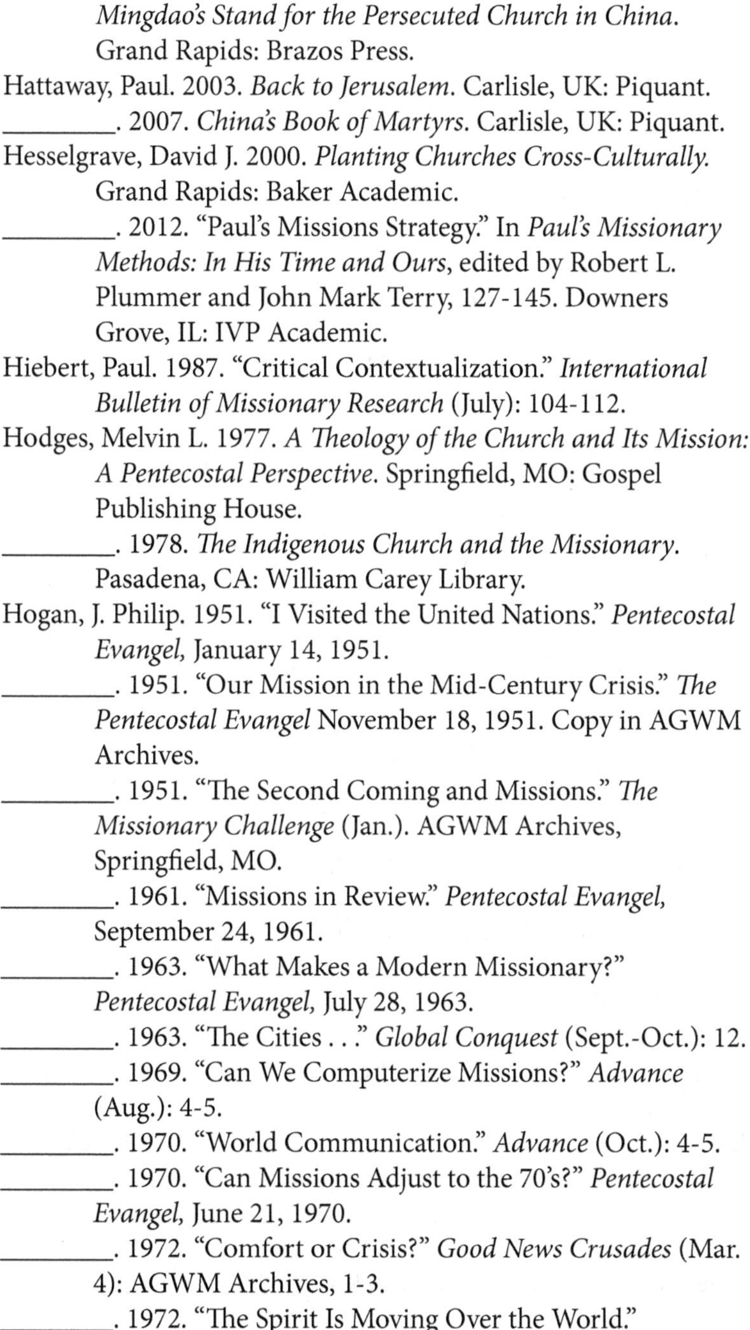

Mingdao's Stand for the Persecuted Church in China. Grand Rapids: Brazos Press.

Hattaway, Paul. 2003. *Back to Jerusalem.* Carlisle, UK: Piquant.

________. 2007. *China's Book of Martyrs.* Carlisle, UK: Piquant.

Hesselgrave, David J. 2000. *Planting Churches Cross-Culturally.* Grand Rapids: Baker Academic.

________. 2012. "Paul's Missions Strategy." In *Paul's Missionary Methods: In His Time and Ours*, edited by Robert L. Plummer and John Mark Terry, 127-145. Downers Grove, IL: IVP Academic.

Hiebert, Paul. 1987. "Critical Contextualization." *International Bulletin of Missionary Research* (July): 104-112.

Hodges, Melvin L. 1977. *A Theology of the Church and Its Mission: A Pentecostal Perspective.* Springfield, MO: Gospel Publishing House.

________. 1978. *The Indigenous Church and the Missionary.* Pasadena, CA: William Carey Library.

Hogan, J. Philip. 1951. "I Visited the United Nations." *Pentecostal Evangel,* January 14, 1951.

________. 1951. "Our Mission in the Mid-Century Crisis." *The Pentecostal Evangel* November 18, 1951. Copy in AGWM Archives.

________. 1951. "The Second Coming and Missions." *The Missionary Challenge* (Jan.). AGWM Archives, Springfield, MO.

________. 1961. "Missions in Review." *Pentecostal Evangel,* September 24, 1961.

________. 1963. "What Makes a Modern Missionary?" *Pentecostal Evangel,* July 28, 1963.

________. 1963. "The Cities . . ." *Global Conquest* (Sept.-Oct.): 12.

________. 1969. "Can We Computerize Missions?" *Advance* (Aug.): 4-5.

________. 1970. "World Communication." *Advance* (Oct.): 4-5.

________. 1970. "Can Missions Adjust to the 70's?" *Pentecostal Evangel,* June 21, 1970.

________. 1972. "Comfort or Crisis?" *Good News Crusades* (Mar. 4): AGWM Archives, 1-3.

________. 1972. "The Spirit Is Moving Over the World."

Pentecostal Evangel, May 21, 1972.

________. 1974. "The Great Commission: A Continuing Mission." *Advance* (Mar.): 4-5.

________. 1977. "Missionary Work Today." *World Pentecost* 7, no. 1: 18-19.

________. 1977. "Proving Ourselves Worthy Ministers." *Advance* (Jan.): 6-7.

________. 1981. "God Omnipotent Reigns in the World." *Pentecostal Evangel,* October 25, 1981.

________. 1983. "China Church Growth—A Story of Danger and Dedication." *Mountain Movers,* Nov., 1983.

________. 1987. "Critical Issues: Missions in This Decade and Beyond." *Advance* (May): 4-5.

________. 1987. "The Church in China." *Mountain Movers,* September, 12-13, 1987.

________. 1994. "The Dust of Shansi." *Pentecostal Evangel,* July 24, 1994.

________. 1996. Letter to Loren Triplett. AGWM Archives in Springfield, MO.

Hsu, Immanuel C. Y. 1990. *The Rise of Modern China*. New York: Oxford University Press.

Hunter, Alan and Kim-Kwong Chan. 1993. *Protestantism in Contemporary China.* Cambridge: Cambridge University Press.

Hurst, Randy. 2001. "Legacy of Compassion." *AG Heritage* 21, no. 1 (Spring): 14-16.

________. 2009. "Christianity in China." *Pentecostal Evangel,* April 5, 2009.

________. 2013. "All He Commands." *Pentecostal Evangel,* January 6, 2013.

Jenkins, Philip. 2008. *The Lost History of Christianity*. New York: Harper.

Jin, Mingri. 2016. *Back to Jerusalem with All Nations: A Biblical Foundation*. Oxford: Regnum Books.

Johnson, Alan. 2009. *Apostolic Function in 21st Century Missions.* Pasadena, CA: William Carey Library.

Jones, Susan Mann, and Philip A. Kuhn. 1978. "Dynastic Decline and the Roots of Rebellion." In *The Cambridge History of China, Volume 10: Late Ch'ing, 1800-1911, Part 1*, edited by Denis Twitchett and John K. Fairbank, 107-162. Cambridge: Cambridge University Press.

Joshua Project. 2016a. "Language: Lisu." Accessed October 19, 2016. https://joshuaproject.net/languages/lis.

Joshua Project. 2016b. "Uyghur in China." Accessed October 15, 2016. https://joshuaproject.net/people_groups/15755/CH.

Joshua Project. 2019. "Kado in China." Accessed March 20, 2019. https://joshuaproject.net/people_groups/18516/CH.

Kaiser, Andrew T. 2016. *The Rushing on of the Purposes of God: Christian Missions in Shanxi Since 1876*. Eugene: Pickwick Publications.

Kane, J. Herbert. 1976. *Christian Missions in Biblical Perspective.* Grand Rapids: Baker.

Ketcher, Cathy. 2015. "The Onesiphorus Man." *Worldview* 1, no. 6 (June): 24-31.

Kendrick, Klaude. 1961. *The Promise Fulfilled: A History of the Modern Pentecostal Movement.* Springfield, MO: Gospel Publishing House.

Kindopp, Jason, and Carol Lee Hamrin, eds. 2004. *God and Caesar in China: Policy Implications of Church-State Tensions.* Washington: Brookings Institution Press.

Klaus, Byron D., and Douglas P. Petersen, eds. 2006. *The Essential J. Philip Hogan*. Springfield, MO: AGTS.

Koetitz, Edward, ed. [1980?]. *William W. Simpson: Missionary to Northwest China, 1892-1949.* Unpublished manuscript in AGWM Archives, Springfield, MO.

Kowalski, Rosemarie Daher. 2014. "What Made Them Think They Could? Ten Early Assemblies of God Female Missionaries." *AG Heritage* 34 (2014): 67-75.

Kraemer, Hendrik. 1947. *The Christian Message in a Non-Christian World.* New York: Harper and Brothers.

Kuhn, Philip. 1978. "The Taiping Rebellion." In *The Cambridge History of China Volume 10, Late Ch'ing 1800-1911, Part 1*, edited by Denis Twitchett and John K. Fairbank, 264-

317. Cambridge: Cambridge University Press.

Lambert, Tony. 1994. *The Resurrection of the Chinese Church.* Wheaton, IL: Harold Shaw Publishers.

________. 1999. *China's Christian Millions.* Grand Rapids: Monarch Books.

Latourette, Kenneth Scott. 1970a. *A History of the Expansion of Christianity, The First Five Centuries.* Vol. 1. Grand Rapids: Zondervan (orig. publ. 1937).

________. 1970b. *A History of the Expansion of Christianity, Three Centuries of Advance.* Vol. 3. Grand Rapids: Zondervan (orig. publ. 1939).

________. 1970c. *A History of the Expansion of Christianity, The Great Century: North Africa and Asia.* Vol. 6. Grand Rapids: Zondervan (orig. publ.1944).

________. 1970d. *A History of the Expansion of Christianity: Advance through Storm, Volume 7.* Grand Rapids: Zondervan (orig. publ. 1945).

________. 2009. *A History of Christian Missions in China.* Piscataway, NJ: Gorgias Press. (Orig. pub. 1929).

Lawless, Chuck. 2012. "Paul and Leadership Development." In *Paul's Missionary Methods: In His Time and Ours*, edited by Robert L. Plummer and John Mark Terry, 216-234. Downers Grove, IL: IVP Academic.

Lazzarotto, Angelo. 1983. "The Communist Party and Religion." *Missiology: An International Review* XI, no. 3 (July): 268-283.

Lee, Lydia. 2001. *A Living Sacrifice: The Life Story of Allen Yuan.* Tonbridge, Kent, United Kingdom: Sovereign World.

Legge, James. 1854. "Letter of July 21, 1854." *General Chronicle* (Oct.): 223.

Lewer, Mary Buchwalter. 1923. "Follower of Christ, What Doest Thou Here?" *Full Gospel Missionary Herald,* January 1923.

________. 1929. "Trophies Worth While in Western China." *Latter Rain Evangel*, December, 1929.

Lewis, Paul W. 2003. "Hodges, Williams, and Contemporary China," Paper, presented at the International Symposium on Pentecostal Missions, Baguio City, Philippines.

________, ed. 2014. *All the Gospel to All the World: 100 Years of Assemblies of God Missiology*. Springfield, MO: AGTS.

Li, Jieren. 2008. *In Search of the Via Media between Christ and Marx: A Study of Ding Guangxun's Contextual Theology*. Lund, Sweden: Lund University.

Li, Ma, and Jin Li. 2018. *Surviving the State, Remaking the Church: A Sociological Portrait of Christians in Mainland China*. Eugene: Pickwick Publications.

Li, Xinyuan. 2003. *Theological Construction—Or Destruction? An Analysis of the Theology of Bishop K. H. Ting*. Streamwood, IL: Christian Life Press.

Lian Xi. 2018. *Blood Letters*. New York: Basic Books.

Lowe, Chuck. 2001. *Honoring God and Family: A Christian Response to Idol Food in Chinese Popular Religion*. Bangalore, India: Theological Book Trust.

Luce, Alice Eveline. 1921a. "Paul's Missionary Methods." *The Pentecostal Evangel*, January 8, 1921.

________. 1921b. "Paul's Missionary Methods." *Pentecostal Evangel*, January 22, 1921.

________. 1921c. "Paul's Missionary Methods." *Pentecostal Evangel*, February 5, 1921.

________. 1922. "Portions for Whom Nothing is Prepared." *Pentecostal Evangel*, December 9, 1922.

Luttio, Mark. 1968. "The Chinese Rites Controversy (1603-1742): A Diachronic and Synchronic Approach." *Worship* 68 (July): 290-313.

MacInnis, Donald. 1989. *Religion in China Today*. Maryknoll, NY: Orbis Books.

Mandryk, Jason. 2010. *Operation World: The Definitive Prayer Guide to Every Nation*, 7th ed. Colorado Springs: Biblica Publishing.

Middleton, Vern. 2011. *Donald McGavran: His Early Life and Ministry*. Pasadena, CA: William Carey Library.

McClung, Grant, ed. 1986. *Azusa Street and Beyond*. South Plainfield, NJ: Bridge Publishing.

________. 2012. *Azusa Street and Beyond*, 2nd ed. Alachua, FL: Bridge-Logos.

McConnell, C. Douglas, ed. 1997. *The Holy Spirit and Mission*

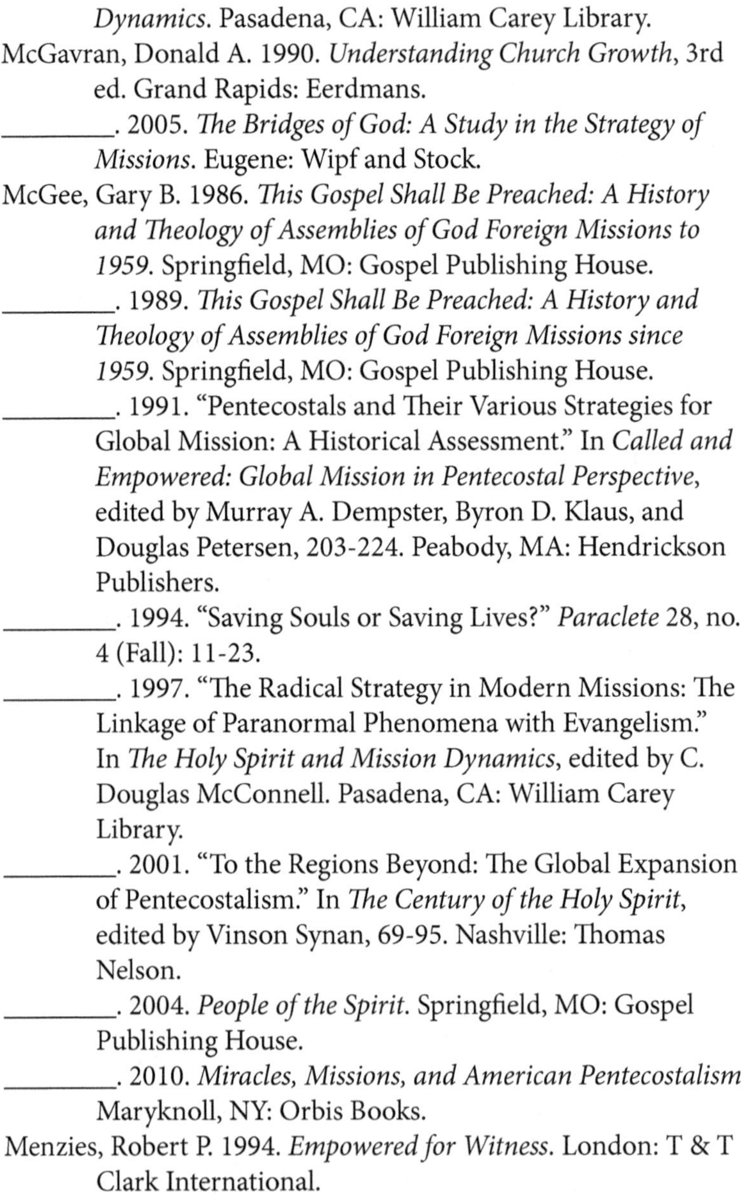

Dynamics. Pasadena, CA: William Carey Library.

McGavran, Donald A. 1990. *Understanding Church Growth*, 3rd ed. Grand Rapids: Eerdmans.

________. 2005. *The Bridges of God: A Study in the Strategy of Missions*. Eugene: Wipf and Stock.

McGee, Gary B. 1986. *This Gospel Shall Be Preached: A History and Theology of Assemblies of God Foreign Missions to 1959*. Springfield, MO: Gospel Publishing House.

________. 1989. *This Gospel Shall Be Preached: A History and Theology of Assemblies of God Foreign Missions since 1959*. Springfield, MO: Gospel Publishing House.

________. 1991. "Pentecostals and Their Various Strategies for Global Mission: A Historical Assessment." In *Called and Empowered: Global Mission in Pentecostal Perspective*, edited by Murray A. Dempster, Byron D. Klaus, and Douglas Petersen, 203-224. Peabody, MA: Hendrickson Publishers.

________. 1994. "Saving Souls or Saving Lives?" *Paraclete* 28, no. 4 (Fall): 11-23.

________. 1997. "The Radical Strategy in Modern Missions: The Linkage of Paranormal Phenomena with Evangelism." In *The Holy Spirit and Mission Dynamics*, edited by C. Douglas McConnell. Pasadena, CA: William Carey Library.

________. 2001. "To the Regions Beyond: The Global Expansion of Pentecostalism." In *The Century of the Holy Spirit*, edited by Vinson Synan, 69-95. Nashville: Thomas Nelson.

________. 2004. *People of the Spirit*. Springfield, MO: Gospel Publishing House.

________. 2010. *Miracles, Missions, and American Pentecostalism*. Maryknoll, NY: Orbis Books.

Menzies, Robert P. 1994. *Empowered for Witness*. London: T & T Clark International.

Menzies, Robert P., and William W. Menzies. 2000. *Spirit and Power: Foundations of Pentecostal Experience*. Grand Rapids: Zondervan.

Miller, Denzil. 2005. *Empowered for Global Mission: A Missionary Look at the Book of Acts.* Springfield, MO: Life Publishers.

Miller, Stuart Creighton. 1974. "Ends and Means: Missionary Justification of Force in Nineteenth Century China." In *The Missionary Enterprise in China and America*, edited by John K. Fairbank, 249-282. Cambridge: Harvard University Press.

Moffett, Samuel Hugh. 1998. *A History of Christianity in Asia.* Vol. 1. Maryknoll, NY: Orbis Books.

________. 2005. *A History of Christianity in Asia.* Vol. 2. Maryknoll, NY: Orbis Books.

Mundis, Greg. 2016. "Vision and Purpose of Assemblies of God World Missions." In *Mission, Vision, and Core Values*, edited by John L. Easter, Paul W. Lewis, Alan Johnson, Anita Koeshall, and Bob Friesen, 21-28. Springfield, MO: AGWM.

Neill, Stephen. 1964. *A History of Christian Missions.* New York: Penguin Books.

________. 1966. *Colonialism and Christian Missions.* New York: McGraw-Hill.

Nevius, Helen S. Coan. 1895. *The Life of John Livingston Nevius: For Forty Years a Missionary in China.* New York: Fleming H. Revell Company.

Nevius, John Livingston. 2015. *The Planting and Development of Missionary Churches,* New York: Foreign Mission Library. (Orig. pub. 1899).

Nienkirchen, Charles W. 1986. "Albert B. Simpson: Fore-runner of the Modern Pentecostal Movement." Paper presented at Society of Pentecostal Studies meeting November 14, 1986.

________. 1992. *A. B. Simpson and the Pentecostal Movement: A Study in Continuity, Crisis, and Change.* Eugene: Wipf and Stock.

Osgood, Howard. 1930. "The Work of the Missionary." *Pentecostal Evangel,* January 4, 1930.

________. 1943. "Thoughts on the Evangelization of China." Missionary Conference in Springfield, MO, March 16-18, 1943.

Paton, David, and Charles H. Long, eds. 1983. *The Compulsion of the Spirit: A Roland Allen Reader*. Grand Rapids: Eerdmans.

Paton, David, ed. 1968. *Reform of the Ministry: A Study in the Work of Roland Allen*. Cambridge, UK: Lutterworth Press.

________. 2011. *The Ministry of the Spirit: Selected Writings of Roland Allen*. Eugene: Wipf and Stock. (Orig. pub. 1960.

Payne, J. D., ed. 2012. "Roland Allen's Missionary Methods at One Hundred." In *Paul's Missionary Methods: In His Time and Ours,* edited by Robert L. Plummer and John Mark Terry, 235-243. Downers Grove, IL: IVP Academic.

________. 2017. *Roland Allen's The Ministry of Expansion: The Priesthood of the Laity.* Pasadena, CA: William Carey Library.

Peterson, Mikeuel Eugene. 2009. "Led by the Holy Spirit: The Missionary Career, Leadership, Thought, and Influence of Alice Eveline Luce." PhD diss., Asbury Theological Seminary.

Platt, Stephen R. 2012. *Autumn in the Heavenly Kingdom: China, the West, and the Epic Story of the Taiping Civil War*. New York: Vintage Books.

________. 2018. *Imperial Twilight: The Opium War and the End of China's Last Golden Age.* New York: Alfred Knopf.

Plummer, Robert L., and John Mark Terry, eds. 2012. *Paul's Missionary Methods: In His Time and Ours*. Downers Grove, IL: IVP Academic.

Pocock, Michael. 2012. "Paul's Strategy: Determinative for Today?" In *Paul's Missionary Methods: In His Time and Ours*, edited by Robert L. Plummer and John Mark Terry, 146-159. Downers Grove, IL: IVP Academic.

Peikou Assembly Church. 1983. "Tribute to a Martyr." *Mountain Movers*. November, 6-7, 1983.

Plymire, David. 1983. *High Adventure in Tibet*, rev. ed. Ellendale, ND: Trinity Print'n Press.

Plymire, Victor. n.d.a. "Brief Synopsis of Pioneering Tangar Mission in Northeast Tibet." Springfield, MO: AGWM Archives.

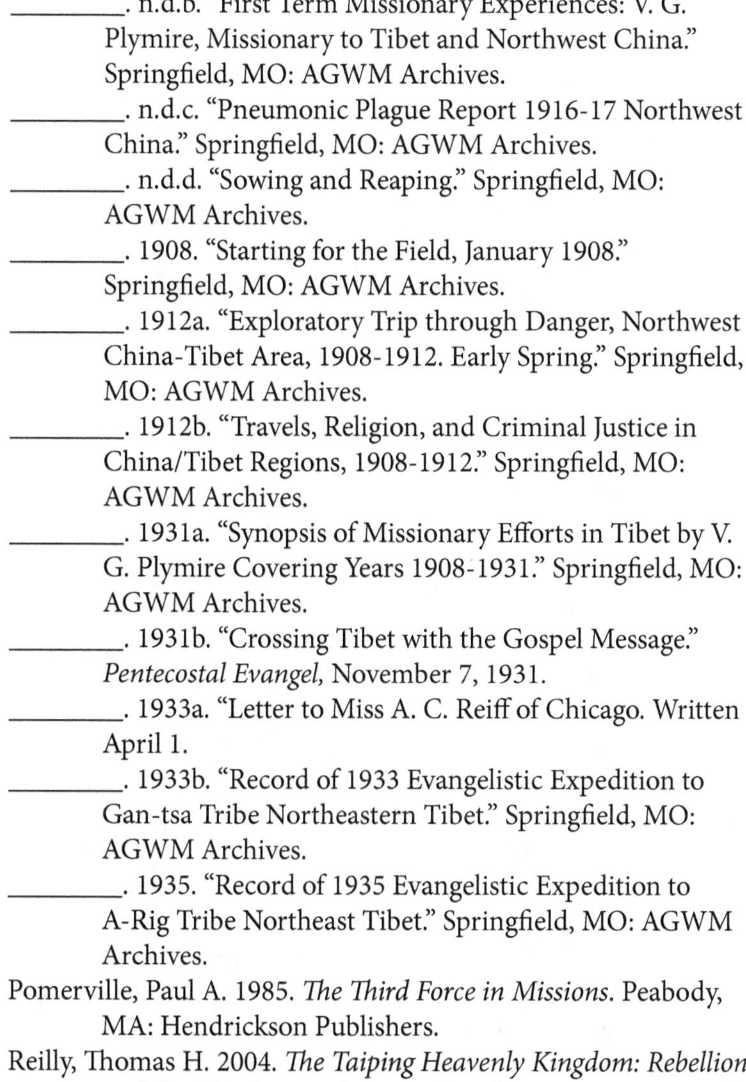

________. n.d.b. "First Term Missionary Experiences: V. G. Plymire, Missionary to Tibet and Northwest China." Springfield, MO: AGWM Archives.

________. n.d.c. "Pneumonic Plague Report 1916-17 Northwest China." Springfield, MO: AGWM Archives.

________. n.d.d. "Sowing and Reaping." Springfield, MO: AGWM Archives.

________. 1908. "Starting for the Field, January 1908." Springfield, MO: AGWM Archives.

________. 1912a. "Exploratory Trip through Danger, Northwest China-Tibet Area, 1908-1912. Early Spring." Springfield, MO: AGWM Archives.

________. 1912b. "Travels, Religion, and Criminal Justice in China/Tibet Regions, 1908-1912." Springfield, MO: AGWM Archives.

________. 1931a. "Synopsis of Missionary Efforts in Tibet by V. G. Plymire Covering Years 1908-1931." Springfield, MO: AGWM Archives.

________. 1931b. "Crossing Tibet with the Gospel Message." *Pentecostal Evangel,* November 7, 1931.

________. 1933a. "Letter to Miss A. C. Reiff of Chicago. Written April 1.

________. 1933b. "Record of 1933 Evangelistic Expedition to Gan-tsa Tribe Northeastern Tibet." Springfield, MO: AGWM Archives.

________. 1935. "Record of 1935 Evangelistic Expedition to A-Rig Tribe Northeast Tibet." Springfield, MO: AGWM Archives.

Pomerville, Paul A. 1985. *The Third Force in Missions*. Peabody, MA: Hendrickson Publishers.

Reilly, Thomas H. 2004. *The Taiping Heavenly Kingdom: Rebellion and the Blasphemy of Empire*. Seattle, WA: University of Washington Press.

Rienstra, M. Howard, ed. 1986. *Jesuit Letters from China: 1583-1584*. Minneapolis: University of Minnesota Press.

Roberts, J. A. G. 1998. *Modern China: An Illustrated History.* Gloucestershire, UK: Sutton Publishing.

Robinson, Charles E. 1940. "Delivering Dope Addicts in China." *Pentecostal Evangel,* April 6, 1940.

Ronan, Charles, and Bonnie B. C. Oh, eds. 1988. *East Meets West: The Jesuits in China, 1582-1773.* Chicago: Loyola University Press, 1988.

Ross, Andrew. 1994. *A Vision Betrayed: The Jesuits in Japan and China, 1542-1742.* Maryknoll, NY: Orbis Books.

Sanneh, Lamin. 2011. "Introductory Essay." In *The Ministry of the Spirit: Selected Writings of Roland Allen,* edited by David M. Paton, iii-xvi. Eugene: Wipf and Stock.

Schirokauer, Conrad. 1982. *Modern China and Japan.* New York: Harcourt Brace Jovanovich Publishers.

Schnabel, Eckard J. 2002. *Early Christian Mission: Jesus and the Twelve.* Downers Grove, IL: InterVarsity Press.

________. 2004. *Early Christian Mission: Paul and the Early Church.* Downers Grove, IL: InterVarsity Press.

________. 2008. *Paul the Missionary: Realities, Strategies, and Methods.* Downers Grove, IL: IVP Academic.

Schwartz, Benjamin I. 1983. "Themes in Intellectual History: May Fourth and After." In *The Cambridge History of China, Volume 12: Republican China 1912-1949, Part 1,* edited By John King Fairbank, 406-451. Cambridge: Cambridge University Press.

Shelton, James B. 1991. *Mighty in Word and Deed: The Role of the Holy Spirit in Luke-Acts.* Eugene: Wipf and Stock.

Sheridan, James. 1983. "The Warlord Era: Politics and Militarism under the Peking Government, 1916-28." In *The Cambridge History of China, Volume 12: Republican China 1912-1949, Part 1,* edited by John King Fairbank, 284-321. Cambridge: Cambridge University Press.

Silbey, David J. 2012. *The Boxer Rebellion and the Great Game in China.* New York: Hill and Wang.

Sills, M. David. 2012. "Paul and Contextualization." In *Paul's Missionary Methods: In His Time and Ours,* edited by Robert L. Plummer and John Mark Terry, 196-215. Downers Grove, IL: IVP Academic.

Simpson, W. W. n.d.a. "Autobiography of William Wallace Simpson." Springfield, MO: AGWM Archives.

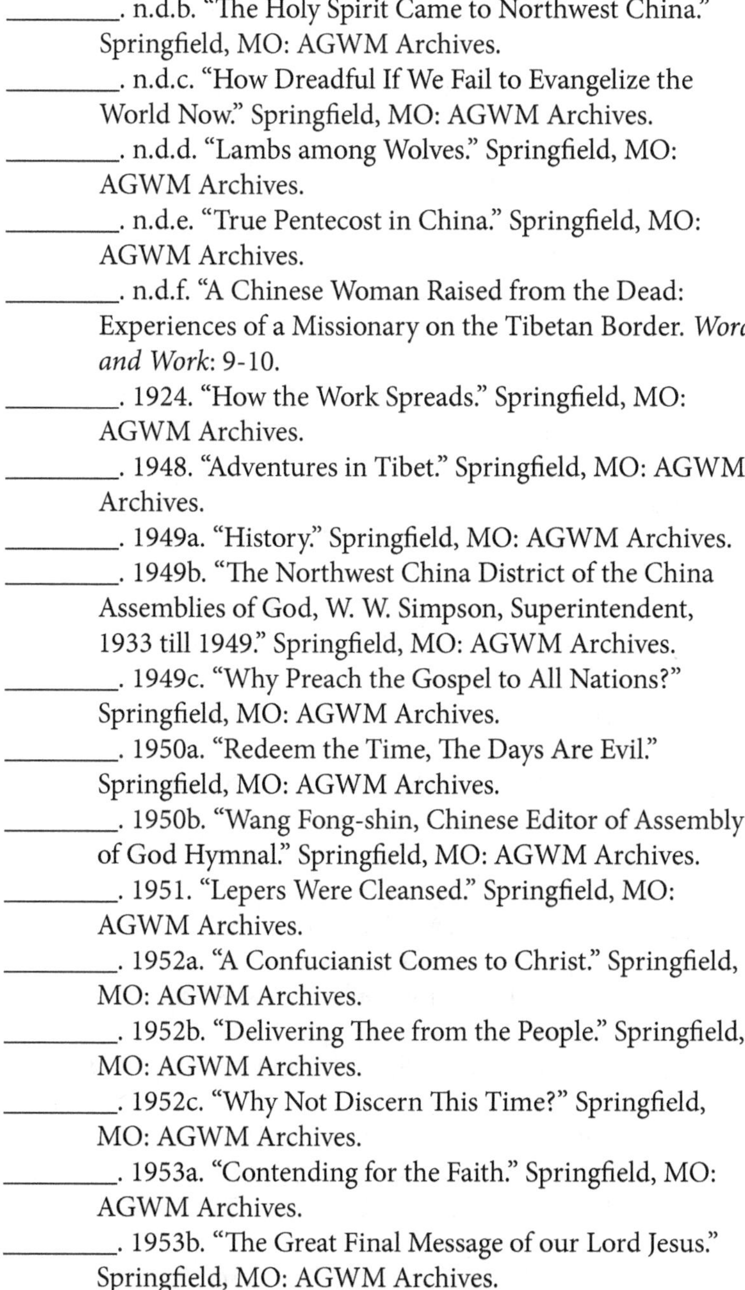

________. n.d.b. "The Holy Spirit Came to Northwest China." Springfield, MO: AGWM Archives.

________. n.d.c. "How Dreadful If We Fail to Evangelize the World Now." Springfield, MO: AGWM Archives.

________. n.d.d. "Lambs among Wolves." Springfield, MO: AGWM Archives.

________. n.d.e. "True Pentecost in China." Springfield, MO: AGWM Archives.

________. n.d.f. "A Chinese Woman Raised from the Dead: Experiences of a Missionary on the Tibetan Border. *Word and Work*: 9-10.

________. 1924. "How the Work Spreads." Springfield, MO: AGWM Archives.

________. 1948. "Adventures in Tibet." Springfield, MO: AGWM Archives.

________. 1949a. "History." Springfield, MO: AGWM Archives.

________. 1949b. "The Northwest China District of the China Assemblies of God, W. W. Simpson, Superintendent, 1933 till 1949." Springfield, MO: AGWM Archives.

________. 1949c. "Why Preach the Gospel to All Nations?" Springfield, MO: AGWM Archives.

________. 1950a. "Redeem the Time, The Days Are Evil." Springfield, MO: AGWM Archives.

________. 1950b. "Wang Fong-shin, Chinese Editor of Assembly of God Hymnal." Springfield, MO: AGWM Archives.

________. 1951. "Lepers Were Cleansed." Springfield, MO: AGWM Archives.

________. 1952a. "A Confucianist Comes to Christ." Springfield, MO: AGWM Archives.

________. 1952b. "Delivering Thee from the People." Springfield, MO: AGWM Archives.

________. 1952c. "Why Not Discern This Time?" Springfield, MO: AGWM Archives.

________. 1953a. "Contending for the Faith." Springfield, MO: AGWM Archives.

________. 1953b. "The Great Final Message of our Lord Jesus." Springfield, MO: AGWM Archives.

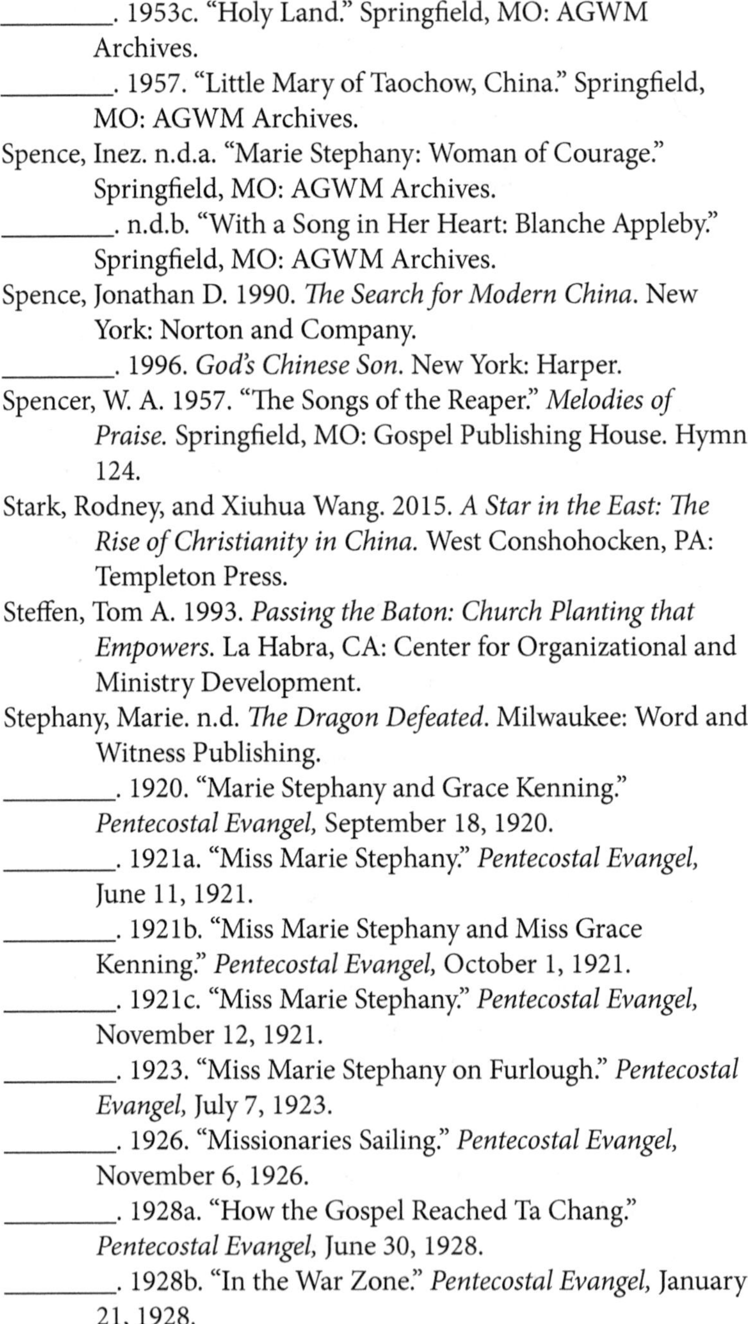

________. 1953c. "Holy Land." Springfield, MO: AGWM Archives.

________. 1957. "Little Mary of Taochow, China." Springfield, MO: AGWM Archives.

Spence, Inez. n.d.a. "Marie Stephany: Woman of Courage." Springfield, MO: AGWM Archives.

________. n.d.b. "With a Song in Her Heart: Blanche Appleby." Springfield, MO: AGWM Archives.

Spence, Jonathan D. 1990. *The Search for Modern China*. New York: Norton and Company.

________. 1996. *God's Chinese Son*. New York: Harper.

Spencer, W. A. 1957. "The Songs of the Reaper." *Melodies of Praise*. Springfield, MO: Gospel Publishing House. Hymn 124.

Stark, Rodney, and Xiuhua Wang. 2015. *A Star in the East: The Rise of Christianity in China*. West Conshohocken, PA: Templeton Press.

Steffen, Tom A. 1993. *Passing the Baton: Church Planting that Empowers*. La Habra, CA: Center for Organizational and Ministry Development.

Stephany, Marie. n.d. *The Dragon Defeated*. Milwaukee: Word and Witness Publishing.

________. 1920. "Marie Stephany and Grace Kenning." *Pentecostal Evangel,* September 18, 1920.

________. 1921a. "Miss Marie Stephany." *Pentecostal Evangel,* June 11, 1921.

________. 1921b. "Miss Marie Stephany and Miss Grace Kenning." *Pentecostal Evangel,* October 1, 1921.

________. 1921c. "Miss Marie Stephany." *Pentecostal Evangel,* November 12, 1921.

________. 1923. "Miss Marie Stephany on Furlough." *Pentecostal Evangel,* July 7, 1923.

________. 1926. "Missionaries Sailing." *Pentecostal Evangel,* November 6, 1926.

________. 1928a. "How the Gospel Reached Ta Chang." *Pentecostal Evangel,* June 30, 1928.

________. 1928b. "In the War Zone." *Pentecostal Evangel,* January 21, 1928.

________. 1928c. "Shansi Province." *Pentecostal Evangel,* August 11, 1928.
________. 1928d. "Shansi Province." *Pentecostal Evangel,* September 1, 1928.
________. 1930a. "Encouragement in Shansi, China." *Pentecostal Evangel,* April 5, 1930.
________. 1930b. "Yu Tsi, Ta Chang, North China." *Pentecostal Evangel,* July 12, 1930.
________. 1931. "Fruit from the Tent Meetings in Ta Chang, China." *Pentecostal Evangel,* May 9, 1931.
________. 1932. "Persecution for the Gospel in North China." *Pentecostal Evangel,* August 13, 1932.
________. 1933. "Dangers and Opportunities in Mongolia." *Pentecostal Evangel,* January 7, 1933.
________. 1934a. "Family of Three Generations Baptized." *Pentecostal Evangel,* August 11, 1934.
________. 1934b. "Manifestation of Holy Spirit Attracts Crowd." *Pentecostal Evangel,* February 24, 1934.
________. 1935. "Have You a Representative?" *Pentecostal Evangel,* March 23, 1935.
________. 1936a. "Communists Invade North China." *Pentecostal Evangel,* June 20, 1936.
________. 1936b. "Jewels for the Master." *Pentecostal Evangel,* November 7, 1936.
________. 1936c. "Victories and Defeats among the Dope Addicts." *Pentecostal Evangel,* March 7, 1936.
________. 1937a. "There Is Power in the Blood." *Pentecostal Evangel,* February 6, 1937.
________. 1937b. "Witnessing in Mongolia." *Pentecostal Evangel,* January 16, 1937.
________. 1938. "A Glimpse of the Work of Marie Stephany and Her Associate Missionaries Henrietta Tieleman and Alice Stewart, Ta Chang, China." *Pentecostal Evangel,* June 11, 1938.
________. 1939. *The Power of the Gospel in Shansi Province.* Springfield, MO: Foreign Missions Department.
________. 1940a. "Last Will and Testament." Springfield, MO: AGWM Archives.

________. 1940b. "Ta Ch'ang Church Dedicated." *Pentecostal Evangel*, March 9, 1940.

Stetzer, Ed with Lizette Beard. 2012. "Paul and Church Planting." In *Paul's Missionary Methods: In His Time and Ours*, edited by Robert L. Plummer and John Mark Terry, 175-195. Downers Grove, IL: IVP Academic.

Stewart, Alice. 1930. "Ta Chang, Shansi, China." *Pentecostal Evangel*, February 8, 1930.

________. 1937. "No Room?" *Pentecostal Evangel*, October 23, 1937.

________. 1945. "Sister Heh's Offering." *Pentecostal Evangel*, November 24, 1945.

________. 1946. "Jesus Loves Me." *Pentecostal Evangel*, August 3, 1946.

________. 1950. "Converts Winning Others." *Pentecostal Evangel*, July 8, 1950.

________. n.d. *Like Zion's Mount in China*. Springfield, MO: AGWM Archives.

Stronstad, Roger. 1984. *The Charismatic Theology of St. Luke*. Grand Rapids: Baker Academic.

Sunquist, Scott, ed. 2001. *A Dictionary of Asian Christianity*. Grand Rapids: Eerdmans.

Synan, Vinson, ed. 1975. *Aspects of Pentecostal-Charismatic Origins*. Plainfield, NJ: Logos International.

________. 2001. *The Century of the Holy Spirit*. Nashville: Thomas Nelson.

Taylor, Mrs. Howard. 1964. *Behind the Ranges: The Story of J. O. Fraser*. Chicago: Moody Press.

Tennent, Timothy. 2007. *Theology in the Context of World Christianity*. Grand Rapids: Zondervan.

Terry, John Mark, and J. D. Payne. 2013. *Developing a Strategy for Missions: A Biblical, Historical and Cultural Introduction*. Grand Rapids: Baker Academic.

Terry, John Mark. 2012. "Paul and Indigenous Missions." In *Paul's Missionary Methods: In His Time and Ours*, edited by Robert L. Plummer and John Mark Terry, 160-174. Downers Grove, IL: IVP Academic.

Tieleman, Henrietta, and Alice F. Stewart. 1938. "At the Land Where Only God's Promises Are Sure." *Pentecostal Evangel,* August 13, 1938.

________. n.d.a. "Heroes of the Conquest." Springfield, MO: Foreign Missions Department.

________. n.d.b. Unpublished biography of Henrietta Tieleman. Springfield, MO: AGWM Archives.

Ting, K. H. 1983. "Evangelism as a Chinese Christian Sees It." *Missiology: An International Review* XI, no. 3 (July): 309-320.

________. 1985. "Concerning Theological Education in China." *Missiology: An International Review* XIII, no. 3 (July): 283-290.

________. 1989. *No Longer Strangers*. Maryknoll: Orbis Books.

________. 2000. *Love Never Ends*. Nanjing: CHINA: Amity Printing Company.

Tucker, Ruth. 2004. *From Jerusalem to Irian Jaya.* Grand Rapids: Zondervan.

Van Houten, Richard, ed. 1988. *Wise as Serpents, Harmless as Doves*. Pasadena, CA: William Carey Library.

Van Rheenen, Gailyn. 2002. "The Missional Helix." Accessed March 9, 2019. http:///www.missionalive.org/ma/index.../83-the-missional-helix-example-of-church-planting.

Wakeman, Jr., Frederic. 1978. "The Canton Trade and the Opium War." In *The Cambridge History of China, Volume 10: Late Ch'ing 1800-1911, Part 1*, edited by Denis Twitchett and John K. Fairbank, 163-212. Cambridge: Cambridge University Press.

Warner, Wayne W., and Darrin J. Rodgers. 2017-2018. *AG Heritage* 37-38 (Winter): 43-49.

Webber, Robert. 2008. *Who Gets to Narrate the World?* Downers Grove, IL: IVP Books.

White, Theodore, and Annalee Jacoby. 1946. *Thunder out of China*. New York: William Sloane Associates, Inc.

Whitehead, Raymond L., ed. 1989. *No Longer Strangers: Selected Writings of K. H. Ting*. Maryknoll, NY: Orbis Books.

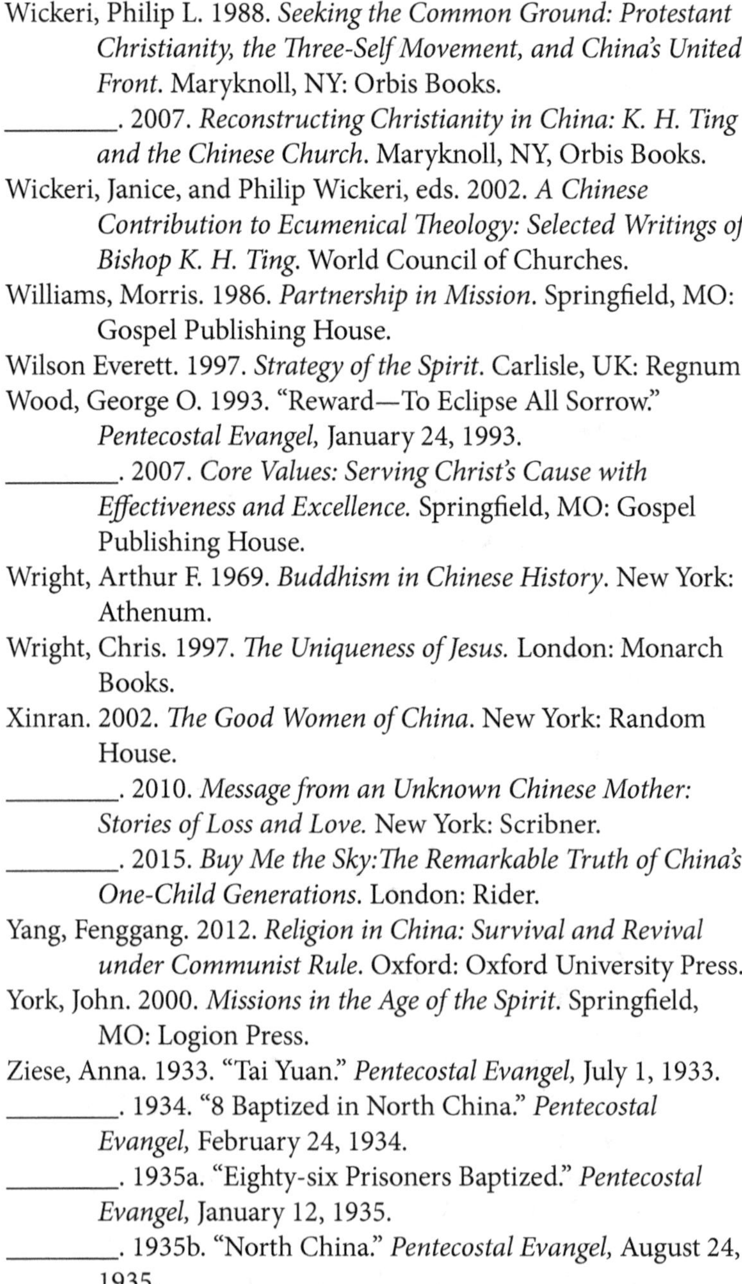

Wickeri, Philip L. 1988. *Seeking the Common Ground: Protestant Christianity, the Three-Self Movement, and China's United Front*. Maryknoll, NY: Orbis Books.

________. 2007. *Reconstructing Christianity in China: K. H. Ting and the Chinese Church*. Maryknoll, NY, Orbis Books.

Wickeri, Janice, and Philip Wickeri, eds. 2002. *A Chinese Contribution to Ecumenical Theology: Selected Writings of Bishop K. H. Ting*. World Council of Churches.

Williams, Morris. 1986. *Partnership in Mission*. Springfield, MO: Gospel Publishing House.

Wilson Everett. 1997. *Strategy of the Spirit*. Carlisle, UK: Regnum.

Wood, George O. 1993. "Reward—To Eclipse All Sorrow." *Pentecostal Evangel*, January 24, 1993.

________. 2007. *Core Values: Serving Christ's Cause with Effectiveness and Excellence*. Springfield, MO: Gospel Publishing House.

Wright, Arthur F. 1969. *Buddhism in Chinese History*. New York: Athenum.

Wright, Chris. 1997. *The Uniqueness of Jesus*. London: Monarch Books.

Xinran. 2002. *The Good Women of China*. New York: Random House.

________. 2010. *Message from an Unknown Chinese Mother: Stories of Loss and Love*. New York: Scribner.

________. 2015. *Buy Me the Sky:The Remarkable Truth of China's One-Child Generations*. London: Rider.

Yang, Fenggang. 2012. *Religion in China: Survival and Revival under Communist Rule*. Oxford: Oxford University Press.

York, John. 2000. *Missions in the Age of the Spirit*. Springfield, MO: Logion Press.

Ziese, Anna. 1933. "Tai Yuan." *Pentecostal Evangel*, July 1, 1933.

________. 1934. "8 Baptized in North China." *Pentecostal Evangel*, February 24, 1934.

________. 1935a. "Eighty-six Prisoners Baptized." *Pentecostal Evangel*, January 12, 1935.

________. 1935b. "North China." *Pentecostal Evangel*, August 24, 1935.

________. 1950. “Letter.” *Pentecostal Evangel,* February 11, 1950.

________. 1966. Letter to Harlan Park. March 22. Flower Pentecostal Heritage Center. https://ifphc.org/. Springfield, Missouri.

APTS PRESS
& ASIAN JOURNAL OF PENTECOSTAL STUDIES

PENTECOST
UNTO THE
Uttermost
2nd Edition
A History of the Assemblies of God in Samoa
Tavita Pagaialii

Pentecostal Theological Education in the Majority World:
The Graduate and Post-Graduate Level
VOLUME 1

THE VERSATILITY OF
PAUL
Artisan Missioner,
Community Developer,
Pastoral Educator
ROBERT BANKS

APTS PRESS
& ASIAN JOURNAL OF PENTECOSTAL STUDIES

A Multimedia Literacy Project
Toward Biblical Literacy in
Bangladesh
TERESA CHAI

Arto Hämäläinen and Ulf Strohbehn
To the Ends of the Earth:
Building a National Missionary Sending Structure
FOREWORD BY
Paul R. Alexander

CRAIG S. KEENER
For All Peoples:
A Biblical Theology of Missions in the Gospels and Acts
Foreword by Wonsuk Ma
Book 2 of the APTS Press Occasional Papers Series

www.ingramcontent.com/pod-product-compliance
Lightning Source LLC
LaVergne TN
LVHW050621100826
845148LV00011B/1674

* 9 7 9 8 3 8 5 2 7 6 0 7 3 *